HUMAN NATURE
from
CALVIN *to* EDWARDS

HUMAN NATURE
from
CALVIN *to* EDWARDS

Paul Helm

Reformation Heritage Books
Grand Rapids, Michigan

Reformation Heritage Books
2965 Leonard St. NE
Grand Rapids, MI 49525
616-977-0889
orders@heritagebooks.org
www.heritagebooks.org

Printed in the United States of America
18 19 20 21 22 23/10 9 8 7 6 5 4 3 2 1

Library of Congress Cataloging-in-Publication Data

Names: Helm, Paul, author.
Title: Human nature from Calvin to Edwards / Paul Helm.
Description: Grand Rapids, Michigan : Reformation Heritage Books, [2018] |
    Includes bibliographical references and index.
Identifiers: LCCN 2018033230 (print) | LCCN 2018042201 (ebook) | ISBN
    9781601786111 (epub) | ISBN 9781601786104 | ISBN 9781601786104
    (paperback :alk. paper)
Subjects: LCSH: Theological anthropology—Reformed Church—History. |
    Reformed Church—History of doctrines.
Classification: LCC BT701.3 (ebook) | LCC BT701.3 .H45 2018 (print) | DDC
    233.088/2842—dc23
LC record available at https://lccn.loc.gov/2018033230

Contents

Preface

The idea of this book is to present a documented account of the anthropology of the Reformed orthodox up to and including Jonathan Edwards. Whether or not it is correct to include Edwards among the Reformed orthodox is debated, and this book addresses some of the debate—the part in which anthropology is relevant. But I do not try to solve that issue here.

It is a characteristic feature of Reformed theology that the fall and its effects on human nature was from a metaphysical point of view "adventitious." Metaphysically it was an accident, though of course not trivial or accidental, which had adverse implications for man's essence, but it did not destroy that essence so much as disorder it.

This book has to do with the nature that lies behind this disordered essence. We shall on occasion advert to its soteriological reordering, but only insofar as it throws light on the essence.

As far as I know there is no other such book; it will not be surprising therefore if this first shot has rough edges, though I have done my best to eliminate these. The individual thinkers that I have chosen could no doubt be improved upon. Certainly it could have been different. But it is my hope nevertheless that this book make a worthwhile start on the systematic study of some of Reformed anthropology.

Richard Muller has encouraged me to attempt this book and argued with me about certain matters in it, in particular whether the views of the Reformed orthodox on human freedom are consistent with compatibilism. Now and again the reader will find an allusion to our divergent views on that matter, which are tangential to the interests of the book. In any case, these differences between us are fewer than they used to be. I have particularly been struck by the friendly and dispassionate way in which he has debated the issues on which we have differed. Richard has also painstakingly read the manuscript and made a number of suggestions, most of which I have taken up. I enjoy his friendship, benefit greatly from his erudition, and owe him an enormous debt of gratitude.

Thanks also to Joel Beeke and Jay Collier, who have superintended the preparation of the book; to James Dolezal and Aza Goudriaan, who read parts of the manuscript; and to Reformation Heritage Books editors for their indispensable editorial skills. Jack Vanden Born graciously allowed me to quote from his unpublished dissertation on Herman Bavinck's book on psychology. John Bolt, Stephen Bishop, Daniel Hill, Michael Lynch, Laurence O'Donnell, and Samuel Renihan have all helped me in various ways, and I thank them too.

The first serious thinking about the book occurred when I held a summer fellowship at the Meeter Center in July 2015, and I thank those concerned with my stay: Karin Maag, the director; Ryan Noppen; and especially Paul Fields.

The website of the Post-Reformation Digital Library has been invaluable in making available old texts. I recommend it to anyone who has interests in the history of Reformed theology.

In writing I have made use of previously published material with permissions, in particular: "'Structural Indifference' and Compatibilism in Reformed Orthodoxy," *Journal of Reformed Theology* 5 (2011): 185–205; "Vermigli, Calvin et l'éthique d'Aristote," in *Contre vents et marées*, ed. Jean-Philippe Bru (Aix-en-Provence: Kerygma, 2014); "Jonathan Edwards, John Locke and Religious Affections," *Jonathan Edwards Studies* 6, no. 1 (2016): 3–15.

Lastly, special thanks to my wife, Angela, for supporting me with her encouragement and patience.

Paul Helm
Cold Aston, Gloucsestershire
England

Introduction

There is very little in print on human nature in Reformed thought. This book is an effort to plug some of that gap by considering the topic historically. It is not intended to be encyclopedic, but selective and typical.

So the main chapters provide a sampler, designed to introduce Reformed anthropology to those who are not aware of the wealth of material there is in treatises and commentaries. The idea is to survey the material in some detail. This is an area where philosophy interfaces with theology, and so there is a good deal of philosophy in what follows. I have no doubt that the range of examples that is cited could be enlarged, as well as the range of topics. My chief aim has been to provide a reasonable and representative range from authors whose writings are available in English. The material, though referring mainly to the period 1550 to 1750, is not presented in chronological order but topically.

This is a selective treatment of anthropology from the late medievalism that John Calvin inherited and more or less adopted, on through to Jonathan Edwards. By "anthropology" is meant the study of man, and in this case the study of man within the Reformed faith. We shall look at "theological anthropology" of a certain kind as it was treated by the Reformed theologians. But it will not be the treatment that this combination of anthropology and Reformed theology usually suggests. Topics such as mankind made in the image of God, the fall and its consequences for mankind, Christ's human nature, and perhaps the resurrection body are what one usually finds. But these subjects are largely absent in what follows, which is concerned simply with human nature. The Reformed of this period believed that grace builds on nature, and their treatment of human nature is central to this.

Given that according to Reformed theology the fall resulted in a loss to created human nature and not to the total destruction of that nature, it is possible to speak of a human nature which endures through all the four states of humankind: as originally created, as fallen, as redeemed in Christ, and as consummated in resurrection. In a recent treatment of man in a fairly comprehensive Puritan theology, for example, there are chapters on the creation of man in a pristine condition, made in God's image, and man in sin. What is missing? There is no treatment of human nature without it being a treatment of either pristine human nature, or as fallen, or as regenerated and restored, or as glorified. There is no treatment of mankind as such, of what is common, what makes these states those of human beings.

Current books on human nature treat it in moral or social or ideological terms, as in Leslie Stevenson's *Seven Theories of Human Nature*[1] or Mary Midgley's *Beast and Man: The Roots of Human Nature.*[2] These are interesting and instructive books. However, we shall be interested in human nature as equivalent to the "soul" in its metaphysics and its powers and capacities, including its relation to the body.

This is not a comprehensive survey of the field nor anything like that. Instead, at its center there is a selective historical treatment of some significant theological documents, without any pretense of covering all the ground. For we shall find that in our period there is a mass of material. So this is a selection, both in terms of topic and of the writers. From it we will identify certain ways of thinking, and from this there is the question of development and change that one usually finds in historical treatments of human life. But there is no claim to finality. Rather, it is a treatment of some themes in human nature at the hands of theologians that I am interested in. There are obvious gaps, as will emerge. It is better to look at a selection of primary sources and to try to make sense of them than try something that aims to be comprehensive but turns out to be rather thin.

Such a treatment nevertheless has certain presuppositions. First, it is a treatment of human nature from an era when it was firmly believed that man had a nature. That may seem to be a truism. But this assumption is much less certain in the Western culture of the twenty-first century.

---

1. Leslie Stevenson, *Seven Theories of Human Nature* (Oxford: Oxford University Press, 1974).

2. Mary Midgley, *Beast and Man: The Roots of Human Nature* (London: Routledge, 2002).

We are aware of forces that mold individuals and groups—consumerism, "man the game player," human beings as nothing other than sexual objects, and of a person's search for his own identity, or for a change of it. We are also aware of other forces that can change personalities: programming, therapy, positive thinking, and so on. And so to us human nature appears more malleable than to those whose views we shall consider. We shall not address these differences head on. But it bears saying that the people we shall discuss were aware of the power of self-deception and of men and women being shaped by forces that they were not aware of. But the aim is not to force these people to speak to us directly, but to look at them and think about them, because what they say is intrinsically interesting and has been influential and may still be.

Our period of study makes certain assumptions. One is that the mind or soul is nonphysical, a spiritual substance. All the people we shall consider assume that the soul is immortal, in sharp contrast to the body. They lived in the light of Plato and the neo-Platonists, and of an Aristotle somewhat modified in the face of overriding Christian requirements. Later, the divergent influences of René Descartes and of John Locke, each of whom features in our discussions, share these assumptions, though modified in significant ways. The other important seventeenth-century influence, Thomas Hobbes, was dismissed by them precisely because his materialism meant that he did not share the prevailing dualistic mind-body assumptions, though he also makes one or two brief appearances in what follows.

It is not my aim to offer an apology for faculty psychology, the dominant psychology of the period. Readers of the literature cited here, as with any literature on human psychology of five hundred years ago, will be struck by the quaintness and outdatedness of the medicine, the outcome of the primitiveness of their understanding of the workings of the human body. They were only beginning to understand the body as an intricate neuro-physiological pump. Some would say that twenty-first-century medicine is only beginning to understand it as well. Nevertheless, the thrust of current research is to assign more and more aspects of the consciousness to the brain. For some this may simply be a methodological requirement of modern medicine, but others identify mind and brain, reducing the one to the other; some others would like to, but are held up by the striking differences between the conceptuality of consciousness and that of the mechanics of neurophysiology. Consciousness is the problem, but it is widely thought that a reduction of mind to brain is only a matter of time. But if, for whatever reason, one thinks that the mind is distinct from the body, then such a one is in the same world of thought as the Reformed orthodox and their fellows in the sixteenth century onward. Their faculty psychology is robustly nonreductionistic. They were struck by the phenomenon of intentionality, the "aboutness" of our consciousness which computers don't have or have only via programs that mimic consciousness, contrived by those who possess it.

The people we will study were puzzled by and marveled at the soul's relation to the body, as we are. The body is not simply a complex tool, but this body is my body and that body is your body. We are both enhanced and limited by having bodies. Our eyes enable us to see myriads of things and to record them in our memories. But our relation to them is not like one we have to a pair of binoculars. They are my eyes, part of me, in a way that a contact lens or magnifying glass could not be. We move and train our eyes to work effortlessly at our bidding. Such actions are what have been called "basic" actions. We do not do anything like reaching for our eyes as we reach for our glasses. We look on the world around us not by performing an action which enables us to look; we do not look by doing anything preparatory—we simply look. (No doubt this would have to be different in the case of a person gradually losing their sight.) This instantaneousness and basicality characterizes our mind in its various powers. But these powers, while they grow apace in childhood and youth, change and decay in midlife and beyond and start to fail to support the mind, as a cancerous brain fails to support it, or as the result of a stroke the brain is suddenly downsized. And we die. That is, Christians typically maintain, our bodies die, and our souls, not unaffected by this death, live on. This closeness of the soul and mind, and yet their distinctness, made many of the Reformed orthodox and other kinds of Christians hospitable to the Aristotelian idea that the soul is the form of the body, and even those who were substance dualists were puzzled and amazed by the present unity formed by the two.

For them a person has a nature—it is not a human construct. But what is it to have a nature? Perhaps we could begin an answer with the following: that A is of nature N if it is born of a pair of individuals having N. This would rule out mules and other similar sterile products having a nature. Evidence for such a nature lies in immune systems and rejection mechanisms and the impossibility of A breeding with an individual of another species or of no species. This kind of biological stubbornness is one kind of fixity which undergirds human nature. Such a human body is necessary in order to be a human being. These factors about bodiliness and breeding provide a causal necessity which verges on metaphysical necessity, but only because of the first Adam and because of the second Adam too. Did the first Adam have a navel? He became the first human and therefore could not have had human parents; the second Adam was fully human without having a human father, unlike his half brother James, for example. But with these clearly identifiable exceptions, a human person is the product of a human father and mother, even allowing for surrogacy of various kinds. This is true even if the first human had parents; his parents could not have been human parents, that's all.

This sort of discussion shows that there is a nature that is human, but not what that nature is. So what else? The product of a human father and mother that was solely in a vegetative state would not be a person in the way in which someone who was born without legs but was otherwise "normal" would be a person, as one who is incomplete, handicapped, or "challenged." A person who is born in a persistent vegetative state (PVS) would be entitled to be cared for and treated decently in life and then in death; that person would have human parents and would be possessed of a characteristically human form and not be a member of any other species; but that one would not be a person, or fully a person nor have the potential to be one. What does the one born in a PVS *ab initio* lack? We might say that he or she—for this one in a PVS would have a biological gender—lacks a mind. If that one could, with help, come to think and to feel sensations and make judgments and perform actions and feel emotions, going beyond the feeling of physical sensations of pain and pleasure, then we'd be correct to call that being a person. I shall venture no further into the question of what we might (or should—a different question, of course) call an individual who had thought and will but no emotions, or thought and emotions but no will; my guess is that individual would in each case be regarded as a severely handicapped human person.

We've gone far enough down this road for present purposes. We have identified a common nature which presupposes embodiment and at least consists in thinking, consciousness and self-awareness, producing emotions or affections, and being able to bring about changes in that individual's relation to the world. So this book will by and large be concerned with such individuals, born of human parents, who have a mind, a repertoire of intellectual, volitional, and emotive or passional powers, and a moral sense. For our purposes this is sufficient to delineate human nature. Such persons would characteristically and typically have a sense of right and wrong both as these terms are applicable to themselves and to others. So the question of conscience will arise. People in the period I am concerned with thought of human beings as natural rather than conventional, as in no sense an artifact, except in the sense of being a divine creation, but of course capable of being influenced by upbringing and education and especially what happened to them in their early lives in human and nonhuman environments.

As this discussion shows, we are in an area in which philosophy and theology interacted and combined, the one brought into the service of the other. In the case of some theologians, the philosophy was adopted; on other occasions a particular philosophical outlook seems to have been so pervasive that it was thought the natural way to think of human beings, for that is the way they are. On still other occasions the philosophical views were adopted as improvements on the past in the sense that they provided a better way (they judged) of looking at theological data. Nearly all the views, if not all of them, handled philosophical data eclectically. That is, they followed or adopted no particular school of philosophy exclusively but took elements from more than one source, including elements from the Christian revelation, which had a controlling interest.

We shall begin our inquiries by considering anthropology as it is found in the earlier church, in Tertullian but more importantly in Augustine (and behind Augustine, Plato) and Thomas Aquinas (and behind him, Aristotle). It was in a rather eclectic mix of these sources, and of Stoicism, that philosophy impacted John Calvin. He was concerned in the *Institutes* to set forth the Christian religion, not Christian theology, the term "theology" being treated by him more often than not with ridicule or disdain. He is not concerned in the *Institutes* to set forth a "scientific" theology in the textbook way that came to be routine in later Reformed theology. Not every locus of theology was treated, and where loci can be discerned in the *Institutes*, each locus does not receive equal treatment.

It is in this operation that Calvin makes use of philosophy in anthropology. He picks and chooses as he sees fit and as suits the manner in which his *Institutes* is written and the needs of his readers. What he concentrates on is an outline of anthropology derived from Plato and a faculty psychology bequeathed by Aristotle and to a lesser extent the Stoics—that is to say, the human self comprised of different sets of powers, or faculties: the intellect, the emotions, and so on. We can observe these powers at work in ourselves and in others. Each set of powers is in relative independence of the others, that is to say they performed various different functions which could be in causal connection with each other. How pervasive and intimate such connections were and what was the extent of these powers itself remained a matter of debate, as we shall see.

It would be misguided to think that the understanding of the human mind by a faculty psychologist has to be flat and simplistic. The early Reformed theologians that we will consider were well aware of mental mechanisms, of fantasy and self-deception, that affect the soul. The prophet Jeremiah asserted that the heart, a biblical term for the psychological and spiritual center of a person as fallen in Adam

> is deceitful above all things,
> And desperately wicked;
> Who can know it?
> I, the LORD, search the heart,
> I test the mind. (Jer. 17:9–10)

And they believed him. Of course as this example shows, the Bible has its own anthropological data in abundance: besides the heart are the soul, the mind and the reason, the will and choice, the conscience, the memory, and the passions and affections. The Reformed may be said to use pagan faculty psychology as a framework, or structure, providing a way or ways in which the unsystematic biblical anthropology may be presented.

They took over from Aristotle and Augustine but especially from the apostle Paul an appreciation of the radical weakness of the human will, its employment of double standards, its inability to motivate the fallen self to good, its capacity to deceive the self, and so on. The possession of a false consciousness was not an invention of Feuerbach or Marx. Nor did they point the finger from a high tower of self-righteousness. For all their concern with high standards of conduct and correct motivations, they were aware—indeed they were confessionally committed to the view—that the best of Christians are but imperfectly re-formed in the image of God. They were well aware of the continued force of fantasy and of worldly ambition. Calvin refers to the fallen mind as a factory of idols. This does not commit him to a Feuerbachian or Freudian worldview. Unlike Feuerbach or Freud, he was not a projectionist. Religion is not a social or personal construct, not the true religion at least. But they knew of the force that willfulness and warped thinking play in the human mind.

In our period of focus, rudimentary science of the brain was slowly advancing, and people were edging toward the modern, secular view that human beings are nothing but machines processing pain- and pleasure-producing states of affairs, giving rise to a range of moral strategies for both cooperating with and curbing the activity of such conditions in society.

So this study is a project on anthropology, on human nature, which begins (in chapter 2) with Calvin and Peter Martyr Vermigli in the second half of the sixteenth century. In subsequent chapters the focus is on the seventeenth century, involving representatives of that busy time—busy, that is, as far as the output of Reformed and Puritan theology is concerned. The educated world was still, to a striking degree, the classical world of Plato and Aristotle and of their influence on late medievalism. That was one reason why the arrival of Descartes on the scene in Holland in the middle of the seventeenth century had such a disturbing effect.

Calvin and Vermigli differed somewhat, in that Calvin was more Platonistically inclined, routinely using dualistic Platonic language, referring to the body as the "prison house" of the soul and stressing the immortality of the soul. The scholastically educated Vermigli held to the Aristotelian idea of the soul as the form of the body. These differences did not prevent the two from being good friends. But they were followed by an explosion of theological activity that was largely scholastic in character. This will occupy us in chapters 3–7. We shall note some of the effects of Descartes on anthropology, particularly but not exclusively in the Netherlands, and end in chapter 8 with John Locke and his influence on the anthropology of Jonathan Edwards, which manifested itself in the first half of the eighteenth century.

In the history of Christian theology, human anthropology may be said to have had *a* beginning—I do not say *the* beginning—with Tertullian's and Augustine's reflections on human nature. I think it is fair to say that Tertullian's views were strongly influenced by the Stoics and did not make an abiding impact on what came later. Augustine in his great work *De Trinitate* saw human nature as revealing God's Trinitarian character. He sees a human as comprising memory, understanding, and will, corresponding to

Father, Son, and Holy Spirit. He experiments with various formulae, but none seems to have satisfied him. Nevertheless, in this way he provides us with a window into his anthropology. Indeed, his outlook seems to have satisfied some Reformed theologians even in the seventeenth century. The latish Puritan theologian Francis Roberts seems satisfied with an anthropology that followed Augustine's Trinitarianism.

But the Reformed orthodox, besides having Augustine in the background, were more immediately the heirs of medieval scholasticism. This was the majority view. The rediscovery of Aristotle and his translation into Latin in the twelfth century, particularly (as far as we are concerned) his work on the soul, *De Anima*, besides much else, led to the adoption of what comes to be known as faculty psychology. Aquinas is a first-rate source for the development of such psychology, modifying Aristotle's views in the light of the New Testament teaching on the conscience and his view of the unity of soul and body in the light of the New Testament teaching of the soul's persistence after the death of the body and prior to its resurrection.

For Augustine the *voluntas* is the seat of the self that is changed in regeneration from worshiping and serving the creature to worshiping and serving the Creator, however imperfectly. In all this, we need to remember that the Reformed adopted and adapted a once-pagan philosophical apparatus to aid them in articulating the biblical data systematically. For most of them, the human soul was metaphysically simple, without parts, whose sets of powers may be grouped under the intellect or reason (or under standing), the will, and the affections, in that order, each dependent on the earlier. The understanding *affects*, or on some accounts, *necessitates* the will, and from the workings of the embodied will in circumstances which either comply with it or bar it the affections may arise. Some made further distinctions between sets of cognitive powers, and though the majority seem to think of the intellect's superiority to the will, others seem to have thought of the understanding and the will as nearly equipollent.

This terminology—intellect, reason, understanding, affections, conscience, and so on—did not necessarily have for the users in our period the connotations that it had later. For example, when our writers use "reason," they do not use it in the normative sense of the Enlightenment and afterward. By reason and reasoning they referred to the soul's belief-forming and belief-endorsing activity, whatever the mix of influences on the reason or understanding may be. All these factors are allowed for in these thinkers' usage of a term such as "reason." That usage has little or nothing directly or exclusively to do with the clear and distinct ideas of Descartes, nor with the Principle of Sufficient Reason of Leibniz, or with conscious judgments of probability, any more than it has to do with the "reasonable man." So its usage was elastic. This is similar with the conscience, a part of the *sensus divinitatis*, though affectable by upbringing and culture. So the conscience has an indelible aspect of the self as well as an aspect that is socially conditioned. It was not the source of nothing but privileged, pure moral intuitions, nor was it simply the purely sociological construct that it has tended to be later.

In the surge in theological writing in the seventeenth century there is by no means a monotonous uniformity. Faculty psychology is sufficiently complex to provide plenty of scope here for individual theologians to finesse their accounts. These variants were distinctions of the reason, distinctions between the soul's various powers. Such powers are not parts of the soul, as arms and legs are parts of the body, for the soul does not have parts, though in discussion of the faculties of the soul, it often seems as if each faculty does have a separate reality, a separate part of the soul. Some readily use this language, the language of *homunculi*, while others are wary of it. That's one significant difference among them.

The individuals we are to consider often have a strong appetite for understanding their faith. Philosophical reflection is to be undertaken for the benefit of faith. The Reformed orthodox take this stance from medieval thinkers whose theology overlaps with theirs. So their psychology, having a theological *telos* in their eyes, benefits from such philosophical reflection.

John Locke, whose views were a general and varied influence on eighteenth-century Anglophone theology, as well as on French Encyclopaedists such as Helvétius and D'Holbach, was also influential on other Reformed theologians. Some, such as Isaac Watts, were enthusiastic; others, such as the Scottish theologian Thomas Halyburton, were cagey and critical, though respectful. Locke held that the newborn mind was a *tabula rasa*, a blank sheet, having no innate ideas. Its cognitive content is stocked and shaped by the ideas it receives, and it is able to make inductive generalizations and abstractions from the particularities of sense experience. How much of this Jonathan Edwards took on is not clear. But he was certainly attracted to what Locke said about the unity of the self, the nature of personal identity, and about the place of pleasure and pain in human action.

Faculty psychology did not immediately fade with Locke, as Edwards's reaction to Locke might lead one to expect. There's a case for saying that our speech is still impregnated with it. Through the work of David Hartley, Locke's discussion of the association of ideas became an important ingredient in the methodology of modern psychology, including experimental psychology. But the influence of anthropology after Locke and its bearing on Reformed theology must be left for others.

Our consideration of Reformed anthropology begins with an account of its roots in classical and medieval philosophy.

CHAPTER 1

Patristic and Medieval Sources
of Faculty Psychology

The aim of this chapter is to set the scene for subsequent chapters which will outline the thinking of Calvin and others in the Reformed orthodox tradition. It is now a commonplace that the Reformers and those who followed them were indebted to late medievalism for their conceptual tools, even though there is scholarly debate about the details of this reception. Here, we will look selectively at the anthropology of two important earlier figures, Augustine of Hippo (354–430) and Thomas Aquinas (1225–1274), both of whose trajectories we will see was followed by the mainstream of Reformed thinkers. Having these influences before us will save us from treating the later Reformed tradition anachronistically or in a starry-eyed way, imagining innovation where there was little or none. In the case of the main theological influences, Augustine prevailed, while it is to Aquinas and the thinkers who came after him that many of the Reformed were indebted for the details of their anthropological outlook.

There was no necessity about this trajectory prevailing as it did. For instance, if those Christians who came before Augustine were included, and had their view prevailed, things may have turned out differently. If the views of Tertullian (145–225) had become dominant, then Christian anthropology would have had a rather Stoic look about it. The Stoic influence on the anthropology of Tertullian, who was widely read, is seen in passages such as this: "The soul we define to be sprung from the breath of God, immortal, possessing body, having form, simple in its substance, intelligent in its own nature, developing its power in various ways, free in its determinations, subject to the changes of accident, in its faculties mutable, rational, supreme, endued with an instinct of presentiment, evolved out of one (archetypal) soul."[1]

---

1. Tertullian, *On the Testimony of the Soul and On the "Prescription" of Heretics*, trans. T. Herbert Bindley (New York: E. S. Gorham, 1914), ch. 22.

If Tertullian's view, as outlined in *Against Hermogenes* and *On the Soul*, had won the day, then the dualism of the existing tradition might instead have been one in which the soul was material, albeit being constituted of material of a rather ethereal kind. Tertullian conceived of the soul as the house of the mind, as the material in-breathing of God that, because it was material, was able to affect and be affected by the material human body without difficulty. That is how Tertullian interprets Genesis 2:7, which is something of a key text about body and soul (we will note other interpretations later). But for Tertullian, the mind is the functioning power of the soul, and he will make copious references to the faculties of that soul. But although Calvin had access to Tertullian's works[2] and quotes him on the resurrection of the body with approval,[3] Tertullian is by no means the chief influence on Calvin's anthropology, as we will see in the next chapter.

Before Augustine, who lived two centuries after Tertullian, were Plato (c. 424–348 BC) and Aristotle (348–322 BC), the historically important developers of faculty psychology, which was to dominate Reformed theology in our period. So, first, some words on Plato.

Plato and His Influence on Augustine
Plato was one of the first, if not the first, to conceptualize human nature in terms of powers, originally a word referring to physical powers. The idea of a power is dispositional, a potential for action or change of some kind. Plants and animals have certain powers or propensities, enabling them to act or be acted upon. So it is by their manifestations that their underlying powers, their dispositions, are identified. In *The Republic*, Plato employs these basic ideas in his tripartite (appetite, reason, spirit) account of the soul. The powers, or faculties, of the soul each have characteristic objects with which they are exclusively correlated, and the faculties are possessed by the embodied soul and work through the body. The embodied soul itself has a set of these powers, understood in psychological terms, enabling it to act in certain ways.[4] Questions arise about their relation to the soul as one thing and to the body as another—two radically different things. The

---

2. See Anthony Lane, *John Calvin: Student of the Church Fathers* (Grand Rapids: Baker, 1999), 168.

3. John Calvin, *Institutes of the Christian Religion*, trans. Henry Beveridge, various editions, III.xxv.7; IV.xvii.29.

4. Plato, *The Republic*, trans. Robin Waterfield (Oxford: Oxford University Press, 1993), bk. IV.

unification of body and soul lies in the faculties being harmonized so that in general the body and soul do not conflict but cooperate in the task of developing virtue. The soul possesses these faculties; it does not consist in them. The rational powers, a fragment of the deity, is what is truly immortal. The other powers, such as the sensory and vegetative powers, have their workings due to embodiment, and they impede rationality. This yields the need for strategies of harmonization of the faculties.

The fact of Plato's influence on Augustine is Augustine's own admission, as he tells us in his *Confessions*. It was the Platonic influence that led Augustine to be emancipated from Manichaeism, a gnostically inclined, dualistic religion, and rid him of Manichean anthropomorphic conceptions of God. Thus, Augustine made the transition to the Christian church partly with the help of Plato, and more exactly of the Neoplatonists.

This transition involved many changes. For example, Augustine came to accept the goodness of the material world as created by God and to accept a new conception of the soul. Souls were present to and provided the principle of life of every living thing: of their growth and nourishment and (in the case of animals, including human beings) their intellectual and sensory life, appetites, and aptitudes, including the ability to move from place to place. The human soul was incorporeal. Augustine obtains from Plato his view of the soul as immaterial, without physical dimensions or properties, but as one whole, a creature.[5] But unlike Plato, Augustine did not hold that the soul is divine, in whole or in part, nor did it preexist its conception and birth. It bore the image of God that was intrinsic to mankind's creation.

The *imago Dei*, which human beings possess, was the incorporeality and rationality of the mind, and the *imago* is further evident, Augustine thought, in the way in which it images the triune God—at least Augustine tried to show that, albeit unsuccessfully, at least in his own estimation. The soul forms a component of the human being, "a substance partaking of reason adapted to ruling the body."[6] Being born such a body-soul composite makes one a human being.[7]

---

5. Augustine, *Letters*, vol. 1 in *The Nicene and Post-Nicene Fathers*, ed. Philip Schaff (Grand Rapids: Eerdmans, 1971), 161.

6. Augustine, *On the Catholic and the Manichean Ways of Life*, ed. R. J. Deferrari (Washington, D.C.: Catholic University Press, 1947), 1.4.6.

7. See R. Teste, "Soul," in *Augustine through the Ages*, ed. Allan. D. Fitzgerald (Grand Rapids: Eerdmans, 1999).

Augustine seems to take the view that the soul, not being a body, is more simple than the body, but that this difference is one of degree. The soul does not have a physical presence, yet it has a spiritual location in the body. When we feel pain in a tooth, Augustine says, the whole soul feels it. "But nevertheless, since in the soul it is one thing to be skilful, another to be indolent, another to be intelligent…since cupidity is one thing, fear another, joy another, sadness another; and since things innumerable, and in innumerable ways, are to be found in the nature of the soul…it is manifest that its nature is not simple, but manifold."[8]

So Augustine was an anthropological dualist, and dualism of one kind or another comes to dominate the Christian theological tradition of anthropology. The human being, the body-soul composite, was a divine creation, and so the body is ethically and spiritually good as are physical aspects of the creation. Augustine rejected his earlier Manichaeism in which the body is darkness, not light.

Augustine's Anthropology: A Fuller Picture

To further elucidate Augustine's anthropology, we will look at parts of his best-known writings, the *De Trinitate*, the *Confessions*, the *Anti-Pelagian Writings*, and *The City of God*. In *De Trinitate*, Augustine first develops in eight books his account of the mystery of the Trinity; and from book 9 onward, as we have already noted, he endeavors to find a trinity in human nature. This project is partly in the interest of confirming how we are to understand that human beings are created in the image of God, partly as an apologetic for the Trinity, and (as was frequent with Augustine) partly because of the sheer interest of such an idea. In *De Trinitate*, Augustine offers several attempts of discerning such a trinity in the human mind, rejecting those he regarded as unsuccessful as he proceeds. For example, he explores the thought that "the mind, itself, and the love of it, and the knowledge of it, are three things, and these three are one; and when they are equal they are perfect."[9]

It is not altogether clear how successful he regarded his various attempts to understand the human mind in Trinitarian fashion or whether he became discouraged in his project. Nonetheless, as far as we are concerned,

---

8. Augustine, *On the Trinity*, trans. A. W. Hadden (Edinburgh: T&T Clark, 1873), VI.6.

9. Augustine, *On the Trinity*, IX.4.

his second attempt (book 10) opens another window on his thinking about human nature, an opinion which endured. In understanding the soul with its threefoldness, Augustine distinguishes between "memory, understanding, and will." That is, according to Augustine, the soul comprises these three powers, or sets of powers.[10] For example, the will, one of these powers, "handles those things that are contained in the memory and understanding, whether it refer them to anything further, or rest satisfied with them as an end. For to use, is to take up something into the power of the will; and to enjoy, is to use with joy, not any longer of hope, but of the actual thing. Accordingly, every one who enjoys, uses; for he takes up something into the power of the will, wherein he also is satisfied as with an end."[11] Here Augustine distinguishes between using and enjoying, as he frequently does (cf. his *De Doctrina*).

Augustine emphasizes not just a threeness but also a oneness in the soul. "Memory, understanding, will, are not three lives, but one life; nor three minds, but one mind; it follows certainly that neither are they three substances, but one substance."[12] He places a strong emphasis on the unity of the soul, just as the three Trinitarian persons are yet one God. Memory is mind, and it is also the life of the mind as far as its own powers are concerned, but also in relation to the other powers of the mind. And so it is with the understanding and will. So for Augustine, "memory," "understanding," and "will"—each is the mind, and they each have a relational character to the other two in turn.

> And hence these three are one, in that they are one life, one mind, one essence; and whatever they are severally called in respect to themselves, they are called also together, not plurally, but in the singular number. But they are three, in that wherein they are mutually referred to each other; and if they were not equal, and this not only each to each, but also each to all, they certainly could not mutually contain each other; for not only is each contained by each, but also all by each.[13]

Augustine occasionally refers to the mind as having "faculties," though he does not employ the term in his *De Trinitate*. Furthermore, his

---

10. Augustine, *On the Trinity*, X.11.

11. Augustine, *On the Trinity*, X.11.

12. Augustine, *On the Trinity*, X.11.

13. Augustine, *On the Trinity*, X.11.

terminology varies. For instance, in debating Pelagius's views in *On the Grace of Christ, and on Original Sin* (418), Augustine employs the conceptuality that Pelagius does: the faculties of capacity, volition, and action. Pelagius argues that only the first of these is granted by God and that God gives to human beings a capacity to be righteous. The other faculties—volition, action, and its result—"proceed simply from ourselves" and require no divine help, whereas the faculty of capacity is always assisted by God.[14]

Additionally, besides his own distinctions in the soul of memory, reason, and will, Augustine also uses the biblical language of "heart" and "spirit," which may be used to refer to the soul itself or to the understanding as it consists in reason and memory. In those cases where it is necessary to stress that God so works on men for good or ill, God works on the *heart* or *spirit* of men, who nevertheless act according to their own will. In all this there is no mention of the body. It is in discussing memory that Augustine notes the effects of the body on the soul.

So the basic idea is that the mind consists in three sets of mutually interpenetrating powers. Of these three powers, Augustine has a very rich and full account of the memory in his *Confessions*. It is not simply a memory of facts, but more than this, of skills and habits, of know-how. For Augustine, memory is a vast storehouse, a "palace," as he calls it. Whatever we think about is stored in the memory and called upon or manifested when needed: "When I am in this storehouse, I ask that it produce what I want to recall, and immediately certain things come out; some things require a longer search, and have to be drawn out as it were from more recondite receptacles. Some memories pour out to crowd the mind and, when one is searching and asking for something quite different, leap forward into the centre as if saying 'Surely we are what you want.'"[15]

Memory stores in its "cavern" various categories of things: colors, sounds, the person whose memory it is, and so on. In Augustine's account in the *Confessions*, memory and mind converge or overlap: "This power of memory is great, very great, my God. It is a vast and infinite profundity. Who has plumbed its bottom? This power is that of my mind and is

---

14. Augustine, *On the Grace of Christ, and on Original Sin*, chs. 4 and 5, in *The Anti-Pelagian Writings of St. Augustine*, vol. 5 in *The Nicene and Post-Nicene Fathers*, ed. Philip Schaff (Grand Rapids: Eerdmans, 1971), 218.

15. Augustine, *Confessions*, trans. Henry Chadwick (Oxford: Oxford University Press, 1991), X.viii, 185.

a natural endowment, but I myself cannot grasp the totality of what I am. Is the mind, then, too restricted to compass itself, so that we have to ask what is which it fails to grasp? How then can it fail to grasp it? The question moves me to great astonishment. Amazement grips me."[16]

But there is more. We memorize not only facts but how to argue, how to debate, to write, all the "innumerable principles and laws of numbers and dimensions." But "none of them have been impressed on memory through any bodily sense-perception."[17] Perhaps Augustine has Plato's *Meno* in mind. He explores the connection between memory and the affections. My remembering my gladness may make me sad, and we experience fear, cupidity, and so on. "We call memory itself the mind. Since that is the case, what is going on when, in gladly remembering a past sadness, my mind is glad and my memory sad? My mind is glad for the fact that gladness is in it, but memory is not saddened by the fact that regret is in it. Surely this does not mean that memory is independent of the mind. Who could say that? No doubt, then, memory is, as it were, the stomach of the mind, whereas gladness and sadness are like sweet and bitter food."[18]

One thing emerges from this fascinating set of reflections on memory in book 10 of the *Confessions*: memory is close to actually being the mind itself. Memory, with all its layers and places, is mind. If so, the mind may be one thing in that it does not have separable parts, but there is incredible complexity in its workings.

To complete this sketch we must consider the will, the *voluntas*. We can find discussion of this also in the *Confessions*. When Augustine considered his state prior to conversion, the problem he then faced was not the mind or the intellect, but the will. As far as his intellect was concerned, the problems about God's nature and the origin of evil, problems that beset him after his break with Manichaeism, were solved. The problem was not a willingness to believe, but his will in a deeper sense. This is how Augustine describes his own will during the time leading up to his conversion:

> The consequence of a distorted will is passion. By servitude to passion, habit is formed, and habit to which there is no resistance becomes necessity. By these links, as it were, connected one to another (hence

---

16. Augustine, *Confessions*, X.x, 187.

17. Augustine, *Confessions*, X.xii, 190.

18. Augustine, *Confessions*, X.xiv, 191.

my term a chain), a harsh bondage held me under restraint. The new will, which was beginning to be within me, a will to serve you freely and to enjoy you, God, the only sure source of pleasure, was yet strong enough to conquer my older will, which had the strength of old habit. So my two wills, one old, the other new, were in conflict with another, and their discord robbed my soul of all concentration.[19]

In this state of conflicting wills, as Augustine explains, "I no longer had my usual excuse to explain why I did not yet despise the world and serve you [Lord], namely, that my perception of the truth was uncertain. By now I was indeed quite sure about it. Yet I was still bound down to the earth. I was refusing to become your soldier, and I was afraid of being rid of all my burdens as I ought to have been at the prospect of carrying them."[20]

Augustine reflects further on his divided will, his "two wills," and what was needed to resolve the tension, indignation, and distress of this situation. To arrive at the destination—that is, to resolve the conflict—"the one necessary condition, which meant not only going but at once arriving there, was to have a will to go—provided only that the will was strong and unqualified."[21] Augustine goes on to describe what he calls the monstrosity of having an indecisive will with respect to God. The mind, in the form of the will, commands that it should will, and yet it does not perform what it commands.[22] If the will were complete, the mind would not need to command the will to exist, for it would already exist.

So in this state of a morbid condition of the mind (as Augustine describes it), the *voluntas* is divided between having the creature and the Creator as its end. As he deliberated serving "my Lord God" in this situation of bondage and conflict, Augustine was neither wholly willing nor wholly unwilling. Augustine took up Paul's letter to the Romans, read verses 13–14 in chapter 13, and said, "I neither wished nor needed to read further.... All the shadows of doubt were dispelled."[23]

More on the will in its fallenness and restoration can be found in Augustine's *City of God*. In chapter 11 of book 14, he deals with the uprightness

---

19. Augustine, *Confessions*, VIII.v, 140.

20. Augustine, *Confessions*, VIII.v, 140.

21. Augustine, *Confessions*, VIII.viii, 147.

22. Augustine, *Confessions*, VIII.ix, 147–48.

23. Augustine, *Confessions*, VIII.xii, 153.

in which man was created: "upright, and so well-willed: otherwise he could not have been upright. And so this good will was God's work, man being therewith created."[24] The good will in question was created. The evil will, when it occurred, was a defect rather than a positive act, a falling away. As created, it was morally and spiritually free. God endowed mankind with that freedom, but it was lost and can only be restored or recovered by God Himself. Christ is both a savior and liberator. He "makes free."[25]

So the fall, as Augustine understands it, brought a change in mankind's outlook at a deep level, reverberating through all that men and women do. It changes the *voluntas* and so alters man's nature.[26] This is the will in a basic, foundational sense, that which expresses the "set" of the entire person. An upright will is *caritas*, love of the good, while a perverse will, a fallen will, is *cupiditas*, selfishness, love of what is bad. So in Augustine's thinking, there come to be two cities, with two sorts of citizens.[27] Those possessing an upright will depart from what is evil, which such a will hates, which is fear. Those who love the good desire and enjoy it. The will, its freedom or bondage, affects the entirety of a person's conative and emotional life. Insofar as the person wills what is evil, that person's love will be evil; and if he wills what is good, then it is good.[28]

> But evil began within them [Adam and Eve] secretly at first, to draw them into open disobedience afterwards. For there would have been no evil work, but there was an evil will before it: and what could begin this evil will but pride, that is "the beginning of all sin" (Ecclus x.13). What is pride but a perverse desire of height, in forsaking Him to whom the soul ought solely to cleave, as the beginning thereof, to make himself seem its own beginning. This is when it likes itself too well, or when it so loves itself that it will abandon that unchangeable Good which ought to be more delightful to it than itself. This defect now is voluntary.... The evil therefore, that is, this transgression, was not done by such as were evil before.[29]

---

24. Augustine, *City of God*, trans. John Healey, ed. R. V. G. Tasker (London: J. M. Dent & Sons, 1945), XIV.xi.

25. Augustine, *City of God*, XIV.xi.

26. Augustine, *City of God*, XIV.xiii.

27. Augustine, *City of God*, XIV.xxvii.

28. Augustine, *City of God*, XIV.xiii.

29. Augustine, *City of God*, XIV.xiii.

So this original transgression was evidence of a will that was basically bent on serving the creature rather than the Creator, and all particular choices thereafter had that character, however they each presented themselves to the agent as being a good. The fall has a ratchet-like character, which means that neither it nor its effects can be undone, except through the operation of the grace of God through Christ. Augustine does not focus on the intellect, but on the will operating in this basic God-defying manner. The intellect was fully functioning, but man rebelled by the misuse of his will.[30]

It is noteworthy that while downplaying the intellect's place in the fall of created human nature, Augustine gives prominence to the emotions, to love and hatred:

> But the quality of man's will is of some moment; for if it be bad, so are all those motions of the soul; if good, they are both blameless and praiseworthy. For there is a will in them all. Nay, they are all direct wills. What is desire, and joy, but a will consenting to that which we affect? And what is fear, and sorrow, but a will contrary to what we like.... Whereof a man that makes God and not man the steersman of his life, ought to love good, and consequently to hate evil. And because none is evil by nature, but all by vice, he that lives after God's love owes his full hate unto the evil; not to hate the man for his vice, nor to love the vice for the man, but to hate the vice and love the man: for the vice being cured, he shall find no object of his hate, but all for his love.[31]

So the fallen understanding is an understanding that is "set" in this rebellious way. And in regeneration, the understanding is "reset," though the effects of this resetting are only partial in this life. Everything turns on the state of the *voluntas*, spiritually speaking. It is central to freedom, grace, and salvation. Only the grace of God can renew the will, preceding all human efforts. Nevertheless, Augustine insists that regeneration does not issue in a state of sinless perfection. This is a major theme in his writings against the Pelagians. See, for example, *On Man's Perfection in Righteousness* (415).[32]

---

30. For a discussion of the will in Augustine's sense, though one that does not appear to appreciate the full significance of the fall, see Albrecht Dihle, *The Theory of Will in Classical Antiquity* (Berkeley: University of California Press, 1982).

31. Augustine, *City of God*, XIV.vi.

32. Augustine, *The Anti-Pelagian Writings of St. Augustine*, vol. 5 in *The Nicene and Post-Nicene Fathers*, ed. Philip Schaff (Grand Rapids: Eerdmans, 1971), 176.

Augustine distills from such accounts the fourfold state of mankind. At creation, Adam was created in a state of perfection, but one that he could depart from, for it was possible for him to sin. After the fall, mankind is in a state in which it is impossible not to sin. Upon regeneration, he is capable of not sinning. Finally, in the beatific vision, he is incapable of sinning. This way of thinking became very influential in Reformed anthropology, as we will see.

Finally is Augustine's understanding of the place of the emotions in the mind. In several of his writings, Augustine is concerned with the Stoics, particularly with their claim that the distinguishing mark of a wise man is to have his emotions tempered by reason. And so the wise man is not subject to the emotions (or passions, affects, or affections—these terms appear to be used interchangeably). The position of the Platonists and Aristotelians, who reckon that the wise man can be affected by the emotions, is contrasted with the Stoics. "But others (as the Stoics) exempt a wise man from any touch of those passions,"[33] though in fact Augustine thinks that differences between the Stoics and other philosophers on this point are merely verbal. All sorts of mental perturbances, part of the mind, occur, and the Christian is charged with subjecting his whole mind to God: "Our doctrine inquires not so much whether one be angry, but wherefore; why he is sad, not whether he be sad; and so of fear."[34]

Here he is in one of his tractates on the gospel of St. John:

Away with the reasons of philosophers who assert that a wise man is not affected by perturbations…. It is plain that the mind of a Christian may be troubled, not by misery, but by pity; he may fear lest men be lost to Christ; he may sorrow when one is being lost; he may have ardent desire to gain men to Christ; he may be filled with joy when such is being done; he may have fear of falling away himself from Christ; he may sorrow over his estrangement from Christ; he may be earnestly desirous of reigning with Christ, and he may be rejoicing in the hope that such fellowship with Christ will yet be his lot. These are certainly four of what they call perturbations—fear and sorrow, love and gladness. And Christian minds may have sufficient cause to feel them, and evidence their dissent from the Stoic philosophers, and all resembling them: who indeed, just as they esteem truth to be vanity,

---

33. Augustine, *City of God*, IX.iv.
34. Augustine, *City of God*, I.256.

regard also insensibility as soundness; not knowing that a man's mind, like the limbs of his body, is only the more hopelessly diseased when it has lost even the feeling of pain.[35]

So, in summary, we see that Augustine's picture of the mind is rather complex. There is a basic Trinitarian pattern of the powers of the soul, and the memory plays a central role as an aspect of the understanding. It is not simply receptive but makes an active contribution to the understanding and the will. There are passions, which are activities of the will that Augustine does not downplay; but he is concerned to point out that they are governed by the will, which affects "the motions of the soul." We may see from this that overall he must be using "will" in two senses: one in the sense of choice between alternatives, and the other in the willedness of the fall and the recreatedness of the will in regeneration. This second is of importance because of the special place that Augustine has for it in the fall. The fall was not the result of a choice between alternatives, like that presented by a fork in the road. It is the choice between cleaving to God and departing from Him, a choice made by one who has uprightness. This choice led to a state of unfreedom. The will, in turning away from God, leaves mankind in a state of turnedness, affecting the entirety of the mind, in particular all future choices, if and until God in His mercy regenerates. In the case of everyday choices, the evil will, enslaved by the fall and its consequences, is nevertheless the power to choose between alternatives. And the Stoic dismissal of the emotions is foolish.

Aristotle and Hylomorphism

Aristotle adds detail and nuance to Plato's account. It was not exactly simply a detail to maintain that the soul is the form of the body, a doctrine that proved somewhat pliable subsequently. But he is much more sophisticated than Plato, such as in his understanding of dispositions and his distinction between potentiality and actuality, which extends powers beyond their initial capacity to change. These are potentialities not only to change but to become, to develop. Hylomorphism, the doctrine that the soul is the form of certain matter, the human body, has to do with actuality and potentiality

---

35. Augustine, *Tractate LX, on John 13:21.* Vol. 4 of *A Select Library of the Nicene and Post-Nicene Fathers of the Christian Church* (repr., Grand Rapids: Eerdmans 1994).

as applied to the soul. The form is what makes this body to be a living soul. So there is no separate identity of the soul, only in reference to the ensouling of certain matter. It is clear that Aristotle's account is what we might call "naturalistic monism"—not materialism as such, because it is not reductionistic, but close, for the soul is part of the form of the human body so that nonhumans like sheep do not have such a soul as humans have but have a soul of a lesser kind.

So just as the Platonic preexistence of the soul is ruled out by Aristotle's account, so is the immortality of the soul. This is natural science, the result of Aristotle's sharp-eyed observation and conceptual creativity taking Plato's faculties as their starting point. Form and matter are inseparable aspects of the same thing, including the same human being. The form of a human being is its faculties. Therefore, there can be neither a soul in separation from the living body nor a living body in separation from its soul. The living body is therefore the only expression of the faculties of the soul. The one exception is thought itself, which does not require a body for its discharge, not even the brain, which Aristotle did not think of as the particular source of thinking. So the study of the faculties is the study of animal and human life in their various forms: vegetative, sensory, and rational. All human activities are derivable from these. They are hierarchically arranged with the higher containing the lower. Later on we will see that Aquinas took this hylomorphism as both a stimulus and a challenge.

There are only a few references to Aristotle in the writings of Augustine. In the *Confessions*, he writes of reading Aristotle's *Categories*, and "Aristotelian" is used adjectivally and unspecifically in his *City of God*. Also, in the meantime much of Aristotle had been absorbed into Neoplatonism, particularly by Iambilichus (245–325). This relative scarcity of reference to Aristotle is because only a few of his writings were translated into Latin in Augustine's day.

The influence of Aristotle on the faculties of the soul and the relation between mind and body on Christian thought had to await the translation of his writings by Arabic scholars. This, the recovery of Aristotle, came roughly between 1150 and 1250. Aristotle's outlook was appropriated by Albert the Great (1206–1280) and his star pupil, Aquinas. Aquinas became dominant in the medieval period and the baseline for all subsequent discussion. William of Ockham and Duns Scotus must be understood as reactions to and modifications of the prevailing intellectualism and realism of Aquinas and his immediate legacy, which we now turn to.

Aquinas, a Modified Aristotle

The identity and powers of things that grow and replicate was discussed in the relation between form and matter. This made for a more complex and nuanced account of human nature than the sharp contrast in Plato between spirit and matter. As we have noted, Aristotelians thought of the human being as matter that is informed by the soul, just as a sheep is matter informed by a sheep soul, the particular characteristics of sheep that inform matter in a certain way and are replicated in their reproduction. So the human soul animates a body, which has characteristic properties. The soul is the substantial form of the body, animating it in its humanness and animating *this* body as *my* body. When the sculptor sculpts a lion from the stone, this becomes its form, but an accidental form, since the stone could have as easily been formed as a lamb. Saying that the soul is a substantial, or essential, form means that it could not but be a human body that its soul informs and must be such a body. The body, though depending on animation by the soul, and not vice versa, is as essential to the human being as the soul is. This idea of the soul as the body's essential form is important in the work of "Christianising" Aristotle, a work begun by Albert the Great but more especially by Aquinas.

When this unity of soul and body begins to come apart, as in the loss of faculties in old age and finally in death, the animation that is characteristically human starts to leave the body. And in its decline into death, the human being may become something more and more solely physical, though no doubt the object of the affection and care of others. Finally, it becomes a corpse.

For Aquinas, the human soul, having sensitive as well as intellectual powers, retains these as potencies when the body dies, and its being an *essential* form ensures a resurrection not only of a body but of the same body. So in death, though the body decays, its soul retains its integrity, and so we may say that it is essential to the bodiless soul *to have* informed a body, and it is also necessary, by a kind of teleological necessity, that it *will* inform a resurrected body identical to that body informed prior to its death and dissolution. But the soul after the death of the body and prior to resurrection must be an "incomplete" substance, an essential aspect of it having been lost.

To say that the soul informs the human body is to claim that it is pervasive in the development of the human being, body and soul. So "soul" has a broader connotation in Aristotle and in Aquinas than in Platonism, which conceives of it as the "motor" of the body in which the soul has become imprisoned. For Aristotle, the human soul, as the body's form, animates its vegetative and sensory life as well as the muscular and nervous changes necessary for the successful performance of skills and routines and upholds a rational or intellectual life that ensures its immortality. No doubt this hylomorphism seemed to carry the prospect of an attractive (though perplexing) account of what has more recently been called the biblical picture of the human being as a "psychosomatic unity."[36]

So there came to be different ways of interpreting the expression "the soul is (nothing other than) the form of the body." Aristotle, untroubled by the demands of providing an account of the resurrection of the body, may interpret the claim as a distinction internal to the human being. The soul is the principle of the human being's animation as a human being, no more and no less. By contrast, Aquinas seems to interpret it more as "the soul has the role of animating the body." When it is distinct from the body, as in the death of the body, its body-animating powers "hibernate." They are retained as sets of dispositions of the soul, which survives. In this state of loss, the soul carries the identity of the person until resurrection.

The resurrection is not a liberation from the "prison house" of the body. Rather, the default position is the human being ensouled with a full range of powers, intellectual, volitional, and sensory. Death is a violent disruption of that unity, but full humanity is resumed at the resurrection, when the soul takes possession of what Paul calls a "spiritual body." After death and before resurrection, the persisting self is in an anomalous state awaiting the resurrection of the body. Thus, in the resurrection the person again becomes completely human, which is not the case in the intermediate state.

---

36. John Cooper notes that "a completely consistent Aristotelianism is untenable for Christians, however. For Aristotle's soul is only the form of the body and not a substance as such. Therefore it cannot survive death as an individual entity. At most its rational capacity might be reassimilated into the eternal universal reason like a drop of water into the ocean." Cooper goes on to say that Aquinas adapted Aristotle's position in a dualistic direction. John W. Cooper, *Body, Soul and Life Everlasting* (Grand Rapids: Eerdmans, 2000), 13.

Nevertheless, it seems that the theologians to be considered later were not too troubled with these particular problems of loss and continuing identity, having confidence in the power and purpose of God "who raises the dead."

So being embodied is essential to being a *human being*, even though it is not essential for a *soul*. Thus the body's death is metaphysically possible, and then the soul lives on as incomplete, "a surviving mental remnant of a person" of the previous body-soul unity, in Peter Geach's memorable phrase.[37] The soul has lost the body and is incapacitated in those matters for which embodiment is necessary.

Incidentally, though sometimes Christian theology is said to have been taken over by the categories of Greek philosophy, we can see from this discussion that this is a rather loose charge. We are outlining a case where the Christian doctrines of creation, human moral accountability, and bodily resurrection exert their own influence on the character and shape of the philosophical anthropology that Christian thinkers have seen fit to appropriate, even if they have inherited this anthropology from the pagan world.

As we have seen, Augustine thought of the mind as including the memory and intellect, the will, and the affections. I think it is fair to say that this arrangement "hardened" through the advent of Aristotelian ideas in Christian theology through scholastics such as Aquinas. It hardened in the sense that the powers of the soul become grouped variously, with greater definiteness. It is noteworthy that in the *Summa Theologiae*, which we are to consider next, on the frequent occasions when Aquinas cites Augustine, he almost invariably defers to him as a theologian in matters of theology. But Aristotle influences his account of human nature.

It's a general view that there is no human intellect as there is a liver or lungs or brain in a human body. It is not an organ or instrument; rather, it is the possessor of collective powers related in incredibly complex ways between itself and the memory, will, and affections based on an awareness of the types of activity of the soul. Reason in a comprehensive sense, being the only soulish faculty that does not require a body, becomes, in Aquinas's account, the bearer of God's image. The intellect includes activities such as counting and assimilating information, inferring (that is, drawing conclusions of various kinds), making plans, and judging (that is, accepting or rejecting various proposals, either that occur to oneself or are made

---

37. Peter Geach, *God and the Soul* (London: Routledge and Kegan Paul, 1969), 22.

by other people). Willing includes the activities of desiring to act, such as intending, choosing, and being strong-willed, or weak-willed. In this dispersal of the activities of the soul into various faculties, the basicness that the *voluntas* had for Augustine as the basic affective and volitional center of the soul is rather masked in Aquinas.

One piece of evidence for this hardening in the Aristotelian way is that the names of these activities become fixed as *faculties* of the soul. They are termed "intellect," "will," and so on. One consequence is that as the appetite for making distinctions grew in scholasticism, the question of the relation between the faculties and the answers offered were in turn debated, sometimes fiercely so, as the activities of the soul entered into theological issues. The temptation to treat these faculties as what might be called "subsouls," or, as *homunculi*, was not always resisted.

The basic pattern for Aquinas and those who followed him is to think of the intellect as hierarchically superior to the will, and the affections as arising from the will and including the impact of bodily states on the mind, producing fear or love, for example. Intellect is not confined to the operations of pure reason but to all the procedures of ratiocination, which encompasses whatever mental factors, normal or abnormal, contribute to a human being addressing a particular situation.

Another general feature that becomes prominent with the influence of Aristotle is that reality as a whole, but particularly human life, is thought of in purposive terms. The soul operates in a means-end way. It is not a machine. Possessing intentions to achieve ends is basic to its operations. It is not as though Augustine thought the soul was mechanistic, but the teleological character of the soul becomes more pronounced with the medievals. This is because the faculty psychologists adopted Aristotle's distinction between theoretical and practical reason as distinct ways of behaving within the creation, which was also ordered in teleological fashion by God in His providence. This has a bearing in determining what a person ought, morally and spiritually, to do or forbear. The theoretical reason is concerned with what to believe; the practical reason, with what to do. The soul has theoretical goals, for it seeks to understand the world outside and within itself. And a person takes means to do this—cognitive means, for instance—by making judgments about what is around him, or what the author of the book he is reading means. So the influence here is on understanding inputs of sensory and other information.

We may understand things for their own sake and also as a guide to our actions and their goals. The practical intellect, or reason, is concerned not with, or not only with, what is true or what it is reasonable to believe about the world but with changing the world, with furthering human action within it. If, for instance, I am presently in place A and want to get to place B, getting to place B is (in this instance) my end or goal. How do I best proceed? Walk? Take some other mode of travel? Here I am appraising possible means to achieve that end. And the end may itself be a proximate means to a more significant end, and so on.

This teleological approach has a good fit with the Christian religion, which portrays believers in Christ as being on a journey to the heavenly city, whose maker and builder is God. How are Christians to equip themselves? First, by using their theoretical reason to give them knowledge from the study of divine revelation and the teaching of the church. Who is God, and what are His revealed character and purposes? And then, a practical question, what does He require of me? In what ways am I to change? The medievals debated these questions. There were debates regarding the extent to which theology is basically a theoretical or practical endeavor. Is its aim simply or chiefly to bring into order the revealed truth of God, which comes to us in a series of documents written over many centuries? Has it as its chief aim the increase of knowledge of that revelation, and of delighting in it? Or is it concerned with living well for God's glory? The first is a theoretical activity; the second, practical. Each emphasis can be found in medieval theology and among the Reformed theologians we shall cover.

So the medieval Christian thinkers modified Platonic dualism, giving greater emphasis to the body and with the integration of body and soul. The human being, body and soul, was created good, and even "very good." The account of the creation implied some kind of dualism. "And the LORD God formed man of the dust of the ground, and breathed into his nostrils the breath of life; and the man became a living being" (Gen. 2:7). So man had a God-given body, and whatever transformed that body into a living soul was equally God given, and so good. But sin has entered the world, and the result of it is disorderly effects on the human being, soul and body.

Aquinas on Human Nature

So we now turn more particularly to the ideas and writings of Aquinas on human nature. We will concentrate on what is in effect a fairly self-contained treatment of human nature within his great (though unfinished) *Summa Theologiae*, in effect his systematic theology, written in Paris in 1269 to 1272. As part of this we will note what he has to say about the conscience, about which Aristotle says nothing.

The style of the *Summa Theologiae* is very different from Augustine's writings. It is more disciplined, orderly, and thorough in its approach. It embodies the style of the *disputatio*, and indeed it helped to form that style of education. It has the following character. A topic is introduced by a question and an assertion (or assertions) offered as the answer. Often these are supported by authorities such as Scripture and doctors of the church, prominent among whom was Augustine. These are followed by counterassertions, often introduced by the phrase "on the other hand." This opposing view may also refer to Scripture and include the citing of various theological authorities. Then follows Aquinas's resolution of the differences by argument and appeal to Scripture; theological authorities, notably Augustine; and philosophical authorities, notably Aristotle, referred to as "the Philosopher."

The reason for considering Aquinas is that according to a growing number of scholars, including John Patrick Donnelly, Christopher Cleveland, and Richard Muller, the influences on the Reformed orthodox were overwhelmingly Thomist when compared with other influences such as those of Duns Scotus or William of Ockham.[38] The Reformed orthodox proposed modifications to Aquinas, but he was the dominant influence on them, as we will see later.

We will first concentrate on what Aquinas has to say in *Summa Theologiae*, the first part, questions 75–89, which is sometimes referred to as a treatise on human nature; then, we will consider the conscience and finally say a little on the passions, which Aquinas discusses in a separate treatise.

Aquinas begins by noting that human nature is a composite of body and soul, with the emphasis (for the theologian) on the soul, its essence, powers, and operations. The soul is the principle of operation of the body. The principle of life of the body cannot therefore be the body itself, but the soul, which is the first principle of life, another kind of mover, something incorporeal which moves the body. The soul is "subsistent"—that is, a substance,

---

38. John Patrick Donnelly, "Calvinist Thomism," *Viator* 7 (1976): 441–55; Richard A. Muller, "'Not Scotist': Understandings of Being, Univocity, and Analogy in Early-Modern Reformed Thought," *Reformation & Renaissance Review* 14, no. 2 (2012): 127–50; Christopher Cleveland, *Thomism in John Owen* (Burlington: Ashgate, 2013).

quoting Augustine.[39] Therefore, the intellectual principle which we call the mind, or the intellect, is a particular substance, a *hypostasis*, a human soul, which is a soul with certain intellectual and sensory powers, and it is the form of a body. This is shown by the fact that the soul has sensations.

This "absolute form," incorruptible but united to a corruptible body, is affected by the fall. The soul has different effects on the human body, the primary principle being its nourishment, sensation, movement, and understanding.[40] A man understands and senses, for example, that he has a body, and it is by his intellect that he understands. So a human being has a body and a soul.

The powers of the soul are divided into sensitive and intellectual powers by which we understand ourselves and the world. The soul itself acts via these various powers, which are distinguishable from each other by their various characteristics and especially by the objects of the various activities. So the vegetative activities of the body are distinct from the intellectual activities of the soul. The soul senses *with* the body, as for example when it feels pain or hunger. It senses *without* the body, as it feels sad or joyful upon hearing something. And the soul senses *apart* from the body, as when it makes some arithmetical or astronomical calculation, for example. And the powers remain active in the soul after the death of the body, though in a reduced way. Things like the memory, some experience of joy and sadness, the calculations, but not of course the bodily senses, may remain until the resurrection of the body.

The intellect moves the body via the *appetites*. Besides the sensitive powers of the soul and the working of the five senses, the soul possesses intellectual powers; and powers are distinguishable by their different objectives. Appetitive power can be classified as partly intellectual and partly sensitive. Aquinas notes that Augustine places the will in the mind, while Aristotle places it in the reason.[41] In Aquinas's view, passions belong to the will. Besides this, the soul's powers can be classified as active and passive. Each soul has a separate intellect. Memory is part of the mind. Aquinas

---

39. Augustine, *On the Trinity*, X.7.

40. Aristotle, *De Anima*, ed. Christopher Shields (Oxford: Oxford University Press, 2016), ii.2.

41. Aristotle, *De Anima*, iii.9.

here is thinking of Augustine's distinction between memory, understanding, and will.

Finally, for Aquinas, the human will is a rational power, and it is always necessarily voluntary, and its activity is the opposite from acting under coercion. Is the will opposed to necessity as such? Aquinas answers this question by noting we must bear in mind that necessity is used in various senses. We may say, for example, that a horse is necessary for a journey, meaning causally necessary for taking this particular journey considered as an end, what Aquinas calls the "necessity of end." This latter is consistent with the operation of the will. He cites Augustine's support.[42] Aquinas's view is that natural necessity does not take away the liberty of the will. The will does not desire of necessity since the last end is the result of the will, the first principles of which are contingent. But certain things are necessarily connected with the last end, with God, in whom alone is all happiness.

So we act *sub specie bono*, what we take to be the good, which judgment may in fact be right or misinformed. And what we attempt we may fail to achieve, but we nevertheless hope to succeed in what is for us desirable, leading perhaps to satisfaction or disappointment at frustration. There may be alternative courses of action to what is desired, means to the end, which we are aware of. We are advised which course to take by our understanding, by what is thought to be the best. Such actions are expressions of our wills. People do what they think is desirable to do, what is good for them. So willing and understanding are inseparable in action, will being an operation of the understanding, the two being in practice interconnected. We don't reflect with our minds and then will as a separate operation; rather, in getting our minds clear we are at the same time forming desires. So our choices are the effect of how we think and reflect our characters, preferences, and weaknesses. It makes no sense for A not to want what A takes here and now to be good. This is the teleological character of the working of the practical reasoning.[43] The good is ultimately the goodness of God, which is God Himself. Of course the process is not infallible, as we are all liable to errors of various kinds. Sin is the neglect of eternal things and seeking solely after temporal things, which are means, as if they are

---

42. Augustine, *City of God*, V.10. (I.155): "If anything is necessary, it is not voluntary."

43. Aquinas, *Summa Theologiae*, various trans. (New York: McGraw-Hill Book Company, 1967–1980), Ia 82.

ultimate ends, upending the God-given structure of means and ends.[44] So the will follows the intellect and is informed by various habits, either virtuous or vicious. The habit which perfects the will is charity. Relatively, the will may be higher than the intellect, since at times the will may have in view a nobler end than the intellect does. Maybe this is one place in which "will" has the connotation of the Augustinian *voluntas*.

Without possessing free will, an appetitive power that is necessarily voluntary, then commands or prohibitions would be in vain. Human beings act from making judgments, judging involving the will. Nonetheless, Aquinas notes that God is the first cause of all actions, of both the natural and the voluntary, "by moving voluntary causes." "[God] does not deprive their acts of being voluntary, but rather he is the cause of this very thing in them. He operates in each thing according to its own nature. It is natural for us to have free will, but the action of free will is not a natural habit. Man is said to have lost free will by falling into sin, not as to natural liberty, which is freedom from coercion, but as regards freedom from fault and unhappiness."[45]

As Robert Pasnau says when commenting on the *voluntas*, Aquinas gives the will a real role in the process of choice.[46] It has long-term dispositions that govern the person day to day. These are subject to higher-order aims or projects that shape us. The will modifies the agent's dispositions or habits, supplanting them with other habits. Reason may tell us to do X, but the *voluntas* will decline it in favor of other objectives or ends. Reason does not operate *de novo* in this situation, but one set of second-order dispositions are (partly) overcome by another set. They displace what was present, forcing it out of its central position. Or they make reason operate in a new way. The theory of action connects with morality and spirituality. Crucial dispositions are capable of modification by the will. Perhaps Pasnau's understanding of "reason" here is better seen as the original moral outlook of the unfallen race.[47]

---

44. See Brian Davies, *Aquinas* (London: Continuum, 2002), 98.

45. Aquinas, *Summa Theologiae*, Ia 85, 109.

46. Robert Pasnau, *Aquinas on Human Nature* (Cambridge: Cambridge University Press, 2008), 228.

47. See on God and theistic determinism, Pasnau, *Aquinas on Human Nature*, 229–31.

Of particular interest is what Aquinas has to say regarding *synderesis*, conscience.[48] This is a notable insertion into Aristotle's outlook of a topic on which he is silent. But this addition is required by the teaching of the New Testament on the conscience, which Aquinas follows closely. He is particularly concerned to categorize it anthropologically and argues that it is a habit, though a habit of a particular sort. *Synderesis* always incites to the good (as the agent perceives it). Citing Augustine, that the judgment assists virtue by the provision of unchangeable rules, Aquinas takes this to be a reference to *synderesis* being higher than the reason, as some have thought, such as Alexander of Hales (1185–1245), whom Aquinas cites. So the conscience is not a power, like the will, but a habit by which we judge the results of our reasoning. The judgments of *synderesis*, the conscience, concern the working of the practical reason; and it is in this connection that *synderesis* incites a person to good (as the agent understands it to be). So it is a special natural habit, a sort of habit of the second order that judges what we have discovered about ourselves. So the conscience cannot be a power, since conscience can be put to one side or overruled; but it applies assessments of what we know we have done or would have done if permitted. And it may act by binding an agent to acts of a certain sort, or freeing him from doing an action, to rebuke, to excuse, or to accuse.

Aquinas regards the passions of the soul, discussed in *Summa Theologiae* II.1.22–48, as the product of the appetitive intellect. Each passion has an object—that is, an intentional object—that makes it the passion it is. So fear is not simply a feeling, but a feeling regarding some real or imagined state of affairs, and so there is a difference between the fear that the dog will bite, and the fear that I have lost my wallet. Each has a different object, generating different fears in each case. The differences in these fears are the products of different beliefs about real (or imagined) fearful states of affairs. In Aquinas's view, such fear is the product of the sensory appetite, not the intellect, which simply indicates a state of affairs that is to be shunned. However, this does not mean that we cannot have passions that we cannot know the reason. He notes the view of the Peripatetics—that is, Aristotelians—that the passions, being the movements of the sensitive appetites, are good when controlled by the reason, and evil when not controlled. The passions are not *per se* diseased, as the Stoics held. Passions

---

48. Aquinas, *Summa Theologiae*, Ia 79.

are not diseased except when not controlled by reason, and so what matters in their evaluation is not their strength or intensity but whether or not they are under such control. When they are contrary to reason, the passions of the soul are inclined to sin; but when controlled by reason, they are inclined to virtue.

We will see later that the Reformed orthodox will want to finesse this to take a fuller account of the infection of the reason itself by sin. For Aquinas, insofar as the passions are controlled by the reason, the good of the act is increased, citing Psalm 83:3. Passion may be a sign of the intensity of the commitment to a good course of action, one guided by good reason. But the goodness or otherwise of a passion is not dependent on its intensity or the lack of it, but on the firmness of the intellectual resolve to a good course of action. So while he may be intellectualist in his general approach, Aquinas nevertheless holds that along with the reason there is the effect of the intensity of the will as shown by the intensity of the sensible appetite.

Other Medieval Influences

Aquinas wrote in the thirteenth century and ushered in medieval scholasticism. Between his death and the start of the Reformation, other intellectual streams are evident, all subordinate to Aquinas in their influence, as already mentioned. To fill out the picture and to mark scholasticism's move into a more speculative phase, we must glance at these. William of Ockham (1285–1347), in accordance with his nominalism, was critical of Aquinas's realism. Ockham thinks of the faculties of the soul as actual states, not potential states. All the faculties "are identical with themselves and with the essence of the soul."[49] Each is nothing but a role that the soul takes on. So unlike Aquinas, for Ockham the soul is not distinct from its faculties. Hence there is in Ockham an emphasis on the oneness of the soul. For him, talk of the faculties as separate is simply nonliteral. They are not distinct powers, not even different modes, but are rather different "lenses" through which we refer to the soul, a single soul which has different roles. This is an example of Ockham's intellectual parsimony, and also that of Duns Scotus (1265/66–1308), who was more speculative than Aquinas, who placed emphasis on the will, choice, and possibility, divine and human, and who influenced some of the Reformed.

---

49. Dominik Perler, ed., *The Faculties* (Oxford: Oxford University Press, 2015), 115.

Perhaps of more interest for the chapters which are to follow is the work of Francisco Suarez (1548–1617), a Jesuit and thus part of the Counter-Reformation. His career was contemporaneous with the second-generation Reformers, and he commented on the early Reformers, such as Luther. In turn, his work is cited by the Reformed orthodox. Besides his work *Disputationes Metaphysicae* (1597), he also wrote a commentary on Aristotle's *De Anima* (1621). In it, Suarez is critical of Ockham, taking an opposite view from him on the soul's unity as the basis for the faculties and rather stressing the reality and separateness of the faculties. He does not mean by this that people possess two or more souls, but that there are separate parts of the soul. The faculties are hierarchically arranged in order to effect certain purposes in the life of the soul. The faculties are caused to be by the soul, on which they continue to depend. So the will is separate from the intellect, and this is shown, for example, that in the case of the (free) will, in a given situation and at a given instant, it is free to choose A or B, or A and not-A. As Suarez puts it when discussing free will in his commentary on the *De Anima*, "Moreover this freedom consists in this, namely, that a power can issue an act or not issue the act, once all the requisites for acting have been posited."[50] Those requisites include the deliverances of the intellect and the senses and anything else that is required for the agent to act. This anticipates Jesuit and Remonstrant views of freedom, often said to be Scotist in origin.

But in general, the bulk of the Reformed orthodox worked in the trajectory of Plato-Augustine-Aristotle-Aquinas. They were educated in this tradition, but there were several other reasons why they found this general orientation congenial, as we will see in due course.

---

50. Francisco Suarez, *De Anima*, in vol. 3 of *Opera Omnia* (Madrid: Fundacion Xavier Zubiri, 1991), disp. 12, q. 2. The translation is by Sydney Penner, www.sydneypenner.ca/suartr .shtml. Accessed January 2018.

CHAPTER 2

The Anthropology of Calvin and Vermigli

I have chosen Calvin and Vermigli not because they were forerunners in the Reformation, two ahead of the pack. They were part of the Reformation. Others of their generation such as Bullinger and Bucer and Zanchius could have figured. John Calvin is perhaps the more foundational character, but Peter Martyr Vermigli was his contemporary, with whom Calvin came to have friendly relations. Each were indebted to the late medieval world—Calvin through his education in philosophy and law, and with it the influence on him of the Platonism of the Renaissance. Vermigli was a scholastically trained Augustinian who broke with Rome later in life when a mature scholar, whereas Calvin was younger when he gave his allegiance to the Reformed.

John Calvin's Anthropology

John Calvin (1509–1564) shows his indebtedness to a Platonized account of the soul. Although educated in philosophy, he was later attracted to the Renaissance, publishing a critical commentary on Seneca's *De Clementia*.[1] He may have taken on elements of Platonism in this period, or from his later study of Augustine.[2] Calvin has a more qualified view of Aristotle than Vermigli, as we will see. He shows indebtedness to Stoicism even in a context such as divine providence in which he condemns Stoic fatalism. So Calvin's overall position might be said to be eclectic, guided very much

---

1. *Calvin's Commentary on Seneca's De Clementia (1532)*, ed., trans., and intro. by F. L. Battles and A. M. Hugo (Leiden: Brill, 1969).

2. But note that he says there is "no solidity to Augustine's speculation that the soul is a mirror of the Trinity, inasmuch as it comprehends within itself intellect, will and memory." Calvin, *Institutes*, I.xv.5.

by Augustine, who was also eclectic but who by his prestigious example bequeathed to posterity a league of philosophers judged in terms of their utility to the Christian thinker. This extended from Plato at the top of the league via Stoicism, to Epicurus, with skeptics and cynics at the bottom.

The structure of the *Institutes* is formed by the aim to possess the knowledge of God and of ourselves, a theme also derived from Augustine. This gives to Calvin's theology overall a thoroughly anthropological cast. From the start of the *Institutes*, mankind, endowed with multiple powers, is a "ruin."[3] At the same time, Calvin does not belittle human nature but rather extols it as possessing the gifts of a wise and beneficent creator. In knowing God, we know ourselves. This is a central Augustinian theme which Augustine himself adapted from the Oracle of Delphi, "Know thyself."[4]

Calvin was not merely eclectic; his use of the philosophers is philosophically underdeveloped in comparison with his contemporary Vermigli, whose education placed him firmly in the tradition of Aquinas, with few competitors. Calvin is both wary and admiring of philosophy, conditioned as he was by his own *Institutes* and the evangelical readership he has in mind. He does not wish theology to be in thrall to any pagan system, even though he believes that the gifts of the pagans are God given. He has no wish to encourage speculation, which is religiously distracting. His *Institutes* were of "the Christian *religion*," after all.

Even in the final 1559 edition of the *Institutes*, Calvin writes about philosophical influences on our understanding of the soul selectively, on a "need-to-know" basis, because in his view the philosophers go into more detail than the theologically informed reader of Scripture needs, strictly speaking. So there is not the fullness of treatment that is met in later anthropology among the Reformed orthodox in the next century.

In *Institutes* I.xv, and undergirding the book as a whole, there is a nuanced distinction between a view of the soul that is influenced by Plato and the Platonic tradition, and one that is filtered through Aristotle. Stretching things a little, we may say that Calvin and Vermigli were representative of these two traditions in the nascent Reformed communities. Both ways of thinking—the Platonic and Aristotelian (modified by Aquinas)—may be

---

3. Calvin, *Institutes*, I.i.

4. Or perhaps he took it from the beginning of Zwingli's *Commentary on True and False Religion* (1525).

said to be dualistic in that in each case the soul is separable from the body at death and to be reunited at the resurrection of the dead. In each, the soul is a unity, without divisible parts, though possessed of distinct powers. In the case of Plato, the soul is the bearer of the human self, and the body is its "prison house," as Plato said and as Calvin frequently repeated.[5] In the phraseology of the New Testament, in the present life, the body is the "tent" of the soul. However, Christian Platonists have no interest in Plato's speculation that the soul is a fragment of divinity which preexisted the body. Rather, the human soul and body were each directly created by God and so are originally good. The soul is now fallen, and the body also subject to decay and death because of the fall, with the prospect of resurrection as a spiritual body.

As we have seen, in the case of Aristotle's hylomorphism, the soul is the form of the body, and so the two are more of a unity than in Plato's account. Calvin occasionally shows his opposition to the first view of the relation of the soul to the body because he thinks it threatens the separability of the soul from the body. So he refers to the "frigid doctrine" (I presume it to be that of Aristotle, but maybe that of the Stoics), which some people use to disprove the immortality of the soul. He writes, "Under the pretext that the faculties of the soul are organized, they chain it to the body as if it were incapable of a separate existence, while they endeavor as much as in them lies, by pronouncing eulogiums on nature, to suppress the name of God. But there is no ground for maintaining that the powers of the soul are confined to the performance of bodily functions."[6] Calvin may have had sympathy with hylomorphism, only objecting to the pre-Aquinas view that the soul is not separable from the body.

Later on in the *Institutes*, Calvin makes a point of stressing the separate (or separable) existence of the immortal soul from the body. He dismisses the Aristotelian view that because "others so attach its powers and faculties to the present life, that they leave nothing external to the body," which

---

5. This expression is found in Plato's *Phaedo* and in *The Republic*. Calvin frequently echoes this, e.g., "as in a house" and "prison house." Calvin, *Institutes*, I.xv.6, 2. However, we must not think that Plato is the sole reference. Calvin has some precedent in the New Testament referring to the body as a "tent" (2 Cor. 5:1, 4), which is shortly to be "put off" (2 Peter 1:14), and other similar expressions.

6. Calvin, *Institutes*, I.v.5. Calvin does not identify those who misuse Aristotle's doctrine in this way.

looks to be a sidelong glance at Aristotle's doctrine that the soul is the form of the human body. For Calvin, the soul is a spiritual essence with accidental properties, not taking up space but which nevertheless "occupies the body as a kind of habitation."[7] So it is certainly separable from the body, and in the early chapters of the *Institutes* and elsewhere, there are repeated references to the soul's immortality.

Behind these negative references, possibly to Aristotle, there is a tradition of medieval debate as to whether Aristotle taught the soul's immortality or whether his views were simply compatible with the assertion of such. There is also the issue of whether the soul's immortality could be established by reason as a philosophical doctrine, or whether it was only derivable from divine revelation and therefore was an exclusively theological preserve. The need to have a view of human nature that manifestly entails the soul's immortality, however this is established, is clearly uppermost in Calvin's mind. This may be said to be part of Calvin's natural theology.

Calvin's account of Genesis 2:7 is revealing as to his anthropology. The divine breathing into the newly formed human body is the in-breathing of life into that body, corresponding to Plato's view that the soul has a physical faculty in which, Calvin thinks, the intellectual soul is lodged. It is this intellectual soul in which the image of God is found. "On this soul God engraved his own image, to which immortality is annexed."[8] The intellectual soul is distinct from the bodily soul, which animates the body. So Genesis 2:7 is not for Calvin an amplification of Genesis 1:16, where there is no mention of the body. He is insistent that the soul is a distinct essence from the animated body, and he makes the point a number of times. The following is evidence of this:

> But the swiftness with which the human mind glances from heaven to earth, scans the secrets of nature, and, after it has embraced all ages, with intellect and memory digests each in its proper order, and reads the future in the past, clearly demonstrates that there lurks in man a something separated from the body. We have intellect by which we are able to conceive of the invisible God and angels—a thing of which

---

7. Calvin, *Institutes*, I.xv.6.

8. From his commentary on Genesis 2:7. John Calvin, *Sermons on Genesis 1–11*, trans. Rob Roy Macgregor (Edinburgh: Banner of Truth, 2009), 145. Thus Genesis 2:7 is not a further comment on 1:16: "For at this point there is no talk of the soul with all its abilities, but of the life force which is in man and which he has in common with the other brute beasts."

body is altogether incapable. We have ideas of rectitude, justice, and honesty, ideas which the bodily senses cannot reach.[9]

"Were not the soul some kind of essence separated from the body," he writes, "Scripture would not teach that we dwell in houses of clay, and at death remove from a tabernacle of flesh."[10] Calvin is very concerned to maintain that the soul is an essence, and not just "a breath of the body which would perish when the body perishes."[11] This is perhaps a passing reference to Stoic views, such as Tertullian favored. Possessing powers that are greater than mere animal powers, it must be an immortal essence. Why is Calvin so committed to the soul's immortality, which only Plato among the heathen had maintained? He clearly thinks that the soul's being the form of the body does not do justice to the separateness of the soul from the body. Calvin would not be prepared to go to the lengths of the Utrecht theologian Gisbertus Voetius (1589–1656), who drew from Aquinas the view that the soul and body are each incomplete substances which together form a substantial unity, the human being (this will be expanded later, in chapter 7). Calvin is emphatic in his repeated assertions that the soul is an immortal essence, and the body its prison house.

If he is insistent on the soul's immortality, Calvin is somewhat relaxed in his enumeration of the faculties of the soul. Mankind's creation in the image of God consists in possession of the intellectual faculty; and though not obliterated by the fall, though corrupted, the image remains. Calvin here anticipates the later Reformed distinction between the image of God in the wider and the narrower senses. So the soul is clearly distinct from the body, the "principal part of man."[12] For this reason, it is vain to seek a definition of the soul from philosophers, not one of whom, with the exception of Plato, distinctly maintained its immortality.

In the *Institutes*, Calvin is somewhat ambivalent with respect to the value of philosophical discussions about the soul. On the one hand, he characteristically wishes to avoid anything that is subtle or speculative. On the other hand, he does not think that philosophical discussions about the soul are worthless. Asking subtle questions about the soul are the province

---

9. Calvin, *Institutes*, I.xv.2.

10. Calvin, *Institutes*, I.xv.2.

11. Calvin, *Institutes*, I.xv.2.

12. Calvin, *Institutes*, I.xv.2. See also I.xv.3.

of the philosophers, yet they are not to be entirely repudiated by the theologian. Yet despite his reservations about including philosophical discussion in the *Institutes*, Calvin nevertheless commits himself to certain philosophical positions. Though the remote influences on Calvin may be Platonism and Augustine, there are also positive references to Aristotle that reveal the proximate influence on him of a more detailed faculty psychology.[13]

> But I leave it to philosophers to discourse more subtilely of these faculties. For the edification of the pious, a simple definition will be sufficient. I admit, indeed, that what they ingeniously teach on the subject is true, and not only pleasant, but also useful to be known; nor do I forbid any who are inclined to prosecute the study. First, I admit that there are five senses, which Plato (in *Theaetetus*) prefers calling organs, by which all objects are brought into a common sensorium, as into a kind of receptacle. Next comes the imagination (*phantasia*), which distinguishes between the objects brought into the sensorium. Next, reason, to which the general power of judgment belongs. And lastly, intellect, which contemplates with fixed and quiet look whatever reason discursively revolves. In like manner, to intellect, fancy, and reason, the three cognitive faculties of the soul, correspond three appetite faculties i.e. will, whose office it is to choose whatever reason and intellect propound; irascibility, which seizes on what is set before it by reason and fancy; and concupiscence, which lays hold of the objects presented by sense and fancy.[14]

There appears to be a pronounced influence of Plato, but much of what Calvin says is also consistent with the Christian Platonism of his era. We saw earlier that Plato introduced the idea of there being organs (or faculties) of the soul. Calvin's approach is to bolt the more developed faculty psychology of Aristotle onto his Platonic view of the soul, as in his early work *Psychopannychia*.[15] The same might have happened with the fourfold causality of Aristotle as it expresses the operation of the practical reason, but there is less evidence, if any, that Calvin adopted this too.

---

13. Aristotle is "a man of genius and learning."

14. Calvin, *Institutes*, I.xv.6.

15. "Plato, in some passages, talks nobly of the faculties of the soul; and Aristotle in discoursing of it, has surpassed all in acuteness." *Psychopannychia*, in *Tracts and Treatises*, in *Selected Works of John Calvin*, ed. Henry Beveridge (repr., Grand Rapids: Baker, 1983), 3:420.

The passage makes clear that despite his disavowal of a philosophical approach to the soul, Calvin is prepared to endorse quite a complex picture of it. But he goes on to say that such complexity ought nevertheless to be passed over in favor of a much simpler set of distinctions.

He prefers a fairly simple account of the soul for theological and pastoral reasons—namely, the need to choose "a division adapted to all capacities."[16] So he contents himself with the distinction between the reason (or intellect) and the appetite (or will).

> Therefore, God has provided the soul of man with intellect, by which he might discern good from evil, just from unjust, and might know what to follow or to shun, reason going before with her lamp…. To this he [God] has joined will [*voluntas*], to which choice [*arbitrium*] belongs. Man excelled in these noble endowments in his primitive condition, when reason, intelligence, prudence and judgment not only sufficed for the government of this earthly life, but also enabled him to rise up to God and eternal happiness. Thereafter choice was added to direct the appetites, and temper all the organic motions; the will being thus perfectly submissive to the authority of reason.[17]

But Calvin also has a deeper reason for dissenting from the philosophical view of man's primitive condition. "For philosophers being unacquainted with the corruption of nature, which is the punishment of revolt, erroneously confound two states of man which are very different from each other."[18] In other words, in Calvin's view, "the philosophers" have no true appreciation of the present depravity of human nature. They think that the present condition of mankind is the normal condition, whereas for Calvin and the Christian church it is radically abnormal. More to the point, the philosophers have a much rosier and more optimistic view of the soul's present powers than Calvin believes Scripture teaches.

Thus, according to Calvin, the philosophers characteristically account for moral conflict in the soul in terms of a clash between the senses, which incline to pleasure, and the understanding, which follows the truth. This is the familiar case of *akrasia*, weakness of will. The understanding is sometimes contemplative or theoretical, and at other times active or practical,

---

16. Calvin, *Institutes*, I.xv.6.

17. Calvin, *Institutes*, I.xv.8.

18. Calvin, *Institutes*, I.xv.7.

giving rise to two sets of appetites. In the human nature, the appetite itself divides into will and concupiscence (that is, lust or excessive desire). Reason should govern the soul. When appetite follows reason, all is well; when appetite overthrows reason, the result is intemperance. Philosophers regard the present activity of both the senses and the understanding as "normal," with moral failure attributed to the clash between the two and nothing more. If appetite obeys the reason, the result is virtuous action. But if it is subjected to the senses, the result is vice. So conflict is not within the soul (as Calvin believes), but between the soul and what is baser, the bodily senses, as the will havers between the attractions of each. But the bodily senses can be subdued by the discipline of reason. However, the idea that the choice between vice and virtue is within our power is too superficial an account for Calvin.

So Calvin departed from this prevailing philosophical account of human nature both because the work of the philosophers is too complex for his needs, and also because he thought that the pagans were ignorant of the corruption of human nature and so superficial. This is a point that recurs in the *Institutes*.[19]

Free Will and the Voluntas

For Calvin, the Augustinian stress on the *voluntas* does not occur until his discussions against Albertus Pighius on the bondage of the will and in the soteriological chapters of the *Institutes* that deal with the emancipation of the will through regeneration. The bondage of the will is of the *voluntas*, not only of the *arbitrium* (or the *electio*), despite the use of *arbitrium* in the title of Calvin's work against Pighius, as we will see later. In the early chapters of the *Institutes*, the term *voluntas* appears. But terminologically there is a conflation between the Augustinian view of *voluntas* as the "heart," the seat of the heart's spiritual "set," and the *voluntas* as *electio*, or *arbitrium* as choice, the purely executive role as the discharger of the judgments of the *voluntas*.

Writing of man as created, Calvin states:

> Therefore choice [*electio*] was added to direct the appetites, and temper all organic motions; the will [*voluntas*] being thus perfectly submissive to the authority of reason. In this upright state, man possessed freedom of will [*arbitrium*], by which, if he chose, he was able

---

19. For example, Calvin, *Institutes*, III.vi.3; III.vii.11.

to obtain eternal life…. Adam, therefore, might have stood if he chose, since it was only by his own will [*voluntas*] that he fell; but it was because his will [*voluntas*] was pliable in either direction, and he had not received constancy to persevere, that he so easily fell. Still he had a free choice [*electio*] of good and evil; and not only so, but in the mind and will [*voluntas*] there was the highest rectitude and all the organic parts were duly framed to obedience, until man corrupted its good properties, and destroyed himself.[20]

So, judged in terms of the order of the distinct "endowments" of the soul, how is the fall to be understood? How are we to understand how these endowments changed? We will see more of the influence of Aristotle at work in Calvin as we attempt to answer that question.

Free Will and the Fall

It is important to realize that, for Calvin, there is a sense in which the fall has changed certain things and left other things as they were. "Therefore," he writes, "since reason, by which man discerns between good and evil, and by which he understands and judges, is a natural gift, it could not be entirely destroyed, but being partly weakened and partly corrupted, a shapeless ruin is all that remains."[21]

Although the fall was calamitous, from the point of view of the metaphysics of human nature it did not strike at the essence of human nature. It is "adventitious":

We say, then, that man is corrupted by a natural viciousness, but not by one which proceeded from nature. In saying that it proceeded not from nature, we mean that it was rather an adventitious event which befell man, than a substantial property assigned to him from the beginning. We, however, call it natural to prevent any one from supposing that each individual contracts it by depraved habit, whereas all receive it by a hereditary law…. Wherefore, if it is not improper to say, that, in consequence of the corruption of human nature, man is naturally hateful to God, it is not improper to say that he is naturally vicious and depraved.[22]

---

20. Calvin, *Institutes*, I.xv.8.

21. Calvin, *Institutes*, II.ii.12.

22. Calvin, *Institutes*, II.i.11. Aquinas says that "adventitious qualities are habits and passions, by virtue of which a man is inclined to one thing rather than to another." *Summa Theologiae*, Ia 83.4.4.

So mankind's faculties are corrupted by the fall, but the faculties are not eliminated. The fall does not have essential anthropological consequences, but accidental, "adventitious" consequences:

> All these, when restored to us by Christ, are to be regarded as adventitious and above nature. If so, we infer that they were previously abolished. On the other hand, soundness of mind and integrity of heart were, at the same time, withdrawn, and it is this which constitutes the corruption of natural gifts. For although there is still some residue of intelligence and judgment as well as will, we cannot call a mind sound and entire which is both weak and immersed in darkness.[23]

By referring to "natural gifts," Calvin means that these are part of the nature or essence of humanity, inseparable from man's nature, and are such that the essence could not have disappeared without men and women losing their nature and becoming bestial. But not every human intention is depraved. Surprisingly, perhaps, Calvin does not subscribe to the view that all fallen actions proceed from an evil intention: "We know too well from experience how often we fall, even when our intention is good. Our reason is exposed to so many forms of delusion, is liable to so many errors, stumbles on so many obstacles, is entangled in so many snares, that it is ever wandering from the right direction."[24]

Here we have a glimpse of the way in which, for Calvin, self-deception or delusion has an important role in the working out of fallenness. Part of his case for human accountability to God is that some knowledge and understanding of what is right remains in fallen human nature. This gives Calvin the resources to develop a theory of agency that is distinctively human, even though mankind is fallen and therefore, in a sense, not fully or properly human.

Man has some good intentions, but they are rendered inoperative by weakness. If, however, as the passages above make clear, certain things have remained despite the fall, certain things have also changed. Reason is now partly weakened and partly corrupted. Reason once motivated unfallen humanity and now motivates the regenerate to the good (although it does not motivate the regenerate elect in all their actions, due to the sin

---

23. Calvin, *Institutes*, II.ii.12.
24. Calvin, *Institutes*, II.ii.25.

remaining in them). It motivates the unregenerate to evil, as a result of the soul's corruption and weakness. Similarly, fallen man retains his will (*voluntas*), though it too is depraved:

> Aristotle seems to me to have made a very shrewd distinction between incontinence and intemperance. Where incontinence reigns he says, that through the passion (*pathos*) particular knowledge is suppressed; so that the individual sees not in his own misdeed the evil which he sees generally in similar cases; but when the passion is over, repentance immediately succeeds. Intemperance (*akolasia*), again, is not extinguished or diminished by a sense of sin, but, on the contrary, persists in the evil choice which it has once made.[25]

It is this sort of distinction in Aristotle that gains Calvin's praise, even though Aristotle has no concept of a fall.

To gain a rounded picture of Calvin's view of the effect of the fall, we need to note what he says on the place of reason in spiritual regeneration and on the nature of the knowledge of the "heavenly things," which he outlines from *Institutes* II.ii.18 onward. There Calvin implies and asserts that human understanding is still present in the fallen race, as when he asserts that "we must now explain what the power of human reason is, with regard to the kingdom of God, and spiritual discernments."[26] Thereby he clearly implies the continued presence and activity of reason. Again, he says, "In short, not one of them even made the least approach to that assurance of the divine favor, without which the mind of man must ever remain a mere chaos of confusion. To the great truth, What God is in himself, and what he is in relation to us, human reason makes not the least approach."[27] Thus, he harkens back to his earlier discussion of human fallenness while making it clear that reason remains a human endowment that is active but in "heavenly things" perversely and ignorantly so.

Institutes II.ii.23–24 contains a particularly interesting passage where Calvin discusses and partly endorses Themistius's paraphrase of Aristotle to the effect that the intellect understands that murder is evil, but when

---

25. Calvin, *Institutes*, II.ii.23. Calvin also refers to Themistius (AD 317–390) in the same context. Themistius wrote commentaries (or paraphrases) on Aristotle's writings, including the *De Anima*.

26. Calvin, *Institutes*, II.ii.18.

27. Calvin, *Institutes*, II.ii.18.

someone plots the death of an enemy he regards that particular murder as something good. The intellect lays down general principles that we often apply perversely or ignore in particular cases, especially when our own interests are vitally involved. Yet Calvin thinks that sometimes what is evil is done as evil, commenting that

> when you hear of a universal judgment in man distinguishing between good and evil, you must not suppose that this judgment is, in every respect, sound and entire. For if the hearts of men are imbued with a sense of justice and injustice, in order that they may have no pretext to allege ignorance, it is by no means necessary for this purpose that they should discern the truth in particular cases. It is even more than sufficient if they understand so as to be unable to practice evasion without being convicted by their own conscience, and beginning even now to tremble at the judgment seat of God.[28]

In his earlier work *On the Bondage and Liberation of the Will*,[29] Calvin tirelessly insists on the fact, against the Roman Catholic theologian Albertus Pighius (1490–1542), that our present lack of free will is not part of our nature, but is a corruption of it. He includes in that book a short excursus, "Coercion versus Necessity,"[30] that establishes the difference. The importance of the distinction for Calvin is that while acting out of necessity is consistent with being held responsible for the action and being praised or blamed for it, being coerced is inconsistent with such praise or blame. In his criterion of praise and blame, he explicitly follows Aristotle: "When Aristotle distinguished what is voluntary from its opposite, he defines the latter as, *to bia e di agnoian gignomenon*, that is, what happens by force or through ignorance. There he defines as forced what has its beginning elsewhere, something to which he who acts or is acted upon makes no contribution (*Ethic.Ni.*3.1)."[31]

---

28. Calvin, *Institutes*, II.ii.24.

29. John Calvin, *De Servitate et Liberatione humani arbitrii* (1543). In translation as *The Bondage and Liberation of the Will*, trans. G. I. Davies, ed. A. N. S. Lane (Grand Rapids: Baker, 1996).

30. Calvin, *Bondage and Liberation*, 146.

31. Calvin, *Bondage and Liberation*, 150.

The Conscience

Calvin does not attempt to place the conscience within the faculties, though it seems to be regarded as a hybrid between the theoretical and the practical reason. He says our understanding of the conscience—its definition—is to be found in the etymology of the word.[32] "For as men, when they apprehend the knowledge of things by the mind and intellect, are said to know, and hence arises the term knowledge or science, so when they have a sense of the divine justice added as a witness which allows them not to conceal their sins, but drags them forward as culprits to the bar of God, that sense is called conscience."[33]

This idea of God knowing the secrets of hearts and of making them known through the conscience, and God's word as the proper "binder" of the conscience—these are prominent ideas in the developing interest in the conscience in the next century. Calvin anticipates this by his interest in conscience in the church and in the "powers that be," the magistrate. Each impinges on and shapes what he understands by "freedom."

Justified sinners possess liberty over the things that are neither commanded nor forbidden by God—that is, indifferent matters. This is a two-way freedom, and hence "indifferent." The rich may live in luxury, but they have liberty not to. Those who like a drink may enjoy one, but it is also a part of their liberty for them to abstain. And so on. "Indifference" rather than "liberty" emphasizes that the expression of such liberty may go either way consistently with a Christian life.

The state is a divinely ordained institution, but its laws are not all divine laws. Nevertheless, they ought to be obeyed. But those who lead the church and regulate its life are not to make laws that go beyond what is required by the word of God. This is a rather surprising result, when you think of it. The church is not free to make new laws, but the state is. But civil laws ought to be kept conscientiously unless they flout the commands of God. So keeping the civil law is to be a case of conscience, not of an indifferent choice. By the same token, laws that the church invents which flout

---

32. See Randall C. Zachman, *The Assurance of Faith: Conscience in the Theology of Martin Luther and John Calvin* (Minneapolis: Fortress Press, 1993).

33. Calvin, *Institutes*, III.xix.15. Cf. IV.x.4, which repeats the earlier section almost verbatim.

the word of God are not to be obeyed. In these ways the Christian citizen expresses his freedom:

> Hence a law is said to bind the conscience, because it simply binds the individual, without looking at men, or taking any account of them. For example, God not only commands us to keep our mind chaste and pure from lust, but prohibits all external lasciviousness or obscenity of language. My conscience is subjected to the observance of this law, though there were not another man in the world, and he who violates it sins not only by setting a bad example to his brethren, but stands convicted in his conscience before God.[34]

Emotions

Finally, lest it be thought that Calvin presents human nature as emotionless (as he himself was supposedly a person without emotions), it is necessary to say a word on this for the sake of the record, if for nothing more. In his account of the soul in the *Institutes*, Calvin offers no account of the emotions. But this does not mean he downplays or ignores them. In his preface to the *Commentary on the Psalms*,[35] he says of the Psalms, "I have been accustomed, I think not inappropriately, to call this book 'An Anatomy of all the Parts of the Soul,' for there is not an emotion of which any one can be conscious that is not here represented as in a mirror." He goes on to praise the psalms as instruments by which the windings of our minds can be made clear to us and our hypocrisies laid bare.

In his treatment of the uses of the doctrine of providence in *Institutes* I.xvii, Calvin's comments are full of references to a range of human emotions and the ways in which meditation can energize the believer against anxiety and give him trust and confidence to calm him amid his fears, removing him from under "the dominion of chance."[36] For some reason, it seems to Calvin better to deal with the emotions as they arise than discuss them in general terms.

---

34. Calvin, *Institutes*, III.xix.16.

35. John Calvin, *Calvin's Commentary on the Psalms*, in *Calvin's Commentaries* (Grand Rapids: Baker, 1979), 1:xxxvi–vii.

36. Calvin, *Institutes*, I.xvii.12.

Peter Martyr Vermigli's Anthropology

In 1542, Peter Martyr Vermigli left his native Italy in a hurry, fleeing to Zurich with the Inquisition breathing down his neck. He was age forty-two and had spent his adult life in scholasticism. He then lectured in Strasbourg from 1542 to 1548 and went to England with Martin Bucer and others. John Calvin had been in Strasbourg from 1538 to 1541 as an exile also, as it turned out. But they narrowly missed each other. Vermigli lectured on Aristotle in 1553 to 1555/6 on his return to Strasbourg from England following the death of Edward VI, alternating with fellow Italian and Reformed Aristotelian Jerome Zanchius (1516–1590), who lectured on Aristotle's *Physics*. He then returned to Zurich as Konrad Pellican's successor and died in 1562. Calvin had a very high opinion of him and described him as "a most excellent man, and my truly honoured brother; may the Lord always stand by you, govern you and bless your labors."[37] There is no evidence that their differences in philosophical outlook ever registered as an issue between them.

Here we will look at several different topics where philosophical issues show themselves but which never became so serious as to threaten the unity in theological outlook. As with Calvin, I have selected topics by concentrating on issues that came to be discussed and unfolded into Reformed orthodox dogmatics as Reformed ministerial education gathered speed and size during the last years of the sixteenth century and into the seventeenth.

The Resurrection of the Body

We will first consider some of Vermigli's long *scholium* on the resurrection to see how his scholasticism operates.[38] The resurrection provides an interesting test case of basic anthropology, displaying the make-up of a human person.

Vermigli's approach to the question of the resurrection of the body is quite orderly and matter of fact. He seeks to place it in an analytic framework of the fourfold Aristotelian causality, a causal scheme which Calvin also occasionally uses.[39] So for Vermigli, resurrection is an action, with an

---

37. Calvin to Vermigli, August 27, 1554, in *Letters*, trans. David Constable, vol. 3 in *Selected Works of John Calvin*, ed. Henry Beveridge (Grand Rapids: Baker, 1983), 60.

38. Vermigli's *scholium* on resurrection is inserted within his commentary on 2 Kings. It is in *Philosophical Works*, vol. 4 in The Peter Martyr Library, ed. Emidio Campi and Joseph C. McLelland (Kirksville, Mo.: Truman State University Press, 1996), 55.

39. The distinction is between *efficient* cause, the *material* cause, the *formal* cause, and the *final* cause. Each corresponds to a sense of "why?" in which some scheme or plan can be

agent and a purposed outcome. Only God could be its efficient cause because only He has the power to resurrect a dead body. But resurrection is not a physical action, such as generation, corruption, or growth and shrinkage in size. Nor is it a case of the exercise of the practical reason, such as building, painting, ploughing, or the casting of metal. Nor is it like a human action such as a virtuous or vicious choice or an economic or political action. Why not? Because all such activities have natural causes. "But the resurrection of the dead is an action completely supernatural."[40]

So what is created or changed in resurrection, which has to do with the human person, which consists of two parts, the soul and the body? Strictly speaking, bodies rise again but souls do not, for they do not die. At death, souls remain, and so since they have not died they do not rise again. Vermigli cites Scripture, for example the parable of the rich man and Lazarus (Luke 16:19–25), and Tertullian. Resurrection is a sort of new birth, citing Matthew 19:28: "So the soul will return and impart its existence to the body just as it did before death."[41] Though the resurrected body will be somewhat different from the body that died, it will nevertheless still be a physical body and will come into being after a gap in time, a new phase of life of the body decayed in death.

Note that while Vermigli searches for a framework in which the resurrection can be understood to some degree, this is not an a priori framework which is then imposed on Scripture. This is not rationalism, therefore, but part of the project of establishing a definition. And such defining is not an act of intellectual imperialism, but is intended to follow the contours of revelation. Vermigli's Aristotelianism seems to be modified (treating a case, resurrection, that was never designed by Aristotle) to reveal a basically dualistic outlook, which he discusses without awkwardness.

So the resurrection is a new union of the body and mind, brought about by God's power, so that people may stand before the last judgment and may receive reward or punishment on the basis of their previous life.[42] The fourfold cause that is central to scholasticism can now be discerned. The *efficient* cause is divine power, as we have seen. The *formal* cause is the

---

brought about. Occasionally there are variants. So for Calvin, faith is the *instrumental* cause of justification, operating like a beggar's outstretched hand for charity.

40. Vermigli, *Philosophical Works*, 55.
41. Vermigli, *Philosophical Works*, 56.
42. Vermigli, *Philosophical Works*, 56.

union of soul and body. The *material* cause is the soul and the body. These are the "materials" on which divine power works. And the *final* cause, the end or objective, is the uniting of soul and body to form a completely resurrected human being.

Vermigli thinks that in this the soul may also be said to be raised, in the sense that it once more informs the body. This is the characteristic scholastic language, of course. The soul animates the body, not in the sense that it works the muscle power of the body or the working of its internal organs. But it enables the body by powers that animate the body to grow and develop sets of skills to be a characteristically human body and the body of a particular human being. In Franz Kafka's short story *Metamorphosis*, the narrator wakes to discover that he no longer has his human body but that of a giant cockroach. Taking this at face value, the person's soul would then have a different kind of body than when he fell asleep. Such a fancy is not possible in Aristoteliansm, for the human soul is the form of the human body, and of that kind of body alone. Similarly for Vermigli. At the resurrection, the soul once more animates the body that was that person's before. It is his again in the resurrection, not a novel or strange body (unlike in Kafka's strange story), and he is once again a complete human being:

> God can do all things which do not involve a contradiction, as they say in the schools. For in general it is impossible for things to coexist when they cancel out and destroy each other. That does not, however, take anything away from God's omnipotence. For God is omnipotent even though he cannot sin or deny himself or make things that happened in the past not to be past events, nor make a human body while it exists not to be a human body and make the number three not to be three. Such things are not impossible because of some defect in him but from the very contradiction in the things.[43]

Vermigli's Lectures

Vermigli's extensive lectures on Aristotle's ethics, though they are incomplete, run to over four hundred pages in translation. Though he provides a summary of all ten books of Aristotle's *Nicomachean Ethics*, the published

---

43. Vermigli, *Philosophical Works*, 55. The fundamental importance of the law of noncontradiction in scholasticism, including Reformed scholasticism, is here evident. However mysterious God and His ways may be, they are never self-contradictory.

commentary itself runs only as far as book 3, chapter 2, perhaps first interrupted by and then suspended permanently by his move to Zurich in 1556, where Conrad Gesner was already teaching philosophy.[44] He may have delivered them there.

Vermigli was ten years older than Calvin and died shortly before him, lecturing in the 1550s extensively on Aristotle's corpus. It is not surprising that a Reformed theologian who was Aristotelian by training (like Vermigli and Zanchius were) should retain a fondness for the Stagirite—what could be more natural?—just as Calvin retained a fondness for the Stoics, for example. Nevertheless, one cannot easily imagine Calvin lecturing on a pagan philosopher.

Richard Muller has pointed out how, by the turn of the sixteenth century, the Reformed churches were becoming institutionalized, and education was having to be provided to a rising generation of would-be Reformed professional men, including ministers.[45] And, it might be added, the Counter-Reformation was in full swing. It is natural, as part of this, to find a curriculum being developed within Reformed seminaries, with attention being given to the teaching of philosophy. But it is somewhat surprising to find such extensive attention being paid to Aristotle fifty years earlier. Maybe the attention was not as extensive as that which subsequently followed, or perhaps the process of institutionalization began early. Certainly it was earlier in Strasbourg and Zurich than in Geneva.

Vermigli has a respectful if not exactly reverential attitude toward Aristotle as compared with Calvin's attitude to the moral philosophy of the Greeks. Calvin's most basic criticism of pagan philosophers and those Christians who were unduly influenced by them, such as later medievals, is in their analysis of free will and virtue:

> Hence the great darkness of philosophers who have looked for a complete building in a ruin, and fit arrangement in disorder. The principle they set out with was, that man could not be a rational animal unless he had a free choice of good and evil. They also imagined that the distinction between virtue and vice was destroyed, if man did not of his

---

44. After Vermigli's death in 1562, the lectures, edited by Santerenziano, were published by his Zurich colleagues. They have now been translated into English for the first time and edited by Emidio Campi and Joseph C. McLelland.

45. Richard A. Muller, *After Calvin: Studies in the Development of a Theological Tradition* (New York: Oxford University Press, 2003), pt. 1.

own counsel arrange his life. So far well, had there been no change in man. This being unknown to them, it is not surprising that they throw every thing into confusion.[46]

As we have already seen, in *Institutes* II.ii.2, Calvin repeatedly inveighs against "the philosophers"—they are referred to five or six times in two short sections[47]—and their view of the "bondage of the senses."

The attitude of Vermigli to pagan moral philosophers, or at least to one moral philosopher, is much less sharp than this, seeing the same philosopher as both "frigid" and yet "the prince of philosophers," as we will see. This is not to say that the outlooks of the two Reformers were antithetical, and it may be that they had different views of philosophical ethics—Calvin seeing in such work a direct challenge to the gospel, and Vermigli seeing it more as an adjunct. Or the differences may be partly explained by the differences in their temperaments.

Vermigli's Attitude to Aristotle

Debating about the hardness of the human heart and the need for grace, Calvin states that Pighius holds that the hardness of the heart was incurred through bad habit—just as if one of the "philosophers' crew" should say that by evil living a person had become hardened toward evil. Calvin's (and Augustine's) view is at odds with the Aristotelian idea—the idea of the "philosophers' crew"—that sinful people become just by doing just acts, prudent by doing prudent acts, and brave by doing brave acts. For if, for example, being just is not simply a matter of habitually or spontaneously doing what is objectively just but also a matter of having the right motives and dispositions in doing so—if, in other words, we take a motivational view of ethical goodness, as Calvin and Augustine very decidedly did—then the first question is how we come to do the just thing in the first place, how we come to be remotivated to love justice. Calvin's answer to this is that we can only do a just act in the first place by having the *habitus* of our minds redirected, a redirecting that must be done for and to us rather than by our doing it.

---

46. Calvin, *Institutes*, I.xv.8.

47. Calvin, *Institutes*, II.xii.2.

In dealing with the same passage[48] in which Aristotle argues that moral virtue is acquired through habit, Vermigli makes the same point as Calvin, though he also provides Aristotle with a get-out-of-prison card. Moral virtues (like intellectual virtues, though distinct from them), though not conatural or innate, are not contrary to nature. Virtues derive from the exercise of the will—"or rather, the will, God, and action; we should also add reason, with which right actions should agree."[49] As is his custom, Vermigli compares what Aristotle says to "holy scripture":

> With respect to vitiated and corrupt nature, however, these statements [of Aristotle's] are true in the normal course of things and according to ordinary reason. Aristotle, however, was unable to see this corruption of nature, since he was left without faith and the light of holy scripture. It is also true that our nature, in its present state, is suited to and capable of receiving the virtues, if we are speaking of the civil and moral kind, although not all people are disposed to them in the same way.[50]

The "civil and moral kind" of virtue is presumably being contrasted with the theological virtues of faith, hope, and charity, though as far as I am aware Vermigli does not use this phrase in this work. But he goes on to refer to the "true virtues, such as faith, hope and charity and the like."[51] He is seeing Aristotle through Aquinas.

Voluntariness and Ignorance

Earlier we noted Calvin in his *Bondage of the Will* discussing Aristotle's criteria of responsibility given in his *Nicomachean Ethics*. Vermigli follows Aristotle on the same passage (book 3.1), but much more closely and in greater detail. The distinction between the voluntary and the involuntary is, for Aristotle, the basis of praise and blame. This is important in view of the "corrupt and spoiled condition of nature."[52] In civil actions, the involuntary

---

48. Book 2, chapter 1 of the *Nicomachean Ethics*. "Habitus" is an important scholastic word, though Calvin rarely uses it.

49. Peter Martyr Vermigli, *A Commentary on Aristotle's Nicomachean Ethics*, vol. 9, in The Peter Martyr Library, ed. Emidio Campi and Joseph C. McLelland (Kirksville, Mo.: Truman State University Press, 2006), 296.

50. Vermigli, *Commentary*, 296–97.

51. Vermigli, *Commentary*, 297 (also 331–37).

52. Vermigli, *Commentary*, 374.

actions and those done through ignorance are to be pardoned according to Aristotle, as also in Scripture (e.g., Deut. 19:5).

The voluntary is understood in terms of the absence of force, an impossible-to-resist or difficult-to-resist impulse, an external force which receives no help from the recipient but which may nevertheless be cooperated with. For example, the highwayman who shouts, "Your money or your life!" may be complied with. Responsibility also depends on knowledge.[53] Vermigli follows Aristotle in showing considerable analytic interest in distinguishing the spontaneous from the voluntary and the range of possible instances of the voluntary, leading to a discussion of cases and also a discussion of the blameworthiness of actions in this range of the voluntary. For example, if one endures evil for an unworthy end, this is blameworthy; if for a noble end—one's country, one's parents, one's wife and children—then it is praiseworthy.[54] Those who act from base motives are not acting involuntarily, though they may claim that they are.[55]

Vermigli goes into all this with great expository skill. He is clear, orderly, and detailed and makes judicious points. And then toward the end of the chapter there is a longer-than-usual discussion of how all these Aristotelian claims accord with Holy Scripture. He cites a number of biblical examples which he says are in line with Aristotelianism. Of particular interest is the way in which Vermigli thinks that scriptural examples of moral action, together with praise and blame, follow the same contours as Aristotle's thinking.

Aristotle famously distinguished between those actions which are fully voluntary and those in which the will is involved which are not fully voluntarily: "Something of this sort occurs in jettisoning goods during a storm. There is no one who, strictly speaking, willingly and voluntarily throws away his own property, but people do it to save themselves and others, if they have any sense."[56] So as regards responsibility, there is a threefold classification: the fully voluntary, the partly voluntary (as in the jettisoning case), and actions done out of ignorance. Vermigli thinks that this is exactly what we find in Scripture.

---

53. Vermigli, *Commentary*, 375.

54. Vermigli, *Commentary*, 379.

55. Vermigli, *Commentary*, 384.

56. Aristotle, *Nicomachean Ethics*, 3.1.11. Quoted in Vermigli, *Commentary*, 376.

First, voluntariness: The faithful are praised for being a willing people (Psalm 111). The woodcutter is excused if his action is accidental because it was not voluntary (Num. 35:18). The devil is compelled to tell the truth and is not praised, nor is Balaam, who is forced at the point of a sword to curse the people of God (Num. 22:1–35).[57] Mixed actions—that is, those where we are constrained, though in doing them we still act of our own accord—are commended in Scripture: for example, self-denial for a greater good, to suffer rather than to sin, to endure persecution.[58] We are praised for such mixed actions, for those who endure persecution are blessed (Matt. 5:10). What should be endured for what? We should endure anything rather than depart from Christ. Base actions may be as voluntary as honorable actions, as Aristotle taught.

But there are issues over which Aristotle and Scripture deviate. For what if the evil we do is due to the presence of original sin? "Supposing someone said that knowledge or awareness is lacking when this sin is contracted and that the sin is caused by the first evil motions of our soul, in which there is no deliberation or choice?" Vermigli's answer is that Aristotle had no knowledge of original sin. It is enough for us that such actions cannot be called compulsory because they proceed from an internal principle. Acting out of original sin is an example of an action that has an internal principle.[59]

Finally, what of ignorance? Aristotle distinguished between those actions done from ignorance, about which we feel remorse when our ignorance is uncovered, and those over which we do not feel remorse. The fact that we do not feel remorse when sin is uncovered does not mean that we committed no sin, if we ought to have known. "Father, forgive them, for they do not know what they do" (Luke 23:34). They had sinned and needed forgiveness. "I know that you did it in ignorance" (Acts 3:17). But if they could not have known what they were ignorant of, this would have ensured their excuse. (Vermigli cites the drunkenness of Noah.) Culpability depends partly on how important and central a matter the ignorance is.[60] Vermigli asserts that actions done when drunk are voluntary, both for Aristotle and Scripture. So the approach here is that what Aristotle says

---

57. Vermigli, *Commentary*, 396.
58. Vermigli, *Commentary*, 397.
59. Vermigli, *Commentary*, 400.
60. Vermigli, *Commentary*, 398.

is true because and insofar as it accords with Scripture. So we might say that Vermigli sees Aristotle as an astute observer of and commentator on human life, as a recipient of "natural light," or "common grace."

Several things are interesting about this treatment. There is no discussion of the metaphysics of human action. Vermigli's reference to original sin presented him with an invitation to discuss these issues, but he does not accept it. There is no attempt to discuss Aristotle's account of the voluntary and the blameworthy in light of Aristotle's own seeming indeterminism and fear of fatalism as is found in his famous account of the sea battle in book 5 of the *De Interpretatione*.

Free Will

It seems that Vermigli, in common with Calvin, is sympathetic to some form of compatibilism—that all human actions are caused ultimately by factors which originate outside the self, and people are responsible for those that they are not coerced in making, but arise from their own wants and plans.[61] In ignoring the questions of the overall consistency or otherwise of Aristotle's moral psychology and his ethics, Vermigli is simply content to help himself to this aspect of Aristotle's thought without bothering about its significance for Aristotle's overall views themselves. (This may be partly at least because, once again, he takes Aristotle to be discussing ethics exclusively from a civil or public angle rather than from the angle of metaphysics, and he may be correct in this.)

In a lecture delivered in 1560 at Zurich which appeared in his *Common Places* in an appendix,[62] Vermigli discusses free will. He begins by defining it. From the Latin *liberum arbitrium*: "[It] appears that we have free will when the appetite is moved by itself toward what the understanding or power of knowing reveals to it. It is indeed in the will, but it takes root in the understanding since it is appropriate that something is judged and measured first, and then follows either refusal or endorsement…. Judgment belongs to the function of understanding but desire belongs to the

---

61. For the verdict that Vermigli is a compatibilist, see Luca Baschera, "Peter Martyr Vermigli on Free Will: The Aristotelian Heritage of Reformed Theology," *Calvin Theological Journal* 12, no. 2 (2007): 325–40

62. The *Common Places* was largely compiled from a series of excursuses that first appeared in Vermigi's commentaries. They were published in Basel in 1586.

will."[63] The reference here to the (intellectual) "appetite" is a direct link to Aquinas and beyond to Aristotle. Vermigli is arguing that free will is the power of the will in itself, not the product of an additional habit, but it is simply a directive and executive force. The direction of such a force is contributed by the will of which appetite is an aspect. At first this may seem a very intellectualistic way of thinking, but by "understanding" Vermigli includes also any factor which contributes in the judgment of the agent to the achieving of happiness, which all men seek. The "understanding" is thus a generic term for any factor which *in the judgment of the agent*, however momentary and ill-judged that understanding may be, establishes or supports an end by being the means to achieve that end. So willing and acting have a means-end, teleological character, intrinsic to the practical reason. And the ends planned may be believed to be contributing as means to further ends. We will find this sort of account in many writers later on.

Habit

Vermigli quickly moves on to a further elaboration of these ends which the understanding discharges. He makes a distinction between lower-order and higher-order ends. Lower-order ends are those matters which are "subject to the senses and human reason" within a person's capacity, such as whether I stay in a place or not, or whether war is declared or not. Other matters are of a higher order, of which we cannot even dream, such as believing in Christ and trusting Him and obeying divine commandments. Such sublime matters are things of the Spirit of God, which the natural man does not perceive.

Besides this distinction between lower and higher ends, there are distinctions between the various states of humanity, the fourfold state of man, drawn from Augustine: the original state of mankind, then fallenness, then regeneration by the Spirit, and finally glorification. As regards the powers of the "natural men," who have limited free will, often reason is overpowered by emotion, so at that point emotion is a factor in the understanding, "nor is restraining reason itself in our power."[64] So even in mundane matters, the emotions and other factors intervene, and free action may be flawed by irrationality in various ways.

---

63. Vermigli, *Philosophical Works*, 272.
64. Vermigli, *Commentary*, 274.

But does not Paul (and Jeremiah) say that the law of God is written on the heart? Vermigli answers by distinguishing between various uses of the law, one of which is to show us what we ought to do. But such a law does not of itself empower to acceptable action. The laws may show us ends that we cannot achieve. "Ought" does not always entail "can." But what may be inferred from the laws concerning those who are not yet renewed by grace? Human powers cannot be proved by this, for such laws may show only that people have a will that has some power to yield or to obey when moved by grace.

Rebirth is not alien to the will, whose nature is such that it may be regenerated by God and obey Him at least with imperfect obedience.[65] So it is implied that in regeneration, grace is given in the form of a new habit of the mind though not so far as to provide moral perfection. (Once again, it is likely that Vermigli is helped by Aquinas at such a point.) In all people, both unregenerate and regenerate, the emotions affect the will for good and evil. For Vermigli, the emotions can cloud the understanding as well as enhance it. The will is "by nature blind"—that is, it does not have an understanding of its own but depends upon the directing power of a distinct understanding. Vermigli is content to say that given the correct distinctions there is partial freedom. In the case of the unregenerate, there is partial success in respect of outward things; in the regenerate, partial freedom in internal things, godly motivation as well, but only partial because of remaining sin.

In regeneration, the intellect is actively predisposed to assent to the assertions and especially the promises of God; but it is passive in respect of the empowering of God that inclines the mind, causing those incapable to be willing pupils of God. The believer may pray for more of such understanding and a strengthening of the will. Such prayers are themselves the product of regenerating grace. So there is no cooperation by humans to the commands of God *ab initio*, but only after regenerating grace is received.[66] Vermigli refers to the "outward and inward word," meaning the communicated word through preaching, reading, and the like, and the Spirit's enlightening work in the mind, which is acquainted with the outward word. Imparting the inward word is not a violent act of coercion or such.

---

65. Vermigli, *Commentary*, 275.
66. Vermigli, *Commentary*, 291.

"For we are created rational, in the image and likeness of God. A passive power of this kind may be rightly called, in the scholastic manner, a power of obedience because we are capable of receiving a divine change when God wills to effect it."[67] Such power is a potentiality to receive something at the behest of another. People have been given a nature that is changeable by God, and such divine activity is pure grace. So there is a clear demarcation between nature and grace at this point.

In the case of acts proceeding from regeneration, Vermigli shows how God works on the mind and will in a fully Augustinian sense, not by cooperating with grace already present, grace of a general kind, but with efficacious grace, the provision of new habits.[68]

Such a discussion shows that Vermigli, even at this stage, due to his use of Aristotelian conceptuality, is able to make distinctions that Calvin, who thinks of regeneration as the first step in conversion, does not make and perhaps cannot do. Vermigli is able to take new steps in the analysis of regeneration. In particular, he is able to make a clear distinction between the divine imparting of a new habit, an event that is purely gracious, and a process, its growth and flourishing at the level of consciousness, in penitence and faith and other graces of sanctification.

Calvin and Vermigli Compared

Different views and emphases did not spoil the unity of the theological outlook that Calvin and Vermigli enjoyed or their regard and friendship for each other. Insofar as they held different views, after their death it was the Aristotelian emphasis of such as Vermigli and others like his colleague Zanchius that prevailed in the Reformed communities. This was due to several external circumstances. The Reformed faith is a catholic faith, holding to the Trinitarian theology and the Christology of the patristic period and subsequently. These were already in place. Therefore, it was natural that the growing Reformed theological community should together embrace a tradition of exposition and defense of these fundamental Christian doctrines. In addition, there was Augustine's influence, who, though not an Aristotelian, made subtle distinctions in anthropology, as we have seen. In addition, there was his memorable way of stating the fourfold state of the human race.

---

67. Vermigli, *Commentary*, 306.
68. Vermigli, *Commentary*, 285–86.

Mankind was created in a state that was *posse peccare*. He was created pure but with the possibility of lapsing from this condition, leading to *non posse non peccare* (it being impossible not to sin). Regeneration by grace brings about *posse peccare aut non peccare* (the possibility of not sinning yet still sinning, the state of sanctification and struggle against remaining sin). And finally, the glorification of the saints is that of *non posse peccare*, the state of sinlessness, the enjoyment of beatific vision. These distinctions made in this way were congenial to a scholastic outlook.

There were also external, institutional forces that led to the adoption of the scholastic outlook. Calvin was exceptional in not having had a monastic education. Most of his fellow Reformed theologians were products of late medieval scholasticism and of institutions in which the characteristic form of education, besides *praelectiones*, lecturing, were *disputationes*, disputations, in which theological students learned to defend some theological claim by reference to Scripture, and in which the making of distinctions was an intrinsic feature. It was natural that when the Reformed communities began to organize theological education these forms of education were employed.[69]

A final significant factor was the need to counter the writings of the Counter-Reformation at and after the Council of Trent, notably the writings of the Jesuits. These writings were themselves scholastic in character, as (later) were the products of the Arminians; and it was natural that if their arguments were to be matched this must be carried out in the conceptuality of their authors. But a common Reformed understanding of the place of philosophy in theological elaboration was to treat it as a good servant though a bad master. This was certainly the common attitude to theological anthropology, as we will see in different emphases exemplified by many confessional Reformed theologians in the next century.

---

69. For further discussion, see Muller, *After Calvin*.

CHAPTER 3

Body and Soul

Like the Augustinian tradition more generally, the Reformed orthodox[1] believed that it is the task of the Christian to understand his faith. They took seriously the place of basic logic, and in particular that no self-contradictory proposition could be true. Statements about God and what He has revealed should be consistent. Bearing in mind that God is transcendent and that the finite cannot encompass the infinite, our statements about what God has revealed should at least be shown not to be inconsistent. As we saw, Vermigli insisted that this does not mean that God is bound by logic in the sense that logic is like a law imposed by the state. Statements about God must be intelligible, and not being demonstrably inconsistent is one mark of intelligibility. Our language about God is necessarily analogical. In explicating his faith, the Reformed theologian should be cautious and careful, and he should use whatever tools are at hand.

One such tool is the use of words and phrases not found in Scripture, such as "Trinity," "by faith alone," "free will," and "faculty."[2] Such expressions may be used to connect the varied data of Scripture. Some of these words are made up, notably in the history of the church *homoousios* to signify the nature of Christ's humanity and divinity. Others are everyday words occurring in Scripture, such as "person" and "nature," that have been given a new or more precise meaning. Bearing in mind Paul's policy in Acts 17 when he used the words of a pagan referring to his god to refer to the living God, the resources of philosophy may be used eclectically to

---

1. I will use "Reformed orthodox" and "Puritan" to refer to Reformed theologians with a confessional commitment and who were more or less influenced by medieval scholasticism.

2. The term "faculty" occurs throughout the book. For different contemporary approaches to it, see appendix C. See also Perler, *Faculties*.

articulate and defend the faith. No philosophical system is revealed as the true system; nevertheless, elements from philosophy may be used. And so we have already seen Augustine using some parts of Platonism and Stoicism and declining to use others, and Aquinas using Aristotle likewise. Calvin and Vermigli followed suit in their different ways.

The Reformed orthodox, among whom were many of the Puritans, shared this outlook. In this chapter, we will see a selection of them at work in articulating what the Bible says about human nature using the resources of scholasticism to do so. Some wrote entire books on the topic, and others make clear their outlook incidentally in the course of writing on a variety of different topics. Our aim is not to repeat the same points from different authors, but to distribute the various topics among them. The emphasis is on straightforward didacticism, noting different emphases in different writers. In chapter 7, we will sample the use of the resources of faculty anthropology in developing arguments defending their confessional faith.

Scholastic theology provided a set of tools like no other for the analysis of theological claims. As a consequence, its proponents seemed more comfortable at analysis than at synthesis, with dissecting issues and separating the wheat from the chaff, than in composing those elements into a synoptic theology. Proceeding in their education from philosophy to theology, the students had in hand numerous sets of distinctions.[3] Consider the concept of justifying faith. Is faith the cause of justification? Is faith the cause of works? Is faith mere belief? Is faith a virtue? Is faith the cause of other virtues, such as hope and love? And so on. As we have noted, scholastic theologians operated with Aristotle's four-cause analysis: the formal cause, the efficient cause, the material cause, and the final cause. So the sculptor's plan is the formal cause of the work; the material case is the marble or granite; the efficient cause is the sculptor's activity of measuring, chiseling, and filing; and the final cause is producing the finished article. What kind of cause is faith? Perhaps faith is not the cause of justification in any

---

3. The Polish Reformed theologian Johannes Maccovius (1588–1644) devoted an entire volume, *Regulae Theologiae ac Philosophicae*, to setting out distinctions in theology and philosophy. It is translated in English as *Scholastic Discourse: Johannes Maccovius (1588–1644) on Theological and Philosophical Distinctions and Rules*, ed. and trans. Willem J. van Asselt et al. (Apeldoorn: Instituut voor Reformatieonderzoek, 2009).

of these senses, but an instrumental cause. And how does an instrumental cause differ from all the four senses mentioned earlier? And what is a primary cause, and how different is it from a secondary cause?[4]

In this first chapter on the seventeenth century, we will look at the basis of Christian anthropology, the relation between soul and body. Just like Calvin and Vermigli, authors began in this task by a study of the data of the Bible itself, by the account of the creation and its language about the soul and the body and resurrection. The volume of theological literature increased greatly in the seventeenth century. In order to reflect this, our selections from the many authors who had things to say about anthropology will be shorter and more varied than was the case in the last chapter. The material is organized in this chapter and subsequent chapters mainly in terms of topic and usually not chronologically.

The Soul as a Whole

I have noted in discussing Augustine that he does not commit himself to the simplicity of the soul. Others have held to the soul's simplicity, and in general this has been to provide an argument for its immortality. In orthodox Christianity, unlike all other creations, the body and soul were created by the mere word of God, but breathed into Adam's body made from the dust and Eve's from Adam's rib, and so man became a living creature (Gen. 2:7). The soul is nonspatial but bounded, being located in the body, but not in any one part of it nor necessarily the whole of it, for a person can still function as a rational animal even if he lacks a limb or limbs. It is not mixed with the body, but it is in union with it. So Petrus van Mastricht (1630–1706) notes that "being purely spiritual the rational essence of the soul is not liable to any dissolution and so has no principle of death."[5] The thought here is that whatever is not simple, but rather composed of parts, is liable to decompose. So the soul, which is not composed of discrete parts, is nevertheless far from being a featureless essence. The essence of the soul

---

4. For a useful introduction to Reformed scholasticism, see Willem J. van Asselt, *An Introduction to Reformed Scholasticism*, trans. Albert Gootjes (Grand Rapids: Reformation Heritage Books, 2011), esp. chs. 7–11.

5. Cited in Heinrich Heppe, *Reformed Dogmatics Set Out and Illustrated from the Sources*, trans. G. T. Thomson (London: George Allen and Unwin, 1950), 226.

is such that it has various powers, particularly intellect and will, in which the image of God resides.

As we saw in the previous chapter, Calvin and Vermigli adapt doctrines of the soul and body, a modified hylomorphic version (to accord with the resurrection of the body) and a modified Platonic version (to eliminate the Platonic doctrine of preexistence). The hylomorphism is due to Aristotle, appropriated by Aquinas, as we have seen. The Platonic account was reinvigorated in the Renaissance and then in a rather different way by René Descartes (1596–1650), as we will see in more detail later. These ways of thinking are dualistic versions of the human being. In each case, the soul, which is incorporeal, is separated from the body at death and is to be reunited at the resurrection of the dead. In each case, the soul is without parts. But in the case of hylomorphism, the soul is the form of the body. In the case of those influenced in a hylomorphic direction, the soul "infuses" the body, animating it at every level, since it informs the body and keeps it formed and active as the human body of some individual person until the death of that body.[6]

As regards the control of the body, there are different stories to tell for different parts. The soul may "ensoul" the pancreas differently from the arms and hands, for we are not aware of controlling the body's internal organs, though often we are aware when they malfunction. We readily perform what are nowadays called basic actions with arms and hands and other members within our direct control. The range of soulish powers as regards the body is affected by the argument: each nonhuman animal such as sheep has a soul, and yet such a soul has purely sensory powers only, and perhaps (in the case of a sheep, for example) a rudimentary memory. A human being has only one soul, which has such vegetative and sensory powers besides its intellectual powers, as its five senses operate singly and in combination on the physical world it inhabits, informing mind and memory. Therefore, the powers of the soul must extend throughout the body, but in some operations that are "nonbodily" and nonspatial. The human self has "phantasms," ideas or sensations, in its consciousness brought about by the operation of the senses.

---

6. For comments on the position of contemporary dualism and the approach to "faculties," see appendix C.

The problem with this is that a human soul which has direct powers over the body looks like its effects will be spatially dispersed through the body and therefore have a sort of spatial complexity as the form of a particular body. To lose an arm is to lose a region in which the soul had operated, and the activity of the body becomes truncated in certain respects. A faculty psychologist will comment that the powers previously exercised before the loss of the arm persist, but in a purely potential form. This may be said to be shown by how a person can activate a prosthetic hand successfully attached to where his lost hand was. This same principle applies, Christian Aristotelianism claims, when there is the loss of the entire body at death. In the interim state, the soul retains its powers exercisable in the body in a dispositional manner, awaiting the resurrection of the body, at which point they will once again become active.

Such a view is, of course, interactive. The body, through the vegetative faculty, also affects the soul. But it differs from Platonism and Cartesianism. (We will consider Cartesianism and its impact on Reformed orthodox anthropology in chapter 7.) In the case of Platonism, the difference between soul and body shows itself by a tendency to be drawn into an ethical contrast between soul and body and with the difficulty or even embarrassment of handling the topic of the resurrection of the dead, which is why it does not usually appear in a fully developed way in writers who hold such a view. But no Reformed theologian is entirely happy with Platonism because the body, being created, is created good. Nevertheless, he may be drawn somewhat in such a direction habitually or subconsciously, as in Calvin's frequent references to the body as the "prison house" of the soul.

The character of the soul is gathered by us a posteriori, via our awareness of the soul's various abilities and the limitations of its particular powers, which are then grouped together and form various different faculties. The powers are real, as are the distinctions based on their perceived differences, for this is not mere nominalism. The distinctions are likewise real but not all physical, just as the soul is located in the body but takes up no space.

John Flavel on Body and Soul

We turn to John Flavel[7] to show us how a well-educated Puritan preacher understood the soul. So he writes of the "infusion" of the soul into the

---

7. A Puritan preacher, John Flavel (1627–1691) was also a voluminous author.

body.[8] This language is rather odd, in that as a person grows, his soul informs a greater and greater area of matter. But the soul does not expand physically. Flavel continues, "We cannot trace the way of the Spirit [that is, the human soul], or tell in what manner it was united with this clod of Earth. But it is enough that he who formed it, did also unite or marry it to the Body. This is clear, it came not by way of natural resultancy from the Body, but by way of inspiration from the Lord; not from the warm bosom of the *Matter*, but from the breath of its *Maker*."[9]

The soul is "a living active being," distinguished from and contrasted with the body, and is the animator of the body. Flavel quotes James 2:26: "Though it has this vital Power in it self, it hath it not from itself, but in a constant receptive dependence upon God, the first Cause both of its Being and Power." Here Flavel draws attention to the immediate effects of divine concurrence in providence. God is the first cause, and souls and their effects are among the secondary causes.

> The word *Substance*, as it is applied to the Soul of Man, puzzles and confounds the dark Understandings of some, that know not what to make of an immaterial substance; whereas in this place it is no more than *substare accidentibus* (i.e.) to be a subject in which Properties, Affections and Habits are seated and subjected. This is a spiritual Substance, and is frequently in Scripture called a Spirit, (Luke 23:46, Acts 7:59) and so frequently all over the Scriptures.[10]

> *A Substance in this use of the word, is that which depends not in respect of its Being upon any other fellow Creature, as Accidents and Qualities do, whose Being is by having their in-being in another Creature as their subject; but this Being, the Soul, exists in itself.*[11]

Two points are worth noting. Flavel is at ease in using scholastic terms— "substance," "subject," "habit," "property"—with a certain amount of familiarity and care and interweaving their use with biblical data in a quite

---

8. John Flavel, *Pneumatalogia, a Treatise of the Soul of Man, the Second Edition* (printed by J. D. for Tho. Parkhurst at the Bible and Three Crowns near Mercers Chappel in Cheapside, 1698), 6. It is highly likely that this material was preached before being written up into the book.

9. Flavel, *Pneumatologia*, 6.

10. Flavel, *Pneumatologia*, 12.

11. Flavel, *Pneumatologia*, 12.

unselfconscious way. The soul is indivisible, with no dimensions or figures (i.e., it is not measurable), and has the "Principle of Life and Motion in itself, or rather it is such a Principle itself."[12] But it cannot be touched (Luke 24:39). When Flavel considers the relation of the soul to the body, he reckons it pervades the body; it dwells in and is wholly in every part and comprehends the body or matter in which it is lodged, itself also forming conceptions of what is immaterial. Not surprisingly Flavel goes on to refer to the simplicity of the soul, but in any case what he already has said about it seems to entail this.[13] He sees the need to think of the soul in terms that do not make it "a particle of God" on the one hand, nor a material substance on the other, nor on having parts like the body. He links simplicity and spirituality to the soul's immortality.

Nevertheless, Flavel refers throughout his work to the soul's close relation to the body and to the relation of the soul to the body as a most natural one. On the question of the soul's relation to the body, Flavel says:

> O the Soul and Body are strongly twisted and knit together in dear bands of intimate Union and Affection, and these Bands cannot be broken without much struggling: O 'tis a hard thing for the Soul to bid the Body farewell, 'tis a bitter parting, a doleful separation: Nothing is heard in that hour but the most deep and emphatical Groans; I say, *emphatical groans*, the deep sense and meaning of which, the living are but little acquainted with.[14]

> Its desire of Re-union continuing still with it in its state of Separation, speaks its love to the Body. As the soul parted with it in grief and sorrow, so it still retains even in glory an inclination to re-union, and waits for a day of re-espousals…. The union of Soul and Body is natural, their separation is not so.[15]

Flavel goes into great detail of the love of the soul for the body and the affections and emotions that arise due to the awareness of dangers to the body, to accidents, wounds, and diseases. These emotions are natural, to be expected: "[The soul is a] whole in every part which it could never doe if it self were material. Yea, it comprehends in its understanding, the

---

12. Flavel, *Pneumatologia*, 13.
13. Flavel, *Pneumatologia*, 15.
14. Flavel, *Pneumatologia*, 126.
15. Flavel, *Pneumatologia*, 129.

Body or Matter in which it is lodged; and more than that, it can and doth form conceptions of pure spiritual and immaterial Beings, which have no Dimensions or Figures; all which shows it to be no corporal, but a spiritual and immaterial Substance."[16]

Flavel does not explicitly avow the Aristotelian view, but he certainly has a very positive and pronounced view of the relation between soul and body, a relation that is regarded as very close. He stresses the unnaturalness of death, that a human being is not complete without a body, and the consequent difficulty we have of conceiving of disembodiment of life after death and before resurrection.

Robert Purnell's Dualism

Here is another example, from the Baptist preacher Robert Purnell (1606–1666), in which the relation between body and soul seems more "dualist," but the indebtedness to scholastic forms of thought are nevertheless visible:

> The soul of man is a sprituall [*sic*] substance, immortall and invisible, endued with memory understanding and will; or the soul is a substance immortall, invisible, united to the body, and endued with many admirable faculties, as life, sense, and reason; to this end principally, that God might be truly honored, and duely worshipped.
>
> Or the soul is a spirituall, invisible and immortall substance, endued with power to understand, and will: this soul is at one instant both created and united to the body, and by the power and faculties of the soul, man is capable of happiness, or of the cheif good, or greatest misery: or thus, the soul of the Saints is a spirituall and immortall substance, created after the Image of God, and renewed after the immortall Image of God in Christ: the soul is a real and very being as the body is, only of a higher kind; the body is of the earth, the soul is immediately from God.[17]

It is interesting that Purnell offers alternative characterizations of the soul, each fuller than the last one, perhaps corresponding to different biblical connotations. The second of these, the soul as source of life, sense, and reason, is quite hylomorphic.

---

16. Flavel, *Pneumatologia*, 14–15.

17. Robert Purnell, *A Little Cabinet Richly Stored with all sorts of Heavenly Varieties, and Soul-reviving Influences* (London: R.W., 1657), 12–13. Purnell was an elder at Broadead Church, Bristol.

Sir Matthew Hale on the Created Soul

A clear account of the human soul consisting of understanding and will, and with the affections dependent on the will, is given by Matthew Hale (1609–1676) in his *A Discourse of the Knowledge of God and of Ourselves*.[18] Hale writes clearly and elegantly, adopting the regular view of the intellect, will, and passions, and of human activity as having a marked teleological structure. Writing of the fall and its effects on humans, he says,

> Upon what hath been said, may appear, wherein lies the *immediate Cause of Man's miscarriage* to his Supream End; it lies in the Defects of his Understanding and his Will. 1. For his Understanding; If this hath either no Light, or a false Light, the Will is misguided: The Soul of Man will be moving to some thing or other under the notion of Good; which either the temper and constitution of the body and fleshly appetite, or the present opportunity suggests and affects, and puts the intention of the Will upon it; as Pleasures, or Profits, or Honours, or empty Speculations.[19]

Here, he writes of man unfallen:

> Touching the Understanding, it is a Faculty receptive of an Object that may be known; but that Object is not of the nature or essence of the Understanding, but distinct from it: so that Man might be created an intellectual Creature, yet till such time as naturally through the Senses or supernaturally by the immediate infusion or demonstration of God, he was not but *rasa tabula*. The first thing therefore, that was put into his Understanding in order to his supream End, was a stock of Knowledge of God, and of that Will of God which concerned Man. And this Will of God concerning Man was that Means, which if known and pursued, would guide a Man to true Happiness.[20]

Hale distinguishes the understanding from its contents. This may be a very strong and emphatic expression of the doctrine of the created soul as a *tabula rasa*, a blank receptive surface, having no innate ideas respecting the knowledge of God, or of ideas which come via the senses. It seems similar

---

18. Published posthumously. Matthew Hale, *A Discourse of the Knowledge of God and of Ourselves* (London: printed by B. W. for William Shrowsbury, 1678). Under Charles, Hale was made first Chief Baron of the Exchequer and then Chief Justice of the King's Bench.

19. Hale, *Discourse of the Knowledge of God and of Ourselves*, 59.

20. Hale, *Discourse of the Knowledge of God and of Ourselves*, 81.

to the rejection of innate ideas which later John Locke more famously also holds, as we will see in due course.

Hale also discusses the effects of the fall on the understanding: "But in Man it is otherwise: the Principles especially in his Understanding, whereby the whole Man is much steered, are extrinsical and adventitious, and so without any essential change in his Nature, those Habits or Principles may be lost. And let us but examine the temper of Mankind, we shall find a general disorder in all his Faculties, and want of those Rules, which should lead him to his Supream End."[21] What we see here is Hale weaving a narrative of the fall (and later, of the restoration) of mankind, having scholastic divisions and expository devices fully at his fingertips, enabling him to do so. In fact, his philosophical and theological outlook seems more Platonic than Aristotelian, judging by the merely passing references to the death of the body and its resurrection. Hale's writing on religion is not as much evidence of scholastic theology influencing a layman (though he is fully informed regarding theology) as evidence of the diffusion of scholasticism in the seventeenth century in the education of a Christian gentleman and of its influence in the law.

Edward Reynolds on the Simplicity of the Soul

A rather different treatment of the understanding, clearly distinguishing between the speculative and the practical understanding, is provided by Edward Reynolds, a prominent Westminster divine, in a book written before the Assembly met. This is a rather elaborate production, *A Treatise on the Passions and Faculties of the Soul* (1640). It principally concerns the emotions, and we will consider Reynolds again when we look at them, but he has things to say regarding the faculties of the soul.

He notes that from the attribute of the soul's spirituality "flows immediately the next of *simplicity*, unity or actuality: for matter is the root of all perfect composition, every compound consisting of two essential parts, matter and form. I exclude not from the soul all manner of composition; for it is proper to God only to be absolutely and perfectly simple: but I exclude all essential composition, in respect whereof the soul is purely actual."[22]

---

21. Hale, *Discourse of the Knowledge of God and of Ourselves*, 84.

22. Edward Reynolds, *A Treatise on the Passions and Faculties of the Soul*, in *The Whole Works of the Rt. Rev. Edward Reynolds*, ed. Alexander Chalmers (London: B. Holdsworth, 1826), 6:254.

Reynolds means that while the soul is not essentially a compound, nevertheless it has separable powers. So for this reason he is prepared to talk of the "parts" of the soul. It has "parts," spirit and form. That is, it is spirit that has a form in the human soul that is different from the form of, for example, angelic souls. Both the matter and form of the soul are spiritual, not material. The acts of the soul are immediate, not requiring any organs. The soul can have the knowledge of universals, such as whiteness, and of angels and God; it can think and reason.

The principal parts of the soul are understanding and will.[23] The understanding's operations *ad intra* concern the will, differently as the understanding has contemplative and practical aspects. "Practical" includes the reception of data from the environment via the senses and intellectual activity concerning these, and "active" in the forming and achieving of goals.[24]

Nicholas Mosley's Hylomorphism

Reynolds's outlook can be compared to that of Nicholas Mosley (1611–1672). Like Sir Matthew Hale, Mosley was a layman. He lived in the Manchester area at the time of the Commonwealth, having, it seems, sided with the Roundheads during the Civil War. Mosley published *Psychosophia, or Natural and divine contemplations.*[25] This has a similar form to Flavel's book, for Mosley offers Christian meditations, his "contemplations," as the practical application of the doctrine of the soul that he unfolds. The purpose of the book is to elucidate the teaching of Christianity with the direct help of Aristotle, whose views are not even mediated through Aquinas in Mosley's treatment. He also wants to make the point, as several others do, that the immortality of the soul, which is a Christian doctrine, is provable by reason—that is, by Aristotle—and is itself a proof of God's existence. Such a proof is part of the standard natural theology of the Reformed orthodox.

---

23. Reynolds, *Treatise on the Passions and Faculties of the Soul*, in *Works*, 6:278.

24. Reynolds, *Treatise on the Passions and Faculties of the Soul*, in *Works*, 6:279.

25. Nicolas Mosley, *Psychosophia, or Natural and Divine Contemplations on the Passions and Faculties of the Soul of Man* (London: printed for Humphrey Mosley, 1653). Mosley was educated in Cambridge and was a supporter of Cromwell. He became a justice of the peace in Lancashire. His brother Oswald was a high official in Cromwell's court, who, acting for him, forced Patrick Gillespie on the University of Glasgow to be its principal. The book gives evidence of acquaintance with such Protestant theologians as Calvin, Ursinus, and Archbishop Hooker.

Mosley thinks there are three faculties: reason, will, and understanding. These three faculties (expanded from the more conventional division into understanding and will) correspond to mind-body activities in the case of the last two, and some mind-mind activities in the case of the first. The entirety is created and upheld by God. The soul is immortal, not backwardly everlasting,[26] but having been created by God and endowed in this state by Him with the property of being self-perpetuating. Perhaps this is what the immortality of the soul means: a created spirit enduring for all times subsequent to the time of its creation—that is, sempiternally—as the result of the creativity and upholding of God. So the soul does not exist necessarily, but only by the will of God, and its everlasting persistence is made possible by its spirituality.

If this is accurate, then there may be a difference in the outlook on immortality between those who seem to stress the soul's natural and inevitable immortality, the absolute necessity of that immortality, which Mosley may be asserting here, and those who affirm the soul's immortality in that it is decreed to be such by God and has only hypothetical necessity as a consequence. This is the view of Gisbertius Voetius (1589–16760), the Dutch Reformed theologian, as we will see later. So there is a difference between the idea of immortality as the inherent character of what is created by God and immortality due to God's decree.

Mosley's outlook on the matter of the soul and the body is a developed and detailed hylomorphism. What Flavel sketches, Mosley fills in with some detail: "The soul of man is produced from above, without any power of matter concurring or intervening; the matter indeed is fitted and prepared to receive the form, but doth not at all produce it, that comes immediately from God."[27]

Besides going directly to Aristotle, whom he refers to as the "Grand Philosopher," for help with all philosophical questions, Mosley invokes the Roman Catholic theologian Suarez, and in considerable detail. Mosley notes, "The soul of man is a simple essence and not to be found in the Predicament of quantity; therefore it admits not of fractions and parts; is not capable of division; if it were corporeal it would be *quanta*, and so divisible

---

26. Mosley, *Psychosophia*, 21.
27. Mosley, *Psychosophia*, 4.

(as quantity is) *in semper divisibilia*; but being a spirit, it is simple, incorporeal, immortal, and so an indivisible substance."[28]

The soul is multipliable; it can beget other souls. But here at least Mosley does not go into the thorny questions of whether the multiplication of souls is traducian or whether each soul's existence is due to a separate act of creation. According to Mosley, the soul fills the whole body, and not by being physically dispersed within it nor taking up room: "And if the body decrease, if any member be cut off or wither, the soul is not diminished or dried up, onely ceaseth to be in that member it was in before, and that without any hurt to or blemish to itself."[29] That is, I suppose, no blemish as to its essence; it is not less that soul than it was. Yet it is hard to suppose its powers are not affected by such changes in the body.

Mosley defines the soul as "*the act, the perfection, and beginning of a Natural Organical, body, endued with life, sense, and understanding.*"[30] Such a definition indicates how integrated soul and body are on the hylomorphic view.

Mosley is quite cautious in his understanding of the faculties. "For when we see and learn these distinct Faculties and operations of the Soul, we are easily drawn to conceit that there are also three distinct Soules in Man."[31] Here's a warning against the *homunculus* view of the soul, a theme which recurs later. The unity of the soul means that there is only one soul per body. "One individual soul onely in man according to *Aristotle*, which not-withstanding hath individual and distinct powers and faculties…. Intellectual; one in respect of its essence, three in respect of its faculties."[32] The author does not pick up a possible allusion here to Augustine's analogies between the soul and the Trinity. The three faculties of reason, understanding, and will are further divided into faculties according to their modes of operation.

In considering Mosley's account of the body and soul, we must first reflect again on hylomorphism. His Aristotelian hylomorphism is nowhere more clearly seen than in his treatment of the vegetative faculty in his

---

28. Mosley, *Psychosophia*, 17.

29. Mosley, *Psychosophia*, 18.

30. Mosley, *Psychosophia*, 29.

31. Mosley, *Psychosophia*, 34. Here Mosley is warning against the temptation to think of the faculties of the soul as *homunculi* (i.e., little souls), as mentioned earlier.

32. Mosley, *Psychosophia*, 36.

Psychosophia as part of his account of the soul. The fundamental tenet of hylomorphism, as we have seen, is that the human soul is the form of the human body, animating it in all respects, not only in spiritual matters. By contrast, the soul is nowadays popularly understood as an exclusively spiritual substance linked to a human body, which the soul informs. This is basically both the position of Platonic and Cartesian dualism, as we have had reason to notice from time to time. In the case of Platonism, the body is ethically inferior to the intellect, though this was modified by such as Augustine in line with the Christian doctrine of creation. In the case of Descartes, the body was understood in autonomous, mechanical terms, as we will see later.

It has to be remembered that, according to Aristotelian hylomorphism, a sheep, for example, has a soul, an immaterial principle that animates it, orders its growth and habits such as its preference for grass and the way it feels pain. But what we ordinarily think of as a soul, a rational and spiritual faculty, is possessed only by human beings (and angels); and a human soul, while it includes both vegetative and sensory activities, is most importantly distinctively intellectual, having intellectual and volitional powers and emotions, as we have been seeing. So a human soul has several layers. Most distinctively, it is in these various ways that it is the form of the body. So the words of Genesis 2:7, God's forming of man from the dust and His breathing into man the breath of life, for hylomorphists is one act, not two, as we saw in the previous chapter was Calvin's view. This does justice, Christian hylomorphists think, to the teaching of Scripture that man is a psychophysical unity, even though the concepts in which this is expressed are of pagan origin.

Mosley proceeds to discuss the immortality of the human soul in respect of the effect on the soul of the death of the body, which he allows is controversial. But he has an Aristotelian way of reconciling the immortality of the vegetative faculty by claiming that after death it is held in potentiality, pending the resurrection: "For the soul is (according to its essence) a Form, and a Form naturally desires the Matter to which it relates, and without the Matter it is but imperfect; for nothing is perfect *ex sola forma,* not by Form alone, but Matter and form together.... otherwise death would not be so terrible if all perfection and happiness consisted in the soul."[33]

---

33. Mosley, *Psychosophia,* 23.

Mosley thus proceeds to consider the soul:

As it hath assumed humane nature, and is the Form of man, and so a part of him who is compounded of Matter and Form…and this nature too we consider not as in the state of integrity in which it was created, but in this lapsed & degenerate condition it groaneth under since the fall of man, and is intombed in the body of weak and sinfull flesh, and operates not but by and with the body: The subject therefore of this Book is Physical, material, and inseparable from the body, as well in its Affections, which we here handle, as in its Essence.[34]

It is not as if the soul is "found" an already prepared body (as in Gen. 2:7), but it is the source of the body's growth from its beginning. The vegetative soul is what humans have in common with all living things, both plants and animals. It is the source of bodily growth and animation. This is the view of the relation between body and soul given by hylomorphism that Mosley presumably derived from Aquinas or from the Christian Aristotelian tradition more generally. Whatever the story, Mosley does not refer to Aquinas, but only to Aristotle. The recognition of the soul's fallenness is one of several places in which Aristotle's philosophy is adapted by the demands of special revelation.

So in line with this, Mosley notes that the various faculties do not work faultlessly: "The operations of Reason and Understanding are impediated [impeded] many waies upon any perturbation of mind, whether by immoderate Love or Anger, Fear or Grief, or the likes, or else by some sickness and distemper of the body; or else by sleep; for then the External Senses rest, neither doth the Understanding that whole work but in all these cases the Phantasie is working."[35] It is not hard to imagine that Christian hylomorphists observed a number of important parallels between the Genesis account of creation and Aristotle's *Physics*.[36] There is the hierarchical order in creation of plants, animals, and mankind. And the key terms in the biblical account of creation—"form," "kind," "spirit," and "soul"—are

---

34. Mosley, *Psychosophia*, 26.

35. Mosley, *Psychosophia*, 79. Mosley holds that the fall was caused by the working of phantasie, when the judgment of the understanding was rejected in favor of the appreciation of phantasie only. Mosley, *Psychosophia*, 80.

36. On this, see David Sytsma, "Calvin, Daneau and *Physica Mosaica*: Neglected Continuities at the Origins of an Early Modern Tradition," *Church History and Religious Culture* 95, no. 4 (2015): 457–76.

also present in Aristotle. There were dissimilarities too, of course. In Genesis, matter is not eternal, but created ex nihilo; and above all there is the display of the sovereignty, power, and wisdom of God and His clear speech to Adam and Eve.

Such hierarchical thinking is evident in Mosley's discussion of the different behavior of the body and the soul. He considers their differences in general terms via a discussion of the two distinct sets of appetites, their various ranges and limitations. Thus, the intellectual appetite may judge the future and past, whereas the sensitive judges only of the present. The intellect knows both material and immaterial things and abstractions from them, as forms; but the merely sensitive soul is not capable of distinguishing form from matter and has to do only with the temporal and the bodily, whereas the intellect can distinguish between form and matter and address spiritual and eternal concerns. The spiritual makes judgments about what it is aware of; the sensitive has to do with the immediate. The soul has three internal senses: common sense, phantasm (that is, sensations or imaginations), and memory. The body has the five external senses of hearing, vision, smell, taste, and touch. The various senses are normally in harmony. These senses are not located in the brain, but in different places. Nonhuman animals go no higher than the reception of phantasms. But for those whose soul possesses the faculty of intellect—for example, human beings—there can be intellectual phantasms of what have never existed, imaginary things. The memory "is the Store-house and Treasury of all Science."[37]

The appetitive faculty consists of powers that require the guidance of other faculties as to what is judged good, whether by reason or phantasm, as in the case of the body's safe movement from place to place. Mosley ascribes much to the vegetative faculty that would now be ascribed to the body itself. For example, it gives the spiritual impetus to physical and organic growth in the body. This seems to be taken as true from Aristotle's belief that nonhuman animals have only sensory and vegetative souls, and since a human being has a body, where else for the vegetative soul to be housed than among the powers of that being's immortal soul?

All this is worked out in further detail in chapter 5, "The Vegetative Faculty and Effects." Corresponding to the three external senses having to do with the body, there are three internal senses, dealt with in chapter 7:

---

37. Mosley, *Psychosophia*, 77.

"The Three Internal Senses, viz., Common Sense, Phantasm, and Memory." Whereas the first three are "outward," seated in the body, the second three are "internal," located in the brain—that is, the brain is their organ of operation. It is what the internal senses use in their various operations, though not knowingly, as one may use one's left arm instead of the right, but not "use" the liver. Mosley offers a further account of where in the brain they operate. I think it is fair to say that he goes into an exceptional degree of detail by comparison with others, theologians and ministers, who are nevertheless committed to scholastic faculty psychology.

This sort of discussion is more characteristic of theologians who are Aristotelian in their metaphysics, but as I noted, even Calvin goes into some of this detail in *Institutes* I.xv and elsewhere. Calvin's reason for curtailing discussion is not that it is worthless, but that it may be beyond his readers' comprehension; and in any case pagan philosophers have no conception of the fall and are consequently led astray. Yet having said this, we must bear in mind Calvin's early work *Psychopannychia* (1542) and his restrained treatment there of the intermediate state.[38]

Mosley's is the fullest exposition of seventeenth-century English hylomorphism I have come across. That he appears to "Christianize" it, not least by basing the "meditations" of the book on it without going through Aquinas, makes it doubly fascinating.

Francis Turretin on Soul, Brain, and Mind

Francis Turretin (1623–1687), the Genevan theologian, has interesting incidental comments on the relation between the soul and the brain, the detail of which is unusual.[39] His remarks show some of the signs of hylomorphism, but not of all. There is no reference to the vegetative faculty, for instance; but nevertheless he argues for a close relation between brain and mind or soul.

---

38. The Reformed treatment of the intermediate state of the redeemed is distinctly positive. When he dies, the believer is "absent from the body, and present with the Lord." The Westminster Confession states that "the souls of the righteous, being then [i.e., at death] made perfect in holiness, are received into the highest heavens, where they behold the face of God in light and glory, waiting for the full redemption of their bodies" (32.1). This is also a prominent theme in Calvin's *Psychopannychia* (1536).

39. Francis Turretin, *The Institutes of Elenctic Theology*, trans. G. M. Giger, ed. James T. Dennison Jr. (Phillipsburg, N.J.: P&R, 1992), 1:485–86.

In the course of arguing for the immortality of the soul, Turretin offers an account of the soul and the brain. It begins with trying to clarify the soul's dependence on the body. He writes, "It is one thing for the soul to depend on the body (as upon a subject and efficient) another to depend upon it as an object and occasion.... Yet on account of its union with the body, the soul does not work through the intellect without first working through the phantasy and at the presence of phantasms, it is excited to work through the intellect."[40] "Phantasms" are products of the senses. He cites the case of the impressions present in one's consciousness that are "traces" of the working of one's senses. If someone says to you, "Imagine a white boat," you immediately have a mental image, a "phantasm" in your "mind's eye." Similarly with smells and sounds and the other senses. We can bring to mind the taste of ginger or the scent of mint. And similarly with certain kinds of memories. The intellect receives these from the body and so depends on the proper working of the bodily senses, which in the form of phantasms facilitate the operation of the intellect. In this sense, the soul depends on its union with the body, Turretin says. So in understanding Turretin's account, a distinction needs to be drawn between the operation of the intellectual soul as the causal source of the physical life of the body—which it is not—and as depending on the operation of the body as an occasion for some working of the soul (as it is in the examples cited).

Further, though the soul can understand certain things without phantasms, and so without the body, it does not follow that in these matters the soul is altogether "released" from the body. Nor would it be possible on the supposition of such a "release" from the body to account for "fury and madness." For according to Turretin, "fury and madness" are malfunctions of the soul that are due to a malfunctioning of the body. In respect of these there is a dependence of the mind on the body too:

> These do not fall upon the soul except by accident on account of the ministering senses and faculties being vitiated and corrupted. Thus the corruption of the brain can cause fury and delirium from the bad disposition of the phantasy of common sense (by which it happens that confused and disturbed objects are presented to the intellect, which being thus preoccupied, can judge nothing rightly). Hence if insanity is sometimes cured by hellebore or other corporeal remedies,

---

40. Turretin, *Institutes of Elenctic Theology*, 1:486.

the entire cure pertains to the injured brain (which must necessarily be healed that the soul may exercise its operations).[41]

Turretin does not say that all mental disorders are due to the malfunctioning of the brain in this way, but he clearly thinks that at least some are. And the hellebore in curing the corruption of the brain permits the soul to operate properly. He broadens this diagnosis to cover general conditions, such as the infirmities of old age and the growth of infants. "Hence it is that in the infant from the beginning, it reasons either little or not at all because either no (or a few) phantasms (on account of the weakness of the organs) are as yet present from which to receive the occasion of reasoning. In decrepit age, it cannot reason any more (or only weakly, as old men in second childhood) because the phantasms are either wholly or in great part destroyed, and what survive are obscurely presented to the intellect."[42]

If Turretin were a full-fledged hylomorphist, such as Mosley and perhaps Flavel, there would surely have been a reference in this passage to the vegetative soul. Perhaps Turretin is favoring a Platonic dualism at this point, modified by Cartesian influence. Contemporaneous with Turretin in the Academy in Geneva was Jean-Robert Chouet (1642–1731), who joined the Academy in 1669 as professor of philosophy and is credited with introducing Cartesian ideas there.[43] Turretin died in 1687. But maybe he expected his readers to fill in the details. So defects in the vegetative faculty can affect the faculty of the understanding, despite the understanding being hierarchically "superior" to the body.

However this may be, Turretin closes the brief discussion of brain and mind with a rather Platonic touch: "It sometimes also happens that, the powers of the body declining, there is a great strength in the soul, and

---

41. Turretin, *Institutes of Elenctic Theology*, 1:486. By "common sense" is meant what the five senses working together deliver to the consciousness or mind. According to Pliny, black hellebore (Christmas rose) was used as a purgative in mania by Melampus, a soothsayer and physician living in 1400 BC. Hence the name of Melampodium applied to hellebore.

42. Turretin, *Institutes of Elenctic Theology*, 1:486.

43. For an account of Chouet's career see Michael Heyd, *Between Orthodoxy and Enlightenment: Jean-Robert Chouet and the Introduction of Cartesian Science in the Academy of Geneva* (The Hague: Martinus Nijhoff, 1982).

the more the body is depressed and weakened, the higher the mind (as if rejoicing to depart from this prison of the body)."[44]

One consequence of the Cartesian philosophy was the reassignment of the various powers of the soul which, according to hylomorphism, animated the human body. Given the principled Cartesian distinction between the soul, a *res cogitans*, a thinking thing, and the body, a *res extensans*, an extended thing, the vegetative powers of the soul were assigned to the body, which, in Descartes's thinking, was a more autonomous (clockwork) arrangement than under hylomorphism. And of course as physiology developed and became neurophysiology, that view of the body became increasingly plausible, though as materialism beckoned it became unattractive to others. In whichever direction one was attracted, the soul was no longer endowed with vegetative and sensory powers, and the problem became how the seamless relation between body and soul could be accounted for.

John Owen on Life and Death

An interesting comparison with Turretin's remarks are John Owen's (1616–1683) comments about the life of the body. In the passage we are about to consider, Owen's main purpose is to expound the doctrine of regeneration, and to do this he takes the New Testament emphasis on regeneration as a new birth and as life from the dead. However, his incidental illustrative remarks are valuable as information as to how he views the soul and the body, the animation of the body, and its death. He takes the position that the rational soul animates the body. He refers to Genesis 2:7, which he understands as God's in-breathing of the total soul, with all its faculties, into the waiting human body—not as Calvin holds, simply the "lower" soul. Owen writes, "[God] creates for him, therefore, a separate, distinct animating soul and infuseth it into the matter prepared by its reception."[45]

Such animation occurs in two sorts of ways. There are, to begin with, acts that flow from life as life. These acts are natural and necessary,

---

44. Turretin, *Institutes of Elenctic Theology*, 1:486. This is one of the few cases I have come across in my study of anthropology that alludes to what I would refer to as cases of mental health or mental handicap.

45. John Owen, *A Discourse Concerning the Holy Spirit*, in *The Works of John Owen*, ed. W. H. Goold (Edinburgh: Banner of Truth, 1966), 3:4.

> as are all the actings and energies of the senses, and of the locomotive faculty, as also what belongs to the receiving and improving of nutriment…. These are acts of life as life, inseparable from it; and their end is, to preserve the union of the whole between the quickening and quickened principles. (2) There are such acts of life as proceed from the especial nature of this quickening principle. Such are all the elicit and imperate acts of our understandings and will; all acts that are voluntary, rational, and peculiarly human.[46]

There are expressions of life that are reflexive and automatic, those to do with eating, walking, and growing, which do not arise from particular volitions. And there are expressions that are brought about in a characteristically human way by the understanding and the will.

And what of death? Death is or involves the separation of the soul from the body. The infusing of the body for all that it does, the whole range of actions, ceases. For it is a principle of life only insofar as it is united to the body. "As a consequence of these [ceasings], there is in the body an impotency for and an inaptitude unto all vital operations. Not only do all operations of life actually cease, but the body is no more able to effect them. There remains in it, indeed, 'potentia obedientialis,' a 'passive power' to receive life again, if communicated unto it by an external efficient cause."[47]

Owen cites the resurrection of Lazarus as a case in point. He is sometimes impatient with scholasticism, as we will see later on; but here we see him (as an illustrative aside in his exposition of regeneration) in full cry as an unabashed scholastic, endorsing a feature of scholastic anthropology that is clearly hylomorphic.

Both Turretin and Owen are well-known Reformed theologians. The fact that their remarks on human life and disorders of various kinds are in places that are incidental to their main purpose is nonetheless revelatory as to their thinking more generally. They are expressions of their general education rather than of theological or philosophical expertise. Nowhere, as far as I know, do they discuss anthropology (as we are approaching it) in its own right at any length. In that sense they are at the other end of the spectrum from Mosley.

---

46. Owen, *Discourse Concerning the Holy Spirit*, in *Works*, 3:284. "Elicit" and "imperate" acts are acts of the will that are either automatic or consciously intended.

47. Owen, *Discourse Concerning the Holy Spirit*, in *Works*, 3:285.

Benedict Pictet's Dualism

Whatever the nature of Turretin's dualism, there is less doubt about Turretin's nephew Benedict Pictet (1655–1724), who followed him as professor of theology in the Academy of Geneva. He was similarly restrained in writing of the state of the soul after death. But he gave a more straightforwardly dualist, even Cartesian, account of body and soul than his uncle Francis, and a cautious account of the intermediate state:

> Nor is the soul, when it survives the body, asleep or insensible, which is a state bordering on annihilation; for this does not appear to be compatible with the nature of a spirit, whose essence cannot be conceived *without* thought. Here we must distinguish between those operations, in which the soul needs the assistance of the body, and its other operations; the former it does not exercise after death, the latter it certainly does; for if it would cease to think, it would cease to exist.[48]

Gisbertus Voetius on Immortality

Earlier we touched on Mosley's view of the immortality of the soul, which seemed to depend for this on the direct will of God. We may now go into this issue in a little more detail.

What is the immortality of the soul grounded in, and what does it imply? We have seen earlier Calvin's insistence on the immortality of the essence of the soul. But he is relatively unforthcoming on the grounding of this state of affairs. A particular clear and strong answer to this question was given by Gisbertus Voetius of Utrecht.[49]

For Voetius, the human soul is immortal from its own nature, not from a separate act of divine goodness. Immortality is not, for example, the gift of Christ to His church. The soul "has not any principle of dissolution or of ending, and therefore its nature demands that it keeps forever the being that it once received." That looks clear: the soul, unlike its body, has the power of indefinite self-persistence from its own nature. It cannot decay. But is it subject to God in this? Otherwise, it might seem that we have an instance of something that when it is brought into existence, God cannot control, being independently immortal.

---

48. Bernard Pictet, *Christian Theology*, trans. Frederick Reyroux (Philadelphia: Presbyterian Board of Publications, n.d.), 348–49.

49. Aza Goudriaan, *Reformed Orthodoxy and Philosophy, 1625–1750* (Leiden: Brill, 2006), ch. 4.

As Aza Goudriaan points out, Voetius is an advocate of the substantial union of body and soul, a view taken directly from Aquinas. His strong doctrine of the immortality of the soul does not have Cartesian sources—he was a firm critic of Descartes's views—but it is a feature of his hylomorphism.[50] The human being is not an accidental connection of soul and body, but the two are both essential to being a human being, uniting as form and matter. But, according to Voetius, the form is immortal, while the matter is mortal, but it is destined to connect up again at the resurrection. The two form one substance, consisting of body and soul. So at death this oneness is compromised somewhat, since one of its essential parts, its body, ceases to function and decays.[51] So the resurrection of the body is thereby necessitated, since the union of a person's body with his soul cannot fail to take place. This arrangement, Voetius thinks, is a matter of God's decree. God could by His absolute power will the permanent dissolution of soul as well as of body, but He will not do so in the case of the soul because of His decree otherwise. So the soul is immortal. It seems that this is no different in principle from God's decree to keep a human being alive for so many years. Certainly God is not necessitated to do what He does, but He does so only by hypothesis. As such it is a necessity of the consequence. The soul does not have independent or intrinsic immortality, therefore.

Is it legitimate to call it immortal by necessity of the consequence, a hypothetical necessity? Yes, but it is hypothetical necessity not of an event or series of such, but of a kind of being, a human soul. It is a kind of natural necessity, the prolongation of the soul indefinitely. The life of the soul could be brought to an end by God's absolute power, and only in that way. But having decreed the soul's neverendingness, God's immutability secures it. Voetius says that the soul "depends on God, it cannot be destroyed, however, by His ordinary power." I suppose by this is meant God's power as exerted in the ordinary course of life. Nevertheless, "God can destroy it by absolute power."[52] So the immortality of the soul is guaranteed by "unchangeableable things"—not two promises, as in Hebrews 6:18, but by two decrees. The immortality of the soul, for Voetius, is a matter of nature,

---

50. Of relevance is J. A. van Ruler, "New Philosophy to Old Standards: Voetius' Vindication of Divine Concurrence and Secondary Causality," *Netherlands Archief voor Kergeschiedenis* 71, no. 1 (1991): 58–91.

51. Goudriaan, *Reformed Orthodoxy and Philosophy*, 238.

52. Goudriaan, *Reformed Orthodoxy and Philosophy*, 242–43.

not of grace, but nonetheless a matter of the will of God. (If it were of grace, then it may have annihilationist consequences for those individuals who do not enjoy grace.) It looks as if Mosley might agree with this.

In this chapter we have looked at the soul and body largely in general terms. In the next chapter we look in more detail at the individual faculties and powers of the soul.

CHAPTER 4

The Faculties and Powers
of the Soul

The understanding is almost universally regarded as the prime faculty. Among the scholastics, it is true there have been voluntarists—Scotists and the like—but they do not figure very markedly among the Reformed.[1] The mind is that which makes sense of what it takes in through the senses and the intellect (a term employed separately from the understanding). The five senses provide the intellect with phantasms (that is, mental and intellectual representations of what they sense), and from other goings-on in the mind, including the memory. And on the basis of these data the intellect judges both what is true or otherwise, in the case of the "contemplative intellect"; and in the case of the "practical intellect," it judges what the individual should do or forbear. Although this book is not only about the theologically significant aspects of the soul, one can hardly discuss the understanding without referring to the theological topic of man created in the image of God. According to the unanimous verdict of the Reformed theologians of this era, to possess an intellect is to possess the image of God. Mankind is distinguished from nonhuman animals not by possessing a soul as such, for sheep, for example, possess souls which animate their bodies, but by possessing an intellect.

So a human person possessing a soul is like a sheep's possession of a soul insofar as they each possess soulish powers that animate their bodies

---

1. The recent attempt to give Duns Scotus a leading role in Reformed anthropology cannot be pronounced a great success. See *Reformed Thought on Freedom*, ed. Willem J. van Asselt, J. Martin Bac, and Roelf T. te Velde (Grand Rapids: Baker, 2010). For discussion, see Paul Helm, "*Reformed Thought on Freedom*: Some Further Thoughts," *Journal of Reformed Theology* 4, no. 3 (2010): 185–207; Paul Helm, "Structural Indifference and Compatibilism in Reformed Orthodoxy," *Journal of Reformed Theology* 5, no. 2 (2011): 184–205; and Richard A. Muller, *Divine Will and Human Choice* (Grand Rapids: Baker, 2017).

and vegetative and sensory appetites. But human beings are superior to sheep in that they have souls that possess understanding and will, the theoretical (or contemplative) intellect and the practical intellect, and the power of choice between alternatives. Man is a rational animal, as Aristotle and Calvin[2] each maintained. And this reflects God's purely spiritual, wise, and holy being. So the Reformed theologians founded the *imago Dei* not on relations between the man and the woman, or social relations more generally, nor in God's Trinitarian character, nor in man's governance of the other creatures, but by having a mind which images God's mind and makes obedience and the exercise of the cultural mandate possible.

The center of the entire ensemble of the faculties, including the conscience (if that were to be regarded as a separate faculty), is variously referred to; but it is more generally referred to as the reason or intellect or understanding or heart. The list of the faculties will sometimes include the intellective faculty and the vegetative faculty, and sometimes not; sometimes the conscience, and sometimes not; sometimes the memory, and sometimes not. In some writers, the term "faculty" is used sparingly, and in others more generously to encompass what we might call subfunctions of the soul.

So within that understanding of the *imago* there are various ways of identifying and enumerating the powers of the soul, some more expansive and detailed than others. We have already seen that there is a difference in whether the soul is thought of in Platonic or Aristotelian ways. But in the case of the faculties of the human soul, the mainstream Reformed orthodox and Puritan thinkers never stray very far from the outlook of Aquinas, and through him to Aristotle. All refer to the understanding and give it primacy, but the details differ.

The charge of some scholars that the growth of Reformed orthodoxy and of Puritanism within it led to the Reformed tradition falling into "rationalism" or "Aristotelian rationalism" is mistaken. And this mistake is at least partly due to the failure to see that when the Reformed orthodox refer to the understanding or intellect or reason, they were treating these terms as descriptions of a faculty in a generic sense, and typically in their treatment they made allowance for its fallenness and for it at best being only partly restored through the regenerating and sanctifying grace

---

2. Calvin, *Institutes*, II.ii.12.

of God. No faculty is in pristine condition. It follows from that fact that the understanding does not operate as it should, much less that the deliverances of the reason were always in the form of sets of clear and distinct ideas to which the primitive supernaturalistic teachings of Scripture are to be subordinated to the reason in a rationalistic fashion. These cautions need to be kept in mind throughout our treatment of the various aspects of anthropology.

On the faculty psychology account of the soul, it is, as we have already noted, spiritual, with no discrete parts as the body has parts. The soul has a range or array of powers which the mind groups as certain activities of the understanding, and others as certain activities of the will. Some thinkers, when working on the organization of the faculties, appear to reify or personalize the faculties. This may perhaps be excused as the employment of figurative language by thinkers for expository effect. A question to have in mind is, Do these seemingly more personal expressions, if that is what they are intended to be, contradict the nature of a faculty and treat it as if it were a personalized "subsoul"? Other thinkers issue warnings about the dangers of doing so.

William Pemble on the Importance of the Understanding

In his book *Vindiciae Gratiae, A Plea for Grace, More Especially Grace and Faith*,[3] William Pemble (1591–1623) has a discussion on the faculties of the soul. He makes the usual distinction between the understanding, the object of which is the truth, and the will, which has its object as the good. So saving faith, for example, is not simply an act of the understanding, since its object is divine revelation, which is a great good. But this is subject to serious qualification. So Pemble cautions,

> Wherefore we affirm that this Assent of Faith is an Act of the Understanding and of the Will, both together approving and allowing the truth and goodness of all Divine things. In which assertion you are to note that we do not make the Habite of Faith to be inherent in

---

3. *Vindiciae Gratiae, A Plea for Grace, More Especially Grace and Faith*, in *The Workes of that Late Learned minister of God's Holy Word, Mr William Pemble*, 4th ed. (Oxford: printed for Henry Hall, for John Adams, Edw. and John Forrest, 1659). The *Workes* is a collection of previously published and hitherto unpublished books and other materials by Pemble, a fellow of Magdalen College, Oxford, who died at the age of thirty-one.

two divers subjects, nor this act of Assent to come from two divers Principles, or two several Faculties of the minde, but we affirm the subject is but one and the same, the intellectual Nature. For I take it with divers of the Learned, yet as they do under correction of the more Learned; that those speculations about the real distinction of the Faculties in such Spiritual Substances as are the Angels and souls of men, are but meer subtilties of the School, without any true ground in nature it self. He that shall in an unpartial search after Truth and full Satisfaction, throughly examine the same Distinction of Faculties in the Sensitive Soul, that the common Sense, Phantasie, and Memorie are three powers of it, really distinct, as in Nature, so in place: let him but examine the weakness of the ground of this distinction, and the inexplicable difficulties that do accompany it, he shall finde upon study of the point, that it is no Heresie in Philosophy to hold, that our grand Master hath been affirmed more than will ever be understood or thoroughly justified by any of his Disciples.[4]

Pemble observes that certain distinctions have been unnecessary as a result of thinking of the spiritual substance of the soul in a way that is true of "material forms." But it is not a case of the division of the soul into separate faculties but of differences in the powers of the one spiritual substance. The things of God are both true and good. But this does not require that they are apprehended by distinct faculties, the understanding and the will. Rather, we must recognize that in some of their activities the understanding and will are involved together.

For the present, we must note this kind of faculty psychology, allowing this language reluctantly when it is used of states of affairs that are not separate but are equally true and good. If we follow Pemble, we must not be led astray so as to assign exclusive powers into separate faculties. We will consider some of the consequence of Pemble's cautions when discussing the intertwining of the faculties in chapter 6. For the moment, we may keep his strictures in mind.

John Flavel on the Understanding and Will

The Puritan pastor John Flavel opens his account of the understanding as follows:

---

4. Pemble, *Vindiciae*, 111–12.

> This is the noble leading Faculty of the Soul: we are not distinguished from the *Brutes* by our *Senses*, but by our *Understanding*. As Grace sets one man above another, so Understanding sets the meanest man above the best of Brutes. Strange and wonderful things are performed by the natural instinct and sagacity of Beasts; but yet, what is said of one is true of them all, *God hath not imparted understanding to them*, Job 39.17. This is a Jewel which adorns none but rational Creatures, Men, and Angels. *It is a Faculty of the reasonable Soul, by which a Man apprehends and judgeth all intelligible things.*[5]

This faculty may be involved, Flavel says, in two kinds of activity:

> It has a two-fold role, the first of which is to distinguish truth from error. It brings things before the soul in a kind of raw state, and then sorts them, and orderly ranks them into their proper *Classes* of *lawful* and *unlawful*, *necessary* and *indifferent*, *expedient* and *inexpedient*, that the Soul may not be damnified by mistaking one for another. And this Judgment of *Discretion* every man must be allowed for himself. No man is obliged to shut the eyes of his own Understanding, and follow another man blindfold.
>
> And secondly *To direct* and guide us in our practice. This faculty is by Philosophers rightly call'd, *the leading faculty*, because the Will follows its practical dictates. It sits at helm, and guides the course of the Soul: Not impelling or rigorously inforcing its dictates upon the Will; for the Will cannot be imposed upon; but by giving a directive light, or pointing, as it were with its finger, at what it ought to chuse, and what to refuse."[6]

This is Flavel's way of pointing to the fundamental place of the understanding (considered as the reason) in theoretical or contemplative matters, in which a person is primarily concerned with acquiring true beliefs, and his understanding is or should be comparatively receptive. And in a parallel way, when the intellect is employed practically in formulating actions to be carried out for the purpose of achieving an end or ends and accomplishing the means to the end or ends, it is engaged more practically. This is the intellect as practical reason, in carrying out a practical task in which it instructs the will to execute actions to achieve these ends, using the data

---

5. Flavel, *Pneumatologia*, 17.
6. Flavel, *Pneumatologia*, 18.

it has acquired. So to take a simple example, a person forms the intention from what he has learned and remembered to visit a certain place; and he undertakes the journey and whatever steps he believes are necessary to get there, avoiding obstacles and false routes as he travels.

So the soul has the power of "thoughts," that is, of thinking, active in the speculative and practical understanding. "When the understanding or mind revolves and meditates the things that come into it, that very Meditation is an inward speaking, or a hidden word in the heart."[7] The mind is not restricted to thinking about the images of the fancy. It can think about God or about itself, spiritual beings; things that are present, and things absent.[8] This power goes with the soul (unlike the fancy, which requires our embodiment).

Flavel says that the conscience also belongs to the understanding, the judgment of a man upon himself. Such judgments have to do with the practical understanding. It is the observer, recorder, and witness to every action; it persists through the death of the body and will be our companion in the world to come. The understanding is the wit, reason, opinion, judgment. It guides the will, and the understanding and will have great influence upon the affections.[9]

To concentrate on the conscience as an aspect of the understanding is Flavel's way of making the distinction between the Aristotelian speculative or contemplative understanding and the practical understanding. But the way in which he presents this shows that he (as a pastor) does not have much interest in understanding human nature for its own sake, but only for those matters that are of practical importance. Further, he wishes to safeguard the conscience from coercion and notes that it should operate voluntarily, the understanding neither coercing or constraining it, but directing it. We will consider the conscience at greater length in chapter 5.

Edward Reynolds on the Understanding

The Westminster divine Edward Reynolds's more polished account goes into more detail but nevertheless shares broadly the same outlook. He distinguishes the understanding's operations between those to do with objects

---

7. Flavel, *Pneumatologia*, 18.
8. Flavel, *Pneumatologia*, 41.
9. Flavel, *Pneumatologia*, 41–42.

and those to do with the will, which employs its cogitations of the understanding for practical purposes. He also has things to say about knowledge and the inferences it is possible to make from what we already know.[10] Knowledge involves apprehension and judgment regarding the particulars of our understanding. This is speculative (or contemplative) knowledge. And it involves the "rational memory" ("that excellent faculty of the mind"). He discusses ignorance of various kinds.[11] The dangers of speculation and the distinction between science (*scientia*) and opinion are made clear. There is a noticeable moralistic tone to his discussion of errors.[12] There follows a discussion of the action of reason in the operation of the understanding, "invention, wit and judgment."[13] A considerable part of Reynolds's discussion has to do with the corruptions of the various uses of the faculties, which he usually illustrates from classical literature.

The understanding informs the will, which otherwise is "blind." "So all the acts of the will necessarily presuppose some precedent guiding acts in the understanding, whereby they are proportioned to the rules of right reason."[14] What compels the understanding, for example, in the case of the valid conclusion of a syllogism is the meaning of the propositions, not the will. The will cannot compel the understanding, only regulate and direct it. It does this by proposing final and intermediary ends of action and means to these ends. (Pemble might comment that to do so it must presumably apprehend those ends, so there is not a clear separation between the operations of understanding and will.)

As we have already seen, in the faculty psychology of the Reformed orthodox, the will is generally regarded as being subordinate to the intellect and executor of the preponderant judgments of the understanding or intellect or reason. Turretin held that the will *must* follow the intellect, understanding this subordination to be metaphysical.[15] This seems to be the general position in Reformed orthodoxy.

As we will shortly see, discussion of the state of the first pair and what occurred in the commission of the first sin, and in particular in what sense

---

10. Reynolds, *Treatise on the Passions and Faculties of the Soul*, in *Works*, 6:281.

11. Reynolds, *Treatise on the Passions and Faculties of the Soul*, in *Works*, 6:289–90.

12. Reynolds, *Treatise on the Passions and Faculties of the Soul*, in *Works*, 6:278–93.

13. Reynolds, *Treatise on the Passions and Faculties of the Soul*, in *Works*, 6:305.

14. Reynolds, *Treatise on the Passions and Faculties of the Soul*, in *Works*, 6:317.

15. Turretin, *Institutes of Elenctic Theology*, 1:663.

the faculties became disordered by and in the fall—these matters were of intense interest to the Reformed. But first we will look again at Flavel and then at Reynolds as samples of the different ways in which the relation between intellect and will were characterized. And then we will consider the different senses that the phrase "free will" may bear.

John Flavel on the Primacy of the Will

Flavel's treatment of the will is rather short compared to the treatment of other areas. He first compares the will's relation to the body and not to the other faculties of the soul, to that of an "absolute Sovereign,"[16] which is his way of expressing the soul's "ownership" of the body. Though, as Flavel points out, the will cannot command the health of the body or its ceasing to exist. It is true, however, that in the sequence of understanding-will-action, it is the will which is the executive faculty, which immediately affects the body, and therefore may be said to be over it. So, as Flavel puts it, the will has a "*political* power" over the faculties and passions of the soul, a power exercised by "*suasion* and *insinuation*."

Flavel seems at points to depart from the then-current orthodoxy regarding the understanding when he says of the will,

> Thus it can oft-times perswade the understanding and thoughts to lay by this or that subject, and apply themselves to the study of another. It can bridle, and restrain the Affections and Passions, but yet it hath no absolute power over the inner, as it hath with the outer man; its weakness and inability to govern the inner man, appears in two things more especially remarkable viz. 1. It cannot with all its power and skill command and fetch off the thoughts from some subjects which are set on at some times with extraordinary weight upon the Soul. However the thoughts may obsequiously follow its beck sometimes, and per-swasions cannot disengage one thought.[17]

If the will truly persuaded the understanding, then it would no longer be blind, as Reynolds earlier claimed. At least it is informed by the intellect. So this passage seems to be rather ambivalent on the will. Sometimes it sovereignly makes the understanding change its attention. But in other respects, it may be subordinate to the understanding. Here Flavel cites the case of

---

16. Flavel, *Pneumatologia*, 22.

17. Flavel, *Pneumatologia*, 23–24.

conversion. Instead of the will disturbing conversion, it also is changed by divine power. Here he stoutly upholds the monergy of the effectual call, but it seems that he gives to the will certain powers similar to that of the understanding. He sees the will's "carnality," its depravity, as having a mind of its own, rather than having a disinclination or aversion to carrying out certain desires to satisfy them, and contrasts it with the "sanctified" will, which in conversion finally triumphs. Nor can the will pacify a raging conscience; it cannot be stilled by an act of the will. "But notwithstanding these exemptions, it is a noble faculty, and hath a vastly extended Empire in the Soul of Man: It is the door of the soul, at which the Spirit of God knocks for entrance. When this is won, the Soul is won to Christ."[18] No doubt Flavel is able to reconcile these views with Augustinianism, but his positive account of the will as maneuverable in this way is unusual.

Edward Reynolds on the Will's Blindness

A view distinct from this, or perhaps more consistent than Flavel's, is given by Reynolds when, toward the end of his treatment of the faculties and passions, he considers the relations of the understanding to the will. For Reynolds, the understanding is a "minister or counsellor" to the will:

> For the will alone is a blind faculty; and therefore as it cannot see the right good it ought to affect, without the assistance of an informing power,—so neither can it see the right way it ought to take for procuring that good, without the direction of a conducting power. As it hath not judgement to discover an end, so neither hath it discourse to judge of the right means, whereby that may be attained. So that all the acts of the will necessary presuppose some precedent guiding acts in the understanding, whereby they are proportioned to the rules of right reason.[19]

This is another good example of a theologian using the faculties while avoiding the *homunculus* fallacy, of thinking that a particular faculty has the powers of a soul within a soul. No, says Reynolds, the will itself does not possess understanding. Rather, it is "blind," and it moves as guided and commanded by the soul's understanding. Thus, the understanding

---

18. Flavel, *Pneumatologia*, 29.

19. Reynolds, *Treatise on the Passions and Faculties of the Soul*, in *Works*, 6:317.

commands the will. Yet the understanding does not have dominion over the will to force it, but simply priority in operation, the will being regulated and directed by the understanding. Although through the fall human faculties are depraved, yet they retain their character in this respect, that what the understanding desires, the will brings to pass. So fallen men and women can delight in evil *sub ratione boni*, as their good.[20] We will see later that some theologians stress a disorderliness in their relation brought on through the fall.

The will is also discussed a great deal in coming to an understanding of the unique event of the disobedience of the first pair. Before we begin to look at these, and particularly at the uses of the expression "free will" or "free choice," it is important to remember the doctrinal background to the discussions.

Adam and Eve were created good, even very good; and theologically this is taken to mean they were created in a state in which they were sinless. But their sinlessness was not as good as it could be. For one thing, possessing it was not guaranteed; it was contingent. The pair were not essentially sinless, since it was possible for them to disobey even in this created state—and they did disobey and so fell. This is characteristically referred to as being created good though *mutable*.

Franciscus Gomarus on Free Choice

When he turned thirty, Franciscus Gomarus (1563–1641) became professor of theology at the University of Leiden, and later at Saumur, and then at Groningen. In a disputation on free choice, one of several that he produced, he shows us how fertile a field free will was for the scholastic Reformed theologian. This is because the concept spanned the fourfold state of man, having a different value in each state, as well as because the topic became a battleground between the Reformed and the Jesuit and Arminian views of grace. We will look at such debates in chapter 7. Here we see Gomarus laying out the relevant distinctions between the senses of free will.[21] He sets out a definition of free choice as "the free power of a mind-gifted nature to

---

20. Reynolds, *Treatise on the Passions and Faculties of the Soul*, in *Works*, 6:320.

21. The translated material of Gomarus is taken from a disputation as published in van Asselt et al., *Reformed Thought on Freedom*, ch. 4.

choose from those [means] leading to a certain goal, one proposed by reason above another, or to accept or reject one and the same means."[22]

This is, in effect, providing the genus of "free choice," from which the four species, corresponding to the four states of mankind, issue. The relation posited between the will and the reason, or the intellect, is prominent, and the teleological framework of choice, which has to do with achieving means to an end, or the end itself, as proposed by the intellect. These points and others related are then discussed in detail and clarified. The result is then applied to the four states: before the fall, the fall into sin, the state of grace, and the state of glory.

In the unfallen state, what can be freely chosen, and what not?[23] Created in righteousness, without stain or blemish in either body or mind, man could continue in a course that was pleasing to God. He was in a condition of being able to continue choosing the good (that is, what is judged by him as a good) but also to veer to evil, and a bad course was chosen. Nevertheless, the fallen faculties are able to do some remaining good in both intellectual and practical matters. Concerning these matters, Gomarus states that the unregenerate can perform such acts with liberty, while in regard to such matters as justification and sanctification, nothing in the fallen state can be performed freely.

Concerning the third state, Gomarus notes,

> It is discussed whether either our will according to its natural and inborn faculty cooperates actively with the divine will in the first conversion toward God, or whether the will is rather passive in the first conversion, in such a way that the will concurs in no way [with the divine will] at the first moment of conversion, but bears (*patiatur*) that this power [*dunamin*] of willing well is being infused to it? The first is claimed by the Roman Catholics, we claim the second, and this with Scripture.[24]

So in the third state the will has to be divinely freed, being passive as God frees it.

---

22. Quoted in van Asselt et al., *Reformed Thought on Freedom*, 128.

23. Quoted in van Asselt et al., *Reformed Thought on Freedom*, 130.

24. Quoted in van Asselt et al., *Reformed Thought on Freedom*, 133.

The Leiden *Synopsis* on the Complexities of Freedom

The Leiden *Synopsis Purioris Theologiae* is a multiple-authored treatment of theological topics in disputational mode, a cycle of disputations by members of the faculty of theology at the University of Leiden responded to by students. There were several such disputation cycles at Leiden, but this was the first to be published in 1625. The student responses were not published. The topics were ordered in the sequence of Scripture, God, creation, providence, the fall, as well as others. The sequence is "interrupted" after the discussions of original and actual sin by a distinct disputation, disputation 17, "Of Free Choice," which clarifies and extends understanding of the free choice arising out of the place played by the human will in the fall.[25] This was a dogmatic crux in disputation with the Jesuits and Arminians and so required exact formulation:

> Human free choice is not free of the creation and providential rule of God, obviously not, but free choice refers to a basic power of alternative choice, a "willing" that is contrasted with action done from coercion, necessitated by force, either physical force (as in torture) or psychological force (as in blackmail), but free and contingent. These words denote the presence and operation of intellectual judgment or choice, a power to do X or to refrain from X.
>
> So the object or the material of free choice is all that is subject to human deliberation, choice and action; or all the good and evil things that concern moral behavior and actions (though not the physical things that our natural desires pursue or shun).[26]

A distinction is drawn between deliberation and action, ascribed in turn to the understanding and the will, and the desire for physical things, the objects of desire. Objects of such deliberation may be human activities such as eating, drinking, walking, resting; others are "civic" activities for the common good in families and in society; and finally, matters to do with the inner spiritual life. These distinctions are important for a proper understanding of free choice. Man's will has the general character as a choice that wills this or that. But given that the condition and status of people vary—the original state of creation, or fall and corruption, or grace and

---

25. This disputation was presented by the theologian Antonius Thysius, and the respondent was Jacobus Adrianus Thetronious.

26. *Synopsis Purioris Theologiae*, ed. Dolf te Velde (Leiden: Brill, 2014), 1:412–13.

restoration, and at last, glory and perfection—so the powers of their choice vary. Hence there is need to draw appropriate distinctions to avoid serious confusion. In the first state, that of original integrity, mankind had freedom in the general sense just discussed, but he could turn himself away from his Maker, freely turning to evil or continuing to choose the good, and in this way freely maintaining his original character. Mankind was created free of sin, but was free to change from the good. The first person made such a change and ruined himself, being as a consequence bound to sin. *Non posse non peccare.*

This original asymmetry is important. As noted earlier, primitive free choice was not exercised in a condition of neutrality between good and evil, since the first pair were created good. As a consequence, though fallen Adam could still make free choices in everyday life, his will is nonetheless evil in that "such actions are not initiated, performed, and directed by the goal of giving God the glory that is owed him." And, "in spiritual and inward matters, the will of the natural, unregenerate man is free only to do evil."[27] But in the state of grace and restoration, God works efficaciously by His Spirit, who infuses a new disposition in the person, goodness in his intellect and will. Man is enlightened savingly and spiritually to receive the word of God, being in this way restored.

So the answer of the Leiden divines to the question, Do human beings possess free will? is somewhat complex. The answer is indexed to different eras of man's state. Although our discussion here has chiefly concerned the will, the faculties of the understanding, conscience, and affections are all similarly affected. The depravity is total, affecting all faculties of the soul, so as to make a person's life a state of disobedience and rebellion and disaffection from the love of God and neighbor.

> Man does not, however, behave with his free choice like some block of wood, for God works in man as a subject endowed with the faculties of mind and will, and He works through His word (Romans 10.17; John 17.20; I Corinthians 1.21). Yet it is not as though the natural man himself allows God to be at work in him (for that is an act of good will). For by nature man is stubborn and opposes God when He uses his word outwardly, with its promise, its warning, and its other means of persuasion (Matthew 23.37; Acts 7.51). But God works in man such

---

27. *Synopsis Purioris Theologiae,* 1:419.

as he is, entirely weakened and bound by his evil character and habits (Ephesians 2.1–3; Titus 3.3).[28]

The Leiden *Synopsis* shows the growing complexity of the discussion of the liberty or freedom of the will.

The Westminster Confession on Freedom and Liberty

An attempt to clarify and standardize the terminology of "free will," "liberty of will," and so on, at least in English, may be found in the Westminster Confession (1647). The Confession begins its account as follows: "God… created man, male and female, with reasonable and immortal souls, endued with knowledge, righteousness, and true holiness, after his own image, having the law of God written in their hearts, and power to fulfill it; and yet under a possibility of transgression, being left to the liberty of their own will, which was subject to change" (WCF 4.2).

In the Confession, the terms "freedom" and "liberty" appear to be chosen with some care. In fact, the variation between "liberty" and "free will" is not merely stylistic, but the two terms are doing two distinct jobs.

We first look at the Confession's use of "liberty." In "Of God's Eternal Decree," WCF 3.1, the Confession notes, "Neither is the freedom or contingency of secondary causes." Again, in "Creation," WCF 4.2: "being left to the liberty of their own will." And finally, "Of Free Will," WCF 9.1: "God hath endued the will of man with that natural liberty."

Now we consider the Confession's use of "freedom," first in various places in "Of Free Will": "Man in his state of innocency, had freedom and power to will and to do that which is good" (WCF 9.2); "He freeth him from his natural bondage under sin, by his grace alone enables him freely to will and to do that which is spiritually good" (WCF 9.4); and, "The will of man is made perfectly and immutably free to do good alone in the state of glory only" (WCF 9.5). The term also occurs in "Effectual Calling," WCF 10.1: "yet so as they come most freely, being made willing by his grace." The usage in WCF 20, "Of Christian Liberty and Liberty of Conscience," is somewhat different. But here "liberty" is being used in a political or social sense as it is in "Liberty, Equality and Fraternity," for example, and is not relevant to our discussion.

---

28. *Synopsis Purioris Theologiae*, 1:421.

This apart, there is reason to think that in the Confession, "freely" has invariably to do with spiritual ability, the enjoyment of the effects of divine, enabling grace, or the absence of such ability. So in heaven the saints have perfect and immutable *freedom* to do good, and those who are effectually called are such as they come to Christ *most freely*, being made willing by His grace. The opposite of such freedom is not a metaphysical state, because in the Confession "freedom" does not denote a metaphysical power of the will but a moral and spiritual state, often referred to as freedom from the "bondage" of the will.

So "freely" in the occurrence of "yet so as they come most freely, being made willing by his grace," is warranted not on the outcomes of metaphysical debates about the will, but on the operations of divine grace and in the usage of the New Testament. For example, "Therefore if the Son makes you free, you shall be free indeed" (John 8:36; see also v. 21); and, "Where the spirit of the Lord is, there is freedom" (2 Cor. 3:17 ESV); and, "The freedom of the glory of the children of God" (Rom. 8:21 ESV). Freedom is linked to certain graciously given states of the people of God.

What about "liberty" in the Confession? When this word is used by the divines, its use is much more general. The context of its use seems uniformly to do with the capacities of human beings in general. "The liberty of second causes" has to do with those individuals endowed with intelligence and will, by comparison with the behavior of animals, insects, and vegetation, other kinds of secondary causation. This is the liberty with which God has endowed men and women. In addition, the Confession states that without divine assistance to keep them on the straight and narrow path, the pair in Eden were "left to the liberty of their own will," whatever the character of that willing may have been. It is not that the pair had freedom to choose good or evil, but that they were created good, and therefore biased toward the good; yet not immutably so. And being left to the liberty of their own wills—that is, without receiving further divine enabling—they lapsed, succumbing to devilish temptation, and "brought death into the world and all our woe." But in the glory to come, the Confession states, "The will of man is made perfectly and *immutably free to do good alone* in the state of glory only" (WCF 9.5). Once again the connection is made between freedom and a state of grace. And mutability, the state in which the pair were created, allowed them liberty to disobey. When it was first exercised, it left them in a position of hostility to God, partly natural, partly penal. They were created in a state that was *posse peccare aut non peccare*, and as a result of their first disobedience they were in the state of *non posse non peccare*, to use the traditional Augustinian phrases already mentioned. So within anthropology more generally, mankind's will, the meaning or meanings of "free will," "liberty of will," and so forth, and the nature of the servitude to sin were extensively discussed by the Reformed orthodox in the seventeenth century.[29]

William Pemble on the Affections

Pemble discusses the order and connectedness of the will, affections, and understanding in a rather compressed fashion. It helps in making the transition from the will to the affections. Pemble is dealing with the blinding of the judgement and perverting of the will. He writes, "The Understanding receives her notice from the fancyes impression: which befriending Passion representeth often to the judgment not true and reall, but apparent and conceited shapes…. The will inclines oftner to passion, then Judgement, because passion is given more to choice and liberty. The Judgement is precise and setled to one part."[30] Pemble is pointing out that the perverted will is more likely to be affected by the passions, which are less controlled than it is by the judgment. And then follows the will's relation to the understanding, including the effect of the affections on the will. Sometimes this is effected by directly ruling, and otherwise by persuading. As often occurs in the literature, Pemble uses political analogies to aid his readers' understanding:

> The seate of the Will is the Heart, where passions reside. As the braine is the seat of the Understanding. The will prosecutes what the understanding judges. The object of it is Good. Of the understanding Truth. Will without passion chooseth the true good: with passion the forged and apparent only. If goods be evident, it affects simply without prayse, if doubted there is first deliberation. It hath 2 parts, 1. Approbation, or willing. 2. Refusal, or nilling. For execution it commandes in men Passions, Faculty of motions. The former it rules by persuasion, as by an Aristocracy or state regiment, whereby governement is not so absolute, but the rest may interpose. 2. The latter it rules by command,

---

29. However, it is interesting that in a Latin translation of the *Confession* by John Field (Cambridge, 1659), *libertas* is used both for "liberty" and "freedom."

30. William Pemble, *A Summe of Moral Philosophy* (Oxford: printed by John Lichfield, 1632), 17. This is not included in his collected works.

> as a Lord over his servant, without relent in the one, or reluctance in the other. The tenents of the will are 2. 1. It affects nothing, but what the understanding hath weighed first and contrarily the Understanding conceits nothing, but the will perswades; their offices are joynt and mutuall. 2. It cannot be constrained being of greatest freedom and liberty: Though we have not freedom of will, to come from worse to better, in matters of grace yet in matters civill we have…from a common motion of goodness conceived by the practicke Understanding. [31]

Pemble is not unique in using the heart, which is of course a biblical word used for the soul or for the source of all the affections, but he seems to be in a minority. But does he here mean the physical heart? He couples its reference with that of the brain being the seat of the understanding. If so, such usage is unusual. These parts of the body may be thought of as the different organs which the soul "targets" for certain of its activities. Passion can divert the will from following the true good into following only the apparent good. It is not, as with some, when it occurs, a state of the will or its effect in operation. But Pemble goes on to state the conjointness of the understanding and will, or their "intertwining." More will be said about the cooperation of faculties in chapter 6. His *Summe of Morall Philosophy*, from which this material is taken, is presented in a very compressed, note-like form, almost as if it was originally Pemble's lecture notes.

In the passage above, he stresses the conjoint operation of understanding and will. As we saw earlier in his work on the grace of faith, he also has rather different things to say regarding the understanding and the will, which he does not consider distinct faculties that may act independently of each other. The will includes the understanding, and the understanding includes the will—because goodness and truth are one. They are known and desired by the same faculty. "The difference lies only in the diverse degree of our apprehension, which varies according to the things apprehended seem to have more or less agreement with our particular uses and necessities."[32]

As we have been seeing, in the case of Puritanism and Reformed orthodoxy, the powers of the soul are distinguishable into distinct groups and distinguished further between their relative priority or posteriority in the soul—between, roughly speaking, intellectualistic, the majority view, and

---

31. Pemble, *Summe*, 62–63.
32. Pemble, *Vindiciae*, 113–14.

voluntaristic positions, the minority. The "passions" or "affections" (both terms are used) are in certain circumstances the product of a faculty, of the will or the intellect.[33] The question is potentially more complex if one takes the view that the intellect and will intertwine, or even if they form one faculty, which was Pemble's position, at least in his work on the grace of justifying faith.

We need to explain how affection is understood in terms of pleasure to be achieved or pain to be avoided or lessened (evoking the generic affections of joy and hope), or pain to be achieved or expected and pleasure lessened (evoking fear and grief). The pleasures and pains may be mental or bodily. In modern usage, "feeling" and "emotion" are often used interchangeably, and "affection" may be used as a milder or more dispositionally based expression of emotion.

A number of preliminary points need to be made to avoid confusion. One is that "feeling" is ambiguous between purely sensory and intellectual uses. The feeling of the smoothness of a surface records the purely sensory effect of touching it. But if a person has a feeling of anger, that feeling typically has an object or objective, a real or imaginary state of affairs that generates anger in the observer. And so the anger at witnessing cruelty is different than the anger felt at some personal failure. The fear of rising inflation is different from the fear of the oncoming pit bull terrier because the respective objects of the fear are different. Sometimes the emotional feeling may be vague, and it may take time to identify its object. And sometimes it is "nameless," difficult to describe or explain; but such cases do not affect the point of principle. For the Reformed orthodox, emotions are feelings understood in these more complex ways, ways involving the intellect and at times the senses. Besides the ambiguity of "feeling," there is another ambiguity. A word such as "peace" can stand for a virtue, that of being peaceable, and also the feeling of peace, peacefulness, and even a legal or moral state, the state of not being at war, and so being at peace. It is sometimes necessary to spend time getting clear an author's usage.

In seventeenth-century discussions of the affections and emotions, Stoicism was an outlook that the Reformed rejected unanimously: the view that the rational or wise person seeks the riddance of all feelings which

---

33. For further discussion on emotion, see Alec Ryrie and Thom Schwanda, eds., *Puritanism and Emotion in the Early Modern World* (London: Palgrave, Macmillan, 2016).

may perturb and obstruct the proper working of the reason. Understanding the relation between reason and passion was important, but Reformed orthodox and Puritans did not aim to solve it by the elimination of all passion and emotion. They would concur with Augustine's remark about the Stoics: "I refute them with two words 'Jesus wept.'" Christ's experience of emotion validated the expression of emotions more generally.

The general view is that the affections are aspects of the will when it reaches a certain strength and encounters either opposition or success in executing the business of the understanding or sympathizes with the hopes and fears of others. The cardinal affections are said to be joy, fear, hope, and grief. All affections are variants of one or other or combinations of these four. The objective of the reason is to modulate such feelings in line with Christian virtues and to make the virtues more achievable. This involves the making of the expression of feelings or emotions fitting and proportionate to the states of affairs that generate them, to prevent them reaching such a pitch that they cloud the judgment or affect the states of the body. The objective is not only controlling those that are excessive, however, but of expressing fully those that are sluggish. Christians are to rejoice and to weep as appropriate. In the case of uncontrollable weeping or laughter or of prolonged weeping or laughter caused by some trivial circumstance, they are to restrain such affections by the understanding, while promoting their activity in situations in which a person knows himself to be unnaturally inclined to impassivity in the face of another's need or distress. In these ways, the affections are said to be modulated by the reason.

There is a further matter: Are the passions or affections essentially a consequence of embodiment? Or are some due to embodiment and others not, so that, in the case of those affections which do not require embodiment, angels and the disembodied may have no such affections or passions? The matter affects the understanding of the intermediate, disembodied state. In our earlier discussion of Augustine and Aquinas, we saw that Augustine was chiefly concerned to combat certain Stoic views and tended to be voluntaristic in his approach, whereas Aquinas was intellectualistic. We will see that to some extent these allegiances were also replicated in the anthropological views of seventeenth-century Puritans and Reformed orthodox.

Edward Reynolds on the Passions

Edward Reynolds's anthropological work is primarily his treatise on the passions, which we have consulted already. When we discussed Aquinas earlier, in the first chapter, it was mentioned that Aquinas's frequent appeals to reason do not sufficiently take into account the way the fall has affected the reason. Reynolds makes the soul's fallenness apparent. The natural passions are rational not from being acts of reason, for they are expressions of the mind's sensible appetite; but they take their character from their dependence on the reason. If the objectives of the soul are seen as good, the appetite desires them, taking pleasure in them. If they are seen as evil, it grieves and sorrows. These reactions are further modified by the distance or nearness of the objective and the difficulty or ease of gaining it. This follows the "natural subordination" of the appetite to the understanding, "whereby the actions of the inferior receive their motion and direction from the influence of the higher."[34] The fall has resulted in the blinding of the understanding, and though it retains some light which governs our actions, the fallen understanding is "able only to convince, but not to reform."[35] Only through divine grace is the dominance of understanding reestablished. Reynolds's concern with the control of the feelings by the reason is shown by his remarks on Christ's passions. He writes, "The passions of Christ are by divines called 'Propassions,' that is to say, the beginnings of passions, than passions themselves; inasmuch as they never proceeded beyond their due measure, nor transported the mind to indecency or excess, but had both their rising and original from reason, and also that measure, bounds, continuance limited by reason."[36] He also notes the ways in which the passions can support virtue by stirring up the spirits and can directly influence the habits and manners of the mind. He notes that reason (comprising the understanding) should play a leading place in their modulation. In the state of corruption, passions that at the creation were reasonable have become beastly and sensual. Such appetites muffle reason, withholding its powers to examine the character of pleasures and

---

34. Reynolds, *Treatise on the Passions and Faculties of the Soul*, in *Works*, 6:36.

35. Reynolds, *Treatise on the Passions and Faculties of the Soul*, in *Works*, 6:36.

36. Reynolds, *Treatise on the Passions and Faculties of the Soul*, in *Works*, 6:40. So Christ was never "beside Himself." The expressions of His affections were always controlled by His reason. It is likely Reynolds took such views of Christ's emotions from Augustine, at places such as *City of God*, XIV.ix.

pains. The passions may directly affect the body by expressions of grief, through tears and palpitations. Reynolds's overriding concern is for the passions to be directed by the reason, both in human behavior generally and in Christian sanctification. "So the agitations of passions, so long as they serve only to drive forward, but not to drown virtue,—as long as they keep their dependence on reason, and run in that channel wherewith they are thereby bounded,—are of excellent service in all the travel of man's life; and such as without which the growth, success, and despatch of virtue would be much impaired."[37]

So also Owen, writing about the place of the affections in sanctification:

> This mortification of our affections toward these things, our love, desire and delight, will produce a moderation of passions about them, as fear, anger, sorrow and the like; such will men be stirred up unto in these changes, losses, crosses, which these things are subject unto.... When the mind is weaned from the world, and the things of it, it will be sedate, quiet, composed, not easily moved with the occurrences and occasions of life: it is dead unto them, and in a great measure unconcerned in them. This is that "moderation" of mind wherein the apostle would have us excel.[38]

Nevertheless, Reynolds notes, "For the corrupt effects of passion in general, they are many more, because there may be a multiplicity as well of evil as of error, when there is but a unity of goodness or of truth. And those effects may be either in respect of themselves, one amongst another; or in references to understanding, will, or body. The effects of them amongst themselves, is in their mutual generating and nourishing of each other: as fear is wrought by love; and anger, by grief."[39]

Reynolds draws a comparison between unruliness as regards the passions when not in control of the understanding, and unruliness in the social order (no doubt having the more radical preachers of his day in mind). He notes,

> And it is true as well in man's little commonwealth, as in greater states, that there are no more pestilent and pernicious disturbers of

---

37. Reynolds, *Treatise on the Passions and Faculties of the Soul*, in *The Works of John Owen*, ed. W. H. Goold (Edinburgh: Banner of Truth, 1966), 6:48.

38. John Owen, *Faith and Its Evidences*, in *Works*, 5:448–49.

39. Reynolds, *Treatise on the Passions and Faculties of the Soul*, in *Works*, 6:48.

the public good, than those who are best qualified for service and employment,—if once they grow turbulent and mutinous, neglecting the common end, for their own private respects, and desirous to raise themselves upon public ruins. And, indeed, it is universally true, things most useful and excellent in their regularity, are most dangerous in their abuse.[40]

John Bunyan on Mansoul

The use of political or social analogies in considering human nature was attractive within the culture of faculty psychology. So in John Bunyan's (1628–1688) allegory *The Holy War*, his account of satanic attack on human nature is likened to the taking captive of the government of Mansoul by Diabolus, who became its ruler, wresting this from Shaddai. The chief men of the town came to do Diabolus's bidding. The name of the mayor of Mansoul is Mr. Understanding, and Mr. Mind is his clerk. Its recorder is Mr. Conscience, and Lord Will-be-will, its chief freeholder, "a man of great strength and courage," whose deputy was Mr. Affection. Bunyan's account of Mr. Affection goes as follows. He was one

> greatly debauched in his principles…he was wholly given to the flesh, and therefore they called him Vile-affection. Now there was he, and one Carnal-lust, the daughter of Mr Mind…that fell in love, and made a match, and were married; and (as I take it) they had several children, as Impudent, Blackmouth and Hate-reproof; these three were black boys. And besides these he had three daughters, as Scorn-truth and Slightgod, and the name of the youngest was Revenge; and these were all married in the town, and also begot and yielded many bad brats, too many to be here inserted.[41]

Here, in the allegory, the character of the affections derives from that of the will. Bunyan cannot be thought of as a scholastic theologian. He was self-educated, a tinker by trade and then a peerless author and a popular preacher, spending several years in Bedford prison for his nonconformist

---

40. Reynolds, *Treatise on the Passions and Faculties of the Soul*, in *Works*, 6:38.

41. *The Works of John Bunyan*, ed. George Offor (Glasgow: Blackie and Son, 1857), 3:262–63. John Owen is reputed to have said to Charles II, "Could I have possessed the tinker's abilities for preaching, please your majesty, I would gladly relinquish all my learning." Peter Toon, *God's Statesman* (Exeter: Paternoster, 1971), 161–62.

convictions. But his writings provide evidence of the way in which faculty psychology became part of the everyday way of speaking of human nature.

John Davenant on the Affections and Disorder

The discussion of passion leads unaware to the treatment of virtue. Sometimes the affections are regarded as a separate faculty, and at other times, as we have noted, an offshoot of the will. However distinguished, the fall affects each faculty, including the affections. In his *Commentary on Colossians*,[42] after mentioning the understanding and will, John Davenant remarks,

> The last remain, which is *akrasia,* disorder in the affections, and rebellion against right reason. Hence the saying of the Poet, *I see and approve the better course; but I follow the worse.* The human mind is so hurried away by corrupt affections, that although it perceives what is good and ought to be done, what is evil and to be avoided, yet it cannot restrain itself from being borne away in a contrary direction. This depravity of the human mind Augustine bewailed and wondered at.... Such a great depravity exists in *the mind*, i.e. in the understanding, the will, and the affections of every man not yet called to Christ Jesus.[43]

So the affections have lost their subjection and take pleasure in overturning the order of things. Here, as with Reynolds, the depravity of the affections is in rebellion against the mind. This is not a natural weakness, nor is it the whole of original sin—as with the Schoolmen, who exempt both the reason and the will (so Davenant claims) from the effects of the fall.

William Fenner on Affections and Passions

In the seventeenth century, not only are the affections handled in connection with ethics and ethical motivation but also with the interior life of the Christian. The affections are handled in connection with feelings, which occur in the privacy of a person's own mind, and are the subject of self-examination, as William Fenner (1600–1640) shows in what follows.

---

42. John Davenant, *An Exposition of the Epistle of St. Paul to the Colossians*, 2 vols., trans. Josiah Allport (London: Hamilton, Adams, and Co., 1831). John Davenant (1572–1641) was Lady Margaret Professor of Divinity in the University of Cambridge, and was appointed by James I to be a delegate to the Synod of Dort (1618) and then to bishop of Salisbury.

43. Davenant, *Colossians*, 1:253.

In his *A Treatise on the Affections*,[44] Fenner understands affections to be "motions of the heart." He writes, "For as the body goes with its feet to that which it loves, so the soul goes out with its affections to that which it loves."[45] "The affections are the Souls horses, that draw her as it were in a Coach to the things that she affects: a man is moved by his affections. By *Anger* he moves out to revenge: by *Desire* he moves out to obtain; by *Love* he moves out to enjoy, by *Pity* he moves out to relieve: the affections are the motions of the Soul."[46]

More exactly, affections are motions of the will, according to Fenner, distinguishing his view from that of Aristotle, who Fenner says placed them in the sensitive part of the soul:

> I know *Aristotle* and most of our divines too, doe place the affections in the sensitive part of the Soul, and not in the will, because they are to be seen in the beasts. But this cannot be so, for a mans affections do most stirre at a shame or disgrace; which could not be, if the affections were in the unreasonable sensitive part: the unreasonable sensitive part of man is not sensible of credit or esteem: call the desires of the appetite greedy and gluttonish; the appetite is senselesse of any disgrace, and therefore the affections must be in the heart.[47]

> I confesse there to be certain animal and analogical affections that be in the sense; there's grief for torment, and fear to touch a serpent or a toad; delight in meats that are pleasant, and hatred in them that are noysome. But the Lord doth not call for these sensitive passions to be seated upon him and on heaven, they are seated aright as they stand, so a moderation be kept they have no need to change objects.[48]

So it seems that Fenner distinguishes between affections and passions. The first are motions of the will. The second are motions of the sensual appetite. One reason why the affections are referred to as passions is that they make the soul suffer by their intensity. By this Fenner means that they have various bodily effects. So the distinction between affection and passion is not one of degree, but of the effects and side effects that certain affections

---

44. William Fenner, *A Treatise on the Affections* (London: printed by A. M. for J. Rothwell, 1650). Fenner was for a time the minister of Sedgeley, Staffordshire.

45. Fenner, *Treatise on the Affections*, 3.

46. Fenner, *Treatise on the Affections*, 3.

47. Fenner, *Treatise on the Affections*, 4.

48. Fenner, *Treatise on the Affections*, 4–5.

may have when they reach a certain level of intensity. So affections may be intense. And finally affections have regard to good or evil. He notes, "Nay, if the apprehension be deep indeed, the affections break out into raptures, *as dancings and leapings of the heart*, which are raptures of joy; *ravishments and enamourings*, which are raptures of love; *meltings and bleedings and breakings of spirit*, which are raptures of grief; astonishments, amazements, which are raptures of fear; confusion and the like, which are raptures of shame; the affections burst forth into these, when the apprehension is deep."[49]

So, as Fenner summarizes, affections are *"forcible and sensible motions of the will, to a thing or from a thing, according as it is apprehended to be evil or to be good."*[50]

John Weemes on Virtue and Passion

John Weemes (Wymess) (1579–1636) was a Scottish Reformed scholastic who in his writings followed Aquinas, among which is *The Portraiture of the Image of God in Man, in His Creation, Restauration and Glorification.*[51] In contrast to Fenner, Weemes regards the passions as housed in the sensitive part of the soul.

The use of the term "passion" in preference to "affection" may itself be an indication of his direct dependence on Aquinas's "Passions of the Soul" in his *Summa Theologiae*. Such close dependence is evident throughout Weemes's work. The sensitive faculty is blind and needs the direction of the understanding in the form of the imagination, which the reasonable faculty does not effect, since reasoning does not of itself bring about an alteration in the body. The passions are between the body and the mind, dependent on each, the mind affecting the body in respect of the changes in it. So the passions are ruled by reason. Weemes observes that the passions that are hardest to control are furthest from the rule of reason. Virtues shape the passions, prompting them when deficient and modulating them when excessive. Virtues are habits which the will has a place in forming. The will plays a strong part in this, as David Sytsma has noted, but this is not

---

49. Fenner, *Treatise on the Affections*, 7.

50. Fenner, *Treatise on the Affections*, 3.

51. John Weemes, *The Portraiture of the Image of God in Man, in His Creation, Restauration and Glorification* (London: printed by T. C. for John Bellamie, 1632).

evidence of Scotus's voluntarism as much as the Augustinian *voluntas*.[52] Weemes distinguishes this procedure from the Stoic approach to passion, which is to "root them out of the nature of man, as altogether sinful." But "if there were not *passions* in the soule, then there should be no *vertues* to moderate them; for take away *feare* and *hardnessse* from fortitude, then fortitude were no more a vertue."[53] In Scripture, the passions are ascribed both to Christ and God and therefore are not to be rooted out.

Nicholas Mosley on Passions and Temperament

We turn again to Mosley, to book 1, chapter 9 of his *Psychosophia*, "Of the Affections and Passions of the Soul."[54] Mosley appears to use the terms "passion" and "affection" interchangeably, but he is not concerned with a Stoic-like elimination of the emotions, but with their moderation. This is an Aristotelian approach. Acceptable emotions are those that are midway between extremes, as Weemes suggested, and are moderated in this midposition by the reason. Once again, passion and virtue are connected. Every person has the capability to express the emotion of anger, but inordinate passion is unreasonable. Such inordinate passions obscure the operation of the understanding and cloud the light of truth. As already noted, the affections may be reduced to four: joy, fear, hope, and grief. An affection is a response to some perceived good or evil present or absent—"which Affections as long as they be but rightly, ordinate, and subject, nor may, nor can be expelled being natural and good, but when they grow heady, sensual, fleshy, & terrene [i.e., earthly], set upon the lusts and pleasures of this stageplay world, are vitious and hurtful, which a wise man & a virtuous will keep under, and not suffer to range and rule; for these are they which are properly called Passions."[55]

Which range of passions a person is open to will depend upon his complexion—that is, temperament. If choleric, then anger, hatred, malice; if melancholic, then sorrow, fear, and grief. This seems to be one of the few

---

52. David Sytsma, "The Portraiture of Thomist Anthropology: John Weemes' Reformed Portrait of the Image of God," ThM thesis, Calvin Theological Seminary, 2008; "The Logic of the Heart: Analyzing the Affections in Early Reformed Orthodoxy," in *Church and School in Early Modern Protestantism*, ed. J. J. Ballor, David S. Sytsma, and Jason Zuidema (Leiden: Brill. 2013).

53. Weemes, *Portraiture of the Image of God in Man*, 158.

54. Mosley, *Psychosophia*, 99.

55. Mosley, *Psychosophia*, 101.

places in discussions of the affections and passions of this era in which a writer refers to different character types.

Note that Mosley makes the strength of affection the test of a passion and also that his concern with the passions lies in the effects on the body of strong affections/passions. From all this it may seem that the relative strength of the anger expressed in a good cause is as evil as anger expressed in an evil one, with moderation in all things as the supreme value. But this is not so. Mosley endorses Jeremy Taylor's view that some affections/passions are good in themselves, as some are "evil" and others "morally indifferent." But even in a good case, presumably, an affection can be excessive and so become a passion, with its adverse effects upon the soul.[56] Here also the language for the affections becomes blurred with that of virtues and vices.

The various faculties of the soul and their modifications produce different effects, either in mental acts and attitudes or changes in the body. So the will may produce certain affections that in turn may affect the body, the pulse and heartbeats, causing blushing, shaking, and so on.

Although we have devoted a separate section to the affections and emotions, they do not comprise a distinct faculty of soul. Rather, they are a sort of subfaculty, by and large thought to depend on the will, and are expressions of the effects that the goals of the will make on the feelings and desires. When their exercise is a good thing, this is because they enliven and promote a virtue or virtues. If they are bad, this is because they promote some vice or vices. Their effects on the body are likewise good or bad. They are generally harmful when they cloud the judgment.

In faculty psychology, a distinction is drawn between powers and habits. Powers (*potentiae*) of the soul are intrinsic to one faculty or another and may be shared between faculties. So the power to choose belongs to the will; the power to decide that something is the case is shared by both intellect and will. Powers may be developed or neglected, and inoperative but not lost. Habits of the mind (*habitus*) are acquired by nature or by grace, by practice or by infusion, and under certain circumstances may be permanent or temporary. They have an importance that habits in the modern sense may not have.[57]

---

56. Mosley, *Psychosophia*, 102–3.

57. See Richard A. Muller, *Dictionary of Latin and Greek Theological Terms* (Grand Rapids: Baker, 1985), s.v., *habitus, potentia*.

John Flavel on the Habits of Grace

Although John Flavel does not seem to be very interested in discussing the affections, he has a good deal to say about the end of human life, the separation of the soul from the body (as we saw). This concentration is perhaps due to his pastoral care for the dying and questions that arose about the human condition after death from those to whom he ministered. But he does have interesting things to say about the habits of grace that the departed soul possesses. These are *acquired* habits—to be more exact, *infused* habits, the effect of saving grace. Such a habit, Flavel says, is "a permanent Quality rendring the subject of it prompt to perform a work with ease."[58] These are properties of faculties, not further faculties. They are deeply laid dispositions, which are not lost even in a deep sleep, as is clear when the person who had them awakes. "*Infused* habits of Grace are as deeply rooted in the Soul, yea, deeper than any acquired habit can be: For when Knowledg and Tongues shall be done away, Love abideth" (1 Cor. 13:8). At death, certain inherent habits will be "reduced" to dispositions when the soul is without the body, awaiting resurrection. To suppose otherwise—that they are extinguished, for example—would be to deny the very habit itself.

And Flavel develops the theme. So faith is a habit that will be exercised in acts of faith, without which there is no justification. Justification is by the act of faith, not by the disposition of faith, the habit.[59] Likewise, all virtues and vices are to be understood dispositionally and to be made actual in specific acts of hatred or love, for example.

Habits which are lodged in the soul are generally permanent features of it. For the soul does not depend on the body, except to make actual its desires and dispositions; and the loss of the body does not affect the dispositions of the soul, Flavel says. So the disposition a person has to play a musical instrument is not lost by death, but opportunities to exercise it cease. It is not clear whether by calling a habit permanent Flavel means that once acquired a habit cannot be lost, or simply that a habit is capable of

---

58. Flavel, *Pneumatologia*, 215.

59. For a contrary view and discussion of habits and their exercise, see Gerrit A. van den Brink, "The Act or Habit of Faith? Alexander Comrie's Interpretation of Heidelberg Catechism Question 40," in *Scottish Reformed Orthodoxy*, ed. Aaron C. Denlinger (London: Bloomsbury Academic, 2015). See also Joel R. Beeke, *Assurance of Faith* (Frankfurt-am-Main: Peter Lang, 1991), ch. 8.

enduring in the soul even when it no longer has a body. Death is like sleep, and when we awake from sleep we still possess the habits we had when we went to sleep. So it will be in the sleep of death when our souls are disembodied for a time.

More important are habits of grace, the fruit of the regenerating work of the Holy Spirit. These are "infused" habits, lying deeper in the soul than any acquired habit. What Flavel understands by an infused habit is a habit that is not acquired through dedication and practice, like the habit of reciting the letters of the alphabet, for example. Here the habit is a product of the activity of reciting and remembering. In infused habits, it is the other way around. The habit of love is a gift of grace, and then it is exercisable in acts of love. Such a soul, relieved of its body, is immediately in the presence of God. And its habits, which are the gift of grace—though not these only—will in due course have unending opportunity for their exercise.

Much of what Flavel writes seems favorable to the hylomorphic view that the soul is the form of the body. However, some of his expressions go in a more Platonic direction—such as these expressions of the soul upon the death of the body:

> In these Faculties and Affections the habits of Grace [are] permanently rooted, which therefore accompany it in its ascension to Glory: an ability to use and exercise these Faculties and Graces, and that in a more excellent degree and manner than it did, or could in this World, the subject and habits inherent, being now both made perfect: The clog of flesh knockt off, and all distance from God removed, by its coming home to him, even as near as the capacity of the Soul can admit.[60]

It is characteristic of hylomorphism to lament the loss of the body at death, but here Flavel seems to have regarded it as a gain.

William Pemble on Infused Habits

Pemble's account of the habit of grace, the reception of the grace of God in regeneration, illustrates how such theologians worked out faculty psychology. But it also illustrates how they reworked faculty psychology in incorporating into it an Augustinian account of grace as effectual. Pemble,

---

60. Flavel, *Pneumatologia*, 216.

along with Flavel and others, holds that one receives grace by it being infused immediately into the soul, and his discussion of this provides an indication of the "structure" of the soul.

As we have been seeing, the soul possesses multiple habits, which are dispositions of certain kinds and give rise to actions—what are sometimes called "administrations" and sometimes also referred to as "potencies." Habits can be infused (in Augustinianism) or acquired. Those arising from regeneration are directly infused, in which the soul is passive, as the Westminster Confession puts it. Indeed, regeneration is the infusion of new habits, whereas those habits that are natural are indirectly acquired through the exercise of the soul and body, as innate aptitudes are developed through learning and developing habits. In this case, the person becomes good by doing good. But in the case of sanctifying grace, the opposite is true. A person develops virtuous habits and actions through the exercise of what, initially, was an infusion of a disposition to perform the habits. It is on account of the infusion of grace that he acts graciously. We will consider further the anthropology of regeneration by grace further in chapter 7.

This is not to say that exercise is not required in the development of the supernatural graces. The Reformed orthodox were fond of the verse, "Work out your own salvation with fear and trembling; for it is God who works in you both to will and to do for His good pleasure" (Phil. 2:12–13). That is, the believer must exert himself, yet the source of that effort and its result is God's work in the heart. Pemble notes, "So is our new man born at once, though he grow by degrees: that is, the soul in our conversion is at once re-invested with the Image of God in all its faculties: so that however the actions of grace do not presently appear in each one, yet the habit, the seed, the root of all divine vertues is firmly re-implanted in them, and by the strength of this grace given, they are constantly disposed to all sanctified operation."[61]

Regeneration is an event, a hidden change in the soul. The exercise and growth of habits are processes. So faith and other virtues are to be understood as both habit and act. Habits are qualities of the distinct faculties of the soul. There is one habit, but a multiplicity of operations. Just as health is one temper, yet it issues in several distinct activities, as healthiness

---

61. Pemble, *Vindiciae*, 18.

manifests itself.[62] The theological point Pemble is making is that faith is one of many fruits of regeneration (others being love, joy, and peace), not the equally necessary conduit of all the others:

> For Grace, as in all parts it works imperfectly during this life, so in divers parts it works diversly: or rather, because habits are not active *per se*, thus, Every faculty having proper operations belonging to it is different from others, which it produceth by the strength of its proper nature: if it be perverted by corruption, it doth that action ill; if it be rectified by grace, it performs it well. As, to know, to assent, to choose, to desire, to joy, to love, etc. are naturall works of the understanding and will, or reasonable appetite. But when they shall put themselves forth to action, nothing will be done in a right manner, nor directed to a right object, unless the faculties be re-indued with their primitive perfection totally, or in part.[63]

Joseph Truman on Licit and Imperate Habits

Joseph Truman (1630–1691), one of the victims of the Great Ejection in 1662, distinguished between *licit* and *imperate* habits and the will.[64] Imperate habits are formed as a result of the activity of the will, taking "imperate" to mean commanded. Licit (permitted) habits are not formed so. Being reflexes, such licit habits are involved in the activity of walking, which is willed, but not each step of which is separately willed by being preceded by each act.[65] So the habit of giving charitably can be formed by reflex, as I see distressing pictures on the TV news; this would be a licit habit. Or I can set out to be a charitable donor by adopting or willing various strategies, and this would be an imperate habit.

Truman draws the distinction between willing to repent and actually repenting.[66] Imperate acts require another power distinct from the will to execute them—for example, a person cannot give without having something

---

62. Pemble, *Vindiciae*, 19.

63. Pemble, *Vindiciae*, 18.

64. Joseph Truman, *A Discourse of Natural and Moral Impotency*, 2nd ed. (London: printed for Robert Clabel, 1675), 45ff. Truman, a minister ejected in 1662 by the Act of Uniformity, was educated at Clare College, but is also listed among the eminent alumni of Queen's College, Cambridge. He was first assistant at St. Peter's, Nottingham, and then vicar of Ruddington. After the Ejection, he lived at Mansfield.

65. Pemble, *Vindiciae*, 50.

66. Truman, *Discourse of Natural and Moral Impotency*, 21.

to give.[67] What Truman seems to be saying is that an imperate act needs "another Power." To be a full or a completed or successful act, one needs not only a charitable or obedient disposition but something to give to another, or an act to obey by. Without that, there can be no charitable or obedient act. Truman then goes on to say that in the case of repenting and believing, God accepts the will or desire for it without a "distinct thing." We cannot bring anything, as in a charitable gift, when we repent and believe. (But maybe I should deny something to myself?) God would grant repentance and faith upon evidence of the desire for it. Otherwise, He would be a "hard" God. Truman's "uses" at the end of the book help to make this clearer, especially objection 4, with expressions such as, "If there be a will in the prevailing degree, the deed will follow if there be the ability and opportunity."[68]

Truman goes into considerable detail regarding the apostolic conflict between flesh and spirit (as in Romans 7), and the general problem of conflict within the self, for the most part wanting A but occasionally wanting B.[69] The book is concerned with setting forth the distinction between natural and moral ability and inability, as we shall see in chapter 5. But the case where a person usually wants to do A but occasionally wants B is difficult to categorize in terms of the natural-moral distinction. Truman says, "We have the Natural power, though not of undoing the sins we have done: yet of unsinning actual obedience for the future; else we should not sin in not performing perfect actual obedience; we onely want [i.e., lack] will: Which may much humble us, would we well consider it."[70] He comments candidly that "the faculties of the Soul [are] such abstruse things."[71] It's what we will that counts, not what we do against what we will. So remembering is not subject to the will, for we cannot always choose the contents of our memory at will.[72]

It is appropriate that at this point we consider agency, including moral and natural potency and impotency.

---

67. Truman, *Discourse of Natural and Moral Impotency*, 21.

68. Truman, *Discourse of Natural and Moral Impotency*, 191–92.

69. Truman, *Discourse of Natural and Moral Impotency*, 38.

70. Truman, *Discourse of Natural and Moral Impotency*, 40–41.

71. Truman, *Discourse of Natural and Moral Impotency*, 42. Truman himself has the disarming habit of when he meets a difficulty, saying so!

72. Truman, *Discourse of Natural and Moral Impotency*, 44.

CHAPTER 5

Morality and Agency

This chapter has to do with various topics that concern human action: its nature and our responsibility for what we do; the nature of moral evil; the distinction between moral and natural ability; and whether human obligations require human abilities. The first is a central matter of concern for the Reformed orthodox, the self-assessment of action via the conscience. We begin with this.

Perkins and Ames on the Conscience

The interest in the conscience, though it is to be found in early Reformed theologians such as Calvin,[1] became of distinct and developing importance due to two influential English theologians, William Perkins of Cambridge (1558–1602) and William Ames (1576–1633), one of Perkins's students who moved to Holland, became the pastor of an Independent congregation, and then a professor of theology at the University of Franeker.

The importance that Perkins and Ames attached to the conscience came to be significant in two areas: in the question of personal assurance of salvation, and in steering one's way through what God commands and forbids. The latter was especially important in the rise of the Puritan party in the Church of England, and Ames and Perkins may be said to be fathers of Puritanism considered as both a pastoral and a church-reforming movement, with a sensitized conscience on these matters as its center.

Though there was a tradition of studying the conscience in the medieval period, it has to be borne in mind that Aristotle did not have a concept of the conscience. And so the Reformed were freer to plot new territory than in what they had generally to say about the faculties of the soul. For

---

1. See, for example, Calvin's treatment of the conscience discussed in chapter 2.

Perkins, the conscience is an aspect of the understanding, having to do with those actions contemplated or performed as a result of the operation of the understanding, the practical reason. However, the working of the conscience is distinct from all other operations of the understanding, "for it determines or gives sentence to things done, by saying unto us, This was done, this was not done; this may be done, this may not be done: this may not be done, this was wel done, this was ill done."[2] He notes,

> The minde thinks a thought, now conscience goes beyond the minde, and knowes what the minde thinks; so as if a man would go about to hide his sinfull thoughts from God, his conscience as another person within him, shall discover all. By meanes of this second action conscience may beare witnes even of thoughts, and from hence it seems to borrow his name, because conscience is a *science* or knowledge joined with another knowledge: for by it I conceive and know what I know.[3]

So for Perkins, conscience is a kind of second-order reflex, telling us what we know about ourselves, such as what we do or intend to do and how we feel, and assessing it in terms of an internal norm or standard. As a power of the soul, the conscience will bear witness forever. Thus, "when the bodie is rotting in the grave, conscience liveth and is safe and sound: and when we shall rise againe, conscience shall come with us to the barre of Gods judgement, either to accuse or excuse us before God, Rom.1,15,16."[4] "Let Atheists barke against this as long as they will: they have that in them which will convince them of the truth of the godhead will they nill they, either in life or death."[5]

But though Perkins stresses the knowledge that the conscience has and may acquire, he also emphasizes the will-like character of its activities. It acts in passing judgment on what it knows, and the conscience may be bound or excused in respect of a certain action or even a certain thought, wish, or intention. So the conscience does not only appraise and assess the understanding; it binds it. It is not simply receptive, but in these ways it is

---

2. William Perkins, *A Discourse of Conscience* (Cambridge: John Legate, printer to the Universitie of Cambridge, 1596), 4.

3. Perkins, *Discourse of Conscience*, 7.

4. Perkins, *Discourse of Conscience*, 8.

5. Perkins, *Discourse of Conscience*, 9.

active. And similarly with the will and the affections, it operates in respect of what men and women want and by what they are affected in certain circumstances. Conscience is the binder of the judgments made or reactions experienced. It has authority over a person, making the mind aware of the sinfulness or inadequacy of what it is thinking, doing, and feeling. Perkins notes, "The Binder is that thing whatsoever which hath power & authority over conscience to order it. To bind is to urge, cause, and constraine it in every action either to accuse for sinne, or to excuse for well doing: or to say, this may be done or it may not be done."[6] That is, conscience is a moral force and may be permissive as well as mandatory. It is this function of freeing the conscience as well as binding it that made it so potent in Puritanism. It was the reform of those practices in the church which are forbidden by the conscience as well those that are permitted by the conscience. For within this sphere of binding, the conscience may also loose. Paul's teaching that the conscience "also [bears] witness, and between themselves their thoughts [accuse] or else [excuse] them" (Rom. 2:15) comes to be a pivotal text. God is Lord of the conscience, and so conscience can only, strictly speaking, be bound by God through His word. Luther's claim that his conscience was captive to the word of God became a dramatic illustration of the conscience's power to bind, even as it freed.

So the conscience must be fitted for its task, not to waver or to be lukewarm or mistaken, but informed, aligning itself with what God requires, permits, and forbids according to His word.[7] A person must strive to form his conscience so that it has a godly shape. The conscience needs to be educated and kept sharp. This is the "practical theology" which became characteristic of Puritanism as a church-reforming movement. Its activity may seem dour and restrictive, but this would be a misunderstanding. In telling us what we may not do, we are also taught by our consciences what we are free to do—namely, the *adiaphora*, those actions that are neither forbidden nor commanded by the word of God. So a rightly formed conscience has also to do with Christian liberty.

So there is liberty of conscience to do or forbear what is neither commanded nor forbidden by the word of God. "God hath given a liberty to the conscience whereby it is freed from all laws of his own whatsoever,

---

6. Perkins, *Discourse of Conscience*, 11.
7. Perkins, *Discourse of Conscience*, 13.

excepting such laws & doctrines as are necessary to salvation."[8] Civil laws are to be obeyed when they do not infringe the law of God because obedience to the magistrate is a divine command and as such should bind the conscience.

When such a conscience is bound by the word of God, it is properly bound; and so its behavior is not merely a reflection of tradition or the culture or upbringing of the person. There are natural laws, generally binding, and moral laws, expressed in the Ten Commandments, and positive laws, binding in some particular time or place or dispensation. And there are various other commands of God in the New Testament, those about the role of the magistrate and the source of his authority, that should also inform the conscience. And those who have never heard the gospel could have had their consciences formed by the word of God, His natural law. The terms of the gospel cannot bind the conscience if they are unknown. As far as I can tell, how the natural law fits with conscience and the revealed law is not separately developed. The thrust of Perkins's work on the conscience can be gleaned from the title of one of his books: *A case of conscience: the greatest that ever was; how a man may know whether he be the child of God or no. Resolved by the word of God. Whereunto is added a briefe discourse, taken out of Hier. Zanchius* (1592).

For Ames, conscience is more prominently linked with natural law than in Perkins. And some standards delivered by the conscience are an ineradicable feature of human life. Conscience is also a judge and therefore not a habit. Ames developed these ideas of what came to be called "practical theology." He has a paragraph or two about this in his book *Conscience and the Power of Cases Thereof* (1639).

> Since also (Gods good providence so disposing it) that I lived out of my owne Countrey,[9] I did observe that in divers Churches, pure both for Doctrine and Order, this Practicall teaching was much wanting, and that this want was one of the chiefe causes of the great neglect, or carelessenesse in some duties which neerely [that is, closely] concerne Godlinesse, and a Christian life. My minde was set on, as it were by violence, to try at least in private, whether I were able to prevaile with some young men that purpose the Ministry, more to apply their

---

8. Perkins, *Discourse of Conscience*, 56.
9. Ames emigrated to Holland in 1610.

mindes to this kinde of handling of Divinity, whence no small fruit was to bee hoped for. Being afterwards called to a publike charge of Teaching in the Universitie, I esteemed nothing better, or more excellent, then to goe before those that were Students for the Ministrie, in this manner of teaching.[10]

Ames differed somewhat from Perkins on the nature of the conscience and its place among the powers of the soul. Yet it can be said that Perkins's general emphases and outlook were exported to Holland and had a welcome among the leading Reformed theologians. Later, Voetius was in many respects a follower of Ames, holding conscience in certain respects to be a habit, and in other respects a power. Voetius, professor of theology at Utrecht, goes to some lengths in warmly approving of the development of such "practical theology."[11]

Ames has this to say about Perkins:

The most grave Divine, *William Perkins*, who only of our Countrymen has set forth a peculiar Treatise of *Conscience*, doth place it among Faculties, and he doth so define it, as he putteth for a generall nature of it a part of the Understanding, that is to say, as he explains himself, *A naturall power or facultie*. He gives this reason of his opinion, namely, because the act of Accusing, Comforting, Terrifying &c. cannot bee ascribed to the Conscience, if itself were an act. But this reason is weake: because in the Scripture, such kinds of effects are attributed to the thoughts themselves which undoubtedly are acts. *Rom. 2.15. Their thoughts Accusing one another, or Excusing.* The reason is, because things done, are the effect not only of the Mover, but also of the motion it selfe. Besides, Master *Perkins* maketh Conscience, Understanding, Opinion, Knowledge, Faith, and Prudence, to be of one kind or sort; but none would define these so, as that they should be taken for different faculties of the soule.[12]

---

10. William Ames, "To the Reader," in *Conscience with the Power and Cases thereof* (n.p., 1639).

11. See Voetius's disputation "Concerning Practical Theology," in *Reformed Dogmatics*, ed. John W. Beardslee III (New York: Oxford University Press, 1965), for his upholding of "practical theology." For an informative account of Voetius and Petrus Van Maastricht's appropriation of the Ames outlook, with slight modifications, see Goudriaan, *Reformed Orthodoxy and Philosophy*, 270.

12. Ames, *Conscience with the Power and Cases thereof*, 2.

We have seen that in the first chapter of his book Ames refers to Perkins, emphasizing that judgments of the conscience are practical judgments, judgments of the practical reason, not contemplative or theoretical syllogisms. "Judgment" can refer to a power or faculty, sometimes a habit, and sometimes an act. The question is, which is it here?[13] Ames notes that Perkins places conscience in the faculties, because it is an agent in its own right. Conscience has the power to accuse or excuse. Some schoolmen—Scotus, Bonaventure, Durand—classify conscience as a habit, following Aquinas, but this can only be part of the story, as conscience has several operations which belong to it. Rather, since the conscience accuses, comforts, and indicates, "(I understand most properly with the best Schoolemen) an act of practicall judgement, proceeding from the Understanding by the power or meanes of a habit."[14]

At this point, Ames refers to the idea of a practical syllogism—that is, a syllogism with a conclusion that is not a proposition, but an action or determination or deliberation. The practical syllogism was integral to Aristotle's ethics, and thus the idea is familiar in medievalism and was noticed occasionally by the Reformers (e.g., Calvin[15]). But here, if not for the first time, then early on, it forms the centerpiece of Ames's work on the conscience. The practical syllogism is, for Ames, "the force and nature of Conscience."[16]

The practical syllogism consists of a major premise of the syllogism, "the Law"; the minor premise, which is an action or belief; and the conclusion, "a Judge"—that is, a judgment. Ames goes on: "That which doth dictate or give the proposition is called *Synteresis*, by the Schoolemen *Synderesis*. The assumption especially and peculiarly is called the *Syneidasis*, the conclusion is the *Krisis* or Judgement."[17] This he takes, or could have taken, from Aquinas.[18] This is the form of a practical syllogism, which Ames says is also the form of the operation of the conscience. "In that

---

13. Ames, *Conscience with the Power and Cases thereof*, 2.

14. Ames, *Conscience with the Power and Cases thereof*, 3. Ames closely follows Aquinas, *Summa Theologiae*, Ia 79.

15. John Calvin, *Sermons on the Hundred and Nineteenth Psalm* (Audubon, N.J.: Old Paths, 1996), 133–34. He writes, "God is merciful to those who have offended. I have offended him, therefore I will call upon him for mercy." There is no mention of the conscience, but the use of the practical syllogism is evident.

16. Ames, *Conscience with the Power and Cases thereof*, 3–4.

17. Ames, *Conscience with the Power and Cases thereof*, 4.

18. Aquinas, *Summa Theologiae*, Ia 79.

Syllogisme alone is contained the whole nature of conscience," says Ames emphatically.[19] So the syllogism has something that is taken to be a divinely given law as a first premise, not simply (as with Aristotle) a statement of what the agent ought to do. So the first premise teaches the law; the assumption (i.e., the second premise) is a particular fact or state; and the conclusion relates what ought to be done. So, in Ames's example, "It belongs to judgement discoursing, because it can not doe its act of Accusing, Excusing, Comforting unless it be through the meanes of some third argument, whose force appeareth only in a Syllogisme, by that which is deduced and concluded out of it."[20] In these words, we have the activity of conscience taking the form of the Aristotelian practical syllogism. There is the major premise, the *synderesis*, or the "law"; and the minor premise, the "*syneidesis*," or the "fact":

> Proposition: "He that lies in sin shall die" (law).
> Assumption: "I lie in sin" (fact).
> Conclusion: "I shall die."

This is, following the apostle Paul, the logic of an "accusing" conscience.

As the title of his book implies, Ames developed Perkins's emphases in the direction of cases of conscience—that is, in the study of those situations in which there is a clash or an apparent clash between a law and what a person believes that he ought to do or may do, and an attempt is made to resolve the conflict. Ames's anthropology was broadly similar to that of his tutor but developed and tightened up and prominently harnessed to the practical syllogism. Operating as a conscience, in its proposition the practical syllogism states a particular state or habit and its consequence, as, "If I (continue in) sin, I shall die." Conscience operates on a man's own actions, not in judging another's. It judges as a God-given arbiter passing sentence, either for some particular state or action or against it. In a natural conscience, the scope of the *synderesis* is to be the principles of the natural law; in an enlightened conscience, the principles are what are prescribed in the Scriptures, which contain both the content of natural and revealed law. In their *sola Scriptura* emphasis, the Puritans differed from the medieval practice.

---

19. Ames, *Conscience with the Power and Cases thereof*, 4.

20. Ames, *Conscience with the Power and Cases thereof*, 3.

The medieval manuals established the major premise, which was usually besides Scripture determined by authorities of the church, indeed was only established after one tradition of authority overcame another. For the Puritans, the law of God drawn from natural law and from Scripture alone binds the conscience. That is, it presents such an authority that the conscience ought to submit itself. The conscience is not subject to any other authority than God's, and no human authority can relieve a person of God's authority exercised through the conscience. When a willing person assents to what God asserts, he is bound by it and seeks to put it into practice. Besides, both the understanding and the will are involved. In matters that are indifferent, the conscience is to discern such and direct the person accordingly. Of course in matters that are indifferent, such courses of actions as are chosen ought to be done for the glory of God. This is the logic that took many a Protestant in England to the stake in the sixteenth century.

So conscience is, as it was called, the voice of God, who knows the secrets of human hearts.[21] Its scope includes thoughts, affections, and actions. The various verdicts of the conscience, excusing or accusing, comforting, constitute the "loosing" and "binding" of the conscience in various ways. Yet it stands apart from the ordinary operations of the mind in the sense that it judges the moral character of its operation of some of its own powers. The person whose conscience it is consents to this work of the understanding. It is interesting that the phrase that both Perkins and Ames use—God as "the Lorde of the conscience"—recurs in the Westminster Confession: "God alone is Lord of the conscience, and left it free from the doctrines and commandments of men which are in anything contrary to his word, or beside it, in matters of faith and worship" (WCF 20.2). For Ames, God alone is the one who also knows the secrets of the hearts of all men and who is the punisher and rewarder of mankind. So there is not an intrinsic obligation to keep a promise, for example, but the obligation arises from the fact that God commands the keeping of promises. That sense of an obligation to keep promises may have arisen by the natural law or been given or reinforced by the moral law in Scripture. Ames notes, "Even a promise, (which in it self is sacred) though it is confirmed by an oath: as it is an act of man doth not properly bind the Conscience, for the former reasons; though men are bound in conscience by God to a strickt and faithfull

---

21. Ames, *Conscience with the Power and Cases thereof*, 7.

keeping of them. For as it hath beene said before of the lawes of men, it may also in some sort be affirmed of all covenants and other conditions, which being made, a man is bound to keep out of Conscience to God."[22]

So for a proper conscience to be formed, a person must first be fully informed regarding his duties and freedoms. The conscience is not, strictly speaking, a faculty of the mind, but the understanding must nevertheless form it. And such formation requires the cultivation of certain virtues, such as the fear of God and of humility, sincerity, zeal, and patience. The object is to gain a tranquil conscience, not one which is deadened, but one which follows the contours of the revealed will of God. There has to be a recognition that many actions are indifferent, being neither commanded nor forbidden by God. The establishing of this area against the encroachment of merely humanly devised rules that do not therefore carry the authority of God is an important aspect of Perkins's outlook. Conscience therefore informs the whole outlook of a person on carrying out his duties to God and neighbor. Toward the end of his treatment in *Conscience with the Power and Cases Thereof*, Ames adopts a marked casuistical tone when discussing various family, civil, and religious relations—everything from marriage and divorce to the waging of war—though he does not discuss many cases of conscience as such. Rather, in these discussions he sees himself as drawing out consequences of the divinely revealed laws to suit a variety of circumstances.

Recognizing that some action is against the conscience is one thing. Being strong or resolved enough to do what the conscience dictates is another. Puritan pastoral ministry was not only intent on helping people to form the conscience but to fortifying the will appropriately.

As we have noted, Ames is aware of following in the footsteps of Perkins, devoting much attention to the conscience in an effort to promote interest in the teaching and practice of practical theology, in which the notion of living according to a reformed conscience was central. But he offers a genuine development of Perkins's views, and they became the standard approach in the seventeenth century.

---

22. Ames, *Conscience with the Power and Cases thereof*, 7.

Richard Bernard on Conscience and God's Law

Richard Bernard (1568–1641)[23] begins by noting the varieties of conception of the conscience. Some affirm it to be a power or faculty; others an act or habit, or a created quality. Divines, he says, place it in the understanding.[24]

> Some doe placing of it in the soul; yet it is distinct from the Understanding, from the Memorie, Will and Heart of Man. It is an other thing created by God, besides all these in mans soule.... It hath differing properties from them all, as shall appear by the offices thereof in this Treatise. Fourthly, Man hath a kind of power (as I may say) over the rest, to set his mind a working, to invent this, or that; so his memory to keep; his will to approve, or disallow. But Conscience is such a thing as he cannot work it to his will and pleasure; it commands him; he hath no rule over it, to make to speak, or silent when he list.[25]

Conscience judges the understanding, either condemning or absolving it. It fashions the will to do what it ought to do. It is present in the heart and among the affections. But being divine, it is mysterious, and we are reduced to guessing what exactly it is. He states that it is "a facultie in the soule, having all the rest attendants, as it commands the whole man in the execution of its offices."[26] So the conscience is given faculty status, and it ranges over the entire rational soul, assessing its activities, at least those that can be evaluated morally. "[The conscience] it selfe knoweth, and manifesteth it selfe, by a distinct act from the mere understanding of a thing, yet not separated from it. For this is certaine, that Conscience acteth beyond that, which the Mind knoweth; which a man neither doth, nor can know without his Conscience."[27]

---

23. Richard Bernard, *Christian See to thy Conscience or A Treatise of the nature, the kinds and manifold cases of conscience...* (London: imprinted by Felix Kingston for Robert Milbourne, 1631). Bernard was "Parson of Batcombe in Somerset-Shire." Another treatment of conscience is William Fenner's *The Souls Looking-Glasse, Lively representing its estate before GOD: With a Treatise of Conscience: Wherein the Definitions thereof are unfolded, and several Cases resolved.* (London: printed by T. R. & E. M. for John Rothwell at the Sun and Fountain in Paul's Church-yard, 1652).

24. Bernard, *Christian See to thy Conscience*, 2.

25. Bernard, *Christian See to thy Conscience*, 4–5.

26. Bernard, *Christian See to thy Conscience*, 9.

27. Bernard, *Christian See to thy Conscience*, 11.

How does the conscience assess? By applying God's law to the person himself regarding good or evil.[28] So it is God's bailiff[29] placed between God and mankind. It knows man via the understanding, which informs the conscience. Memory helps by applying a rule.[30]

Only once does Bernard draw attention to the syllogistic way in which conscience witnesses to us,[31] citing various biblical instances. Since he published his book before Ames's *Conscience* appeared (in English) in 1639, Bernard could have directly depended only on Perkins. And he seems to be similar to Perkins in placing conscience apart from the faculties of the soul. This is similar to what we saw when Ames objected to Perkins's practice of connecting the conscience directly with the understanding: "among *Faculties*, and he doth so define, as he putteth for a general nature of it a part of the Understanding."

Bernard makes a reference to the law of God, outlining something of its character.[32] It is given secondary place in Bernard's exposition, since his first responsibility is for his Christian congregation, and the natural law rules principally for those to whom the gospel has not reached.[33] Conscience does not simply inform and assess; it also binds.[34] Through its activities a person comes to know more of himself. As God's friend, the conscience is God's registrar for the judgment.[35] Yet conscience itself needs informing in order to be God's faithful witness. It can be dull, or over-particular. These are corrupt extremes.[36] Plenty of room for error, therefore.

Wilhelmus à Brakel on Conscience and False Belief

The idea of a formed conscience may imply that it cannot err. In his treatment of the conscience, Wilhelmus à Brakel (1635–1711), a Dutch minister

---

28. Bernard, *Christian See to thy Conscience*, 17.

29. Bernard, *Christian See to thy Conscience*, 32.

30. Bernard, *Christian See to thy Conscience*, 34, 38.

31. Bernard, *Christian See to thy Conscience*, 40. This seems sufficient to establish a Perkinsian pedigree. Bernard was educated at Christ's College, where he matriculated in 1592, during Perkins's time.

32. Bernard, *Christian See to thy Conscience*, 43–45.

33. Bernard, *Christian See to thy Conscience*, 47.

34. Bernard, *Christian See to thy Conscience*, 56.

35. Bernard, *Christian See to thy Conscience*, 83.

36. Bernard, *Christian See to thy Conscience*, 118–19.

and theologian, in his *The Christian's Reasonable Service*[37] takes the conscience to be a constituent element of the intellect, as the term implies. "The conscience is man's practical judgment concerning himself and his deeds, to the extent he is subject to God's judgment."[38] It has three elements: knowledge, the idea of witness, and that of acknowledgment. The acknowledgement is that God is witness to this awareness, indeed that He has brought this awareness about and will hold the person to account. The activity of conscience is the bringing about of a conjunction or concurrence between what oneself ought to do and what one does or does not do in fact. One's appropriate sensitivity to the state of affairs acknowledged, whether negative or positive, indicates a conscience appropriately at work.

À Brakel stresses this in his comments on 1 Corinthians 8, on Paul's reference to the false belief that an idol is important and needs to be honored. "Someone is said to have an evil conscience whenever the commission of abominable deeds fills one with anxiety, fear and remorse."[39] But to have an evil conscience in this sense is not to say that the conscience is evil. Rather, it is doing its job. The fear and remorse is produced by the conscience when a person comes to realize that he has permitted evil actions. Only if the conscience fails in doing its job, approving what God disapproves and disapproving what He approves, is it evil.

Conscience errs when it represents a matter as the command of God when it is not, or vice versa. In these circumstances, the conscience is in error, upholding the act as good when it is evil. For example, if the conscience erroneously advises that person an idol is "something"—that is, it is a representation of a god that really exists—and as a consequence his conscience is in a weakened state, then conscience is in error at that point. "Is this not a very serious error? The conscience can be 'emboldened' in its error in order to persevere in the sin of idolatry with all the more freedom."[40] Such a person is a "weaker brother" in that respect. He is to be treated with care, and someone is to attempt to guide him. A good conscience, properly informed, ought to produce a sense of peace and thankfulness.

---

37. Wilhelmus à Brakel, *The Christian's Reasonable Service*, trans. Bartel Elshout, ed. Joel R. Beeke (repr., Grand Rapids: Reformation Heritage Books, 2012), vol. 1.

38. À Brakel, *Christian's Reasonable Service*, 1:317.

39. À Brakel, *Christian's Reasonable Service*, 1:318.

40. À Brakel, *Christian's Reasonable Service*, 1:319–20.

William Pemble on the Permanence of Conscience

Pemble has a chapter on conscience in his *Summe of Morall Philosophy*. "Conscience is the immediate act of our soul arising from a natural apprehension of good, and avoidance of evil. It cannot be totally extinguished in any."[41] He also portrays the workings of conscience by means of a syllogism:

> No evil is to be committed
> This particular is evil,
> Ergo, not to be committed.

"The Major," Pemble notes, "is drawn from the practicke understanding out of the rules of Nature. The minor ariseth from view of particulars, which are variable, and may often deceive; if our apprehensions of them be false, our Conscience must needs erre."[42]

Pemble then lists the sources of error in the conscience, factors such as ignorance, negligence, and pride. He says nothing about conscience's relation to the various faculties of the soul. In this work of moral philosophy, Pemble restricts the workings of conscience to natural light or natural law and does not extend its workings to God's special revelation.

Franciscus Junius on Natural Law

The products of the *sensus divinitatis* came to be the backdrop from which the Reformed attitude to natural theology was begun. This was not a program of natural theology from premises acceptable to any rational person, but an argument for God's existence from the *semen religionis*.[43] And this was also the starting point for the Reformed account of the conscience and morals. To be more exact, it is with the *fallen sensus divinitatis* that the Reformed work on conscience and law started. The fall did not erase the endowment that created mankind enjoyed; but as a result of the fall, it became twisted or perverted. The redemptive grace of God may operate on these twisted faculties and the remnants of the loss of the *imago Dei*. In this sense, grace builds upon nature; it does not bypass or supplant it.

---

41. Pemble, *Summe*, 58.

42. Pemble, *Summe*, 59.

43. For discussion of the *semen religionis* and its bearing on natural theology, see Michael Sudduth, *The Reformed Objection to Natural Theology* (Farnham: Ashgate, 2009).

In his treatise on the Mosaic polity, *De politiae Mosis observatio* (1593),[44] a work on the nature of law, Franciscus Junius (1545–1602) starts from this original position. Junius was a Frenchman who received his theological education in Geneva and, after pastoral work, became a professor of theology at Leiden in Holland in 1592. He died of the plague at age fifty-seven before he could take up a new post in Saumur.

The present work itself is in the form of a set of theses; and his observations of the creation and fall and its effect on the created endowment of mankind is the first thesis, "The Correct Definition and Division of Law." As we will see, Junius is very scholastic in his outlook. Take the natural endowment, natural law. He says that the *efficient* cause of this human endowment is God; the *material* cause is "the lawful and unlawful thing that pertain to reason"; the *formal* cause is the ordering; the *end* is the common good.[45] Three things of special importance must be borne in mind: "(1) the principle, which is spoken of as *innate to creatures endowed with reason*; (2) the action, which *informs* these creatures *with the imago dei in its wider sense. This endowment may therefore be common notions of nature*; and (3) the mode of that law and of actions, namely, that they *adumbrate the eternal law by a certain participation.*"[46]

The natural law to which Junius refers is not an abstract notion, a secular legal creation, but part of the image of God and then affected by the depravity of the fall, first in the purity of the original creation and then in the depravity of fallenness. It is part of the *imago Dei* in its wider sense, surviving the loss of the true knowledge of God and original righteousness. It is this surviving sense of natural law that is Junius's concern. Natural law is among what philosophers call the "common notions." They are universally— if unevenly—distributed among all men and women.

The natural law, being given for mankind's good, is part of the practical reason, and so it is teleological in its operation. The "end to which we act by the natural law"[47] informs the goal or goals of the practical reason. Good is to be pursued and evil avoided, and the natural law tell us which is which. Some of these notions are universal; some, common to living beings; and

---

44. This has been translated as Franciscus Junius, *The Mosaic Polity*, trans. Todd M. Rester, ed. Andrew McGinnis (Grand Rapids: CLP Academic, 2015).

45. Junius, *Mosaic Polity*, 46.

46. Junius, *Mosaic Polity*, 44.

47. Junius, *Mosaic Polity*, 45.

some, to the reason of human beings. There would appear to be an overlap here, since those common to living beings—such as marriage and the rearing of children—obviously involve the reason. Those that are distinctively human involve principles, norms or values, and conclusions, the ends of the practical reason. The principles are basic, indemonstrable principles, such as that God exists, and life is to be preserved. Conclusions are such as that God is to be worshipped, and that human life must be cared for. So that the enduing of the natural law in these ways is a feature of what would later be called God's general or common grace.

In creation, natural law consisted in conformity to God's eternal law.[48] The law was perfect for unsullied mankind. But human beings are finite and creaturely, and because the natural law is the product of infinite goodness and wisdom, it is only imperfectly apprehended. Thus, it is best to say that such awareness of the natural law was an imperfect adumbration of the perfect natural law. Given our fallenness, such natural law was supplemented through the grace of God by further revelations, new "editions" of the law, fencing us in from what would otherwise be an inevitable deterioration.[49] And then there is "the law of that way, truth and life" by which God exalts the redeemed above nature through the work of the Mediator, Jesus Christ. (Some equivocation on "law" may be discerned here.) So the concept of law pervades both the everyday life of the fallen, and their "supernatural and eternal perfection" through Christ.[50] Part of the bringing about of new life in Jesus Christ is the "infusing" of the natural law. So Junius's thesis 6 reads, "The divine Law is that which is inspired by God, infused in rational creatures, and informs them with common and individual notions beyond nature for the purpose of transmitting them to a supernatural end by a supernatural leading."[51] This formulation makes it clear that for Junius "grace perfects nature; grace does not, however, abolish it."[52]

The question that we will next consider is not what are evil actions, but what is the metaphysical nature of the evil of evil actions? It was of interest to

---

48. Junius, *Mosaic Polity*, 47.

49. Here I take it that Junius's reference is to the Old Testament Mosaic law, one of whose functions was, according to Paul, to hedge in and protect the people of God from their enemies (Gal. 4:3).

50. Junius, *Mosaic Polity*, 48.

51. Junius, *Mosaic Polity*, 49.

52. Junius, *Mosaic Polity*, 38.

those who wrestled with the charge that God's decree over all has the consequence that it makes God the author of sin. Sin, they responded, is principally a defect, a lack, and so not something that God could have created.

Theophilus Gale on God's Relation to Moral Evil

As just noted, the question of God's relation to moral evil was an important topic in Reformed theology ever since the Jesuits accused Augustinian theology of making God the author of sin. One line of response to that accusation harkened back to Augustine's view that God cannot do evil, since evil is a lack, a defect like blindness, only a more general failure. In a sense, when evil occurs, there is nothing for God to have been the author of. (Calvin had commented that Augustine's *privatio boni* was a little too neat, showing "an acuteness of argument which to many, may not be satisfactory."[53]) But the Reformed orthodox that followed made good use of it.

The English theologian Theophilus Gale (1628–1678) made much of this point in his work *The Court of the Gentiles*.[54] Like a handful of other British Reformed divines of the seventeenth century, such as William Twisse (1578–1646) and Samuel Rutherford (1600–1661), Gale was thoroughly versed in the scholasticism of late medievalism, both in its Roman Catholic and Reformed expressions, though unlike Twisse and Rutherford, Gale wrote in English.

The Court of the Gentiles shows his immense learning. His own scholasticism is genuine, even though he says he has a low estimate of the work of his opponents who use scholastic distinctions to further their Pelagian tendencies.[55] Part IV of book III of the work, the last part (published in 1678), appears to have been written as an addendum to the earlier parts. In it, Gale seems to express disappointment that the earlier exposition of his

---

53. See the brief discussion in Paul Helm, *John Calvin's Ideas* (Oxford: Oxford University Press, 2004), 117.

54. Theophilus Gale was the author of *The Court of the Gentiles*, the parts of which were published successively. *Part I Of Philologie* (Oxon: Printed by Hen. Hall for Tho. Gilbert, 1669); *Part II Of Philosophie* (London: Will Hall for Tho. Gilbert, 1671); *Part III The Vanity of Pagan Philosophy* (London: A. Maxwell and R. Roberts, for T. Cockeril, at the sign of the Atlas in Cornhil hear the Royal Exchange, 1677); *Part IV Of Reformed Philosophie* (London: for John Hill at the Black Lyon in Fleet-street, and Samuel Tidmarsh at the King's-Head in Cornhill, 1678).

55. Gale, *Court of the Gentiles*, IV.iii.2.

views (particularly in chapters 7, 9 and 11 of book I of part IV of *The Court of the Gentiles*, published in 1677)[56] had not had the impact that he had hoped for. He takes the Scottish Reformed theologian John Strangius as an opponent.[57] Gale believes Strangius has views similar to his own, making it easier for him to pinpoint their differences. However, we will look only at some of the preparatory work for this debate, not the debate itself.

In Part IV, entitled *Of Reformed Philosophie*, Gale is concerned with how God's providence, particularly His predetermination of and concurrence in the creation (including evil human actions), can be upheld without Gale being guilty of the charge that God is the author of sin. Following Gale himself, our aim is not to dwell on the polemical context, insofar as this can be avoided, but rather to focus on the exposition of his own approach. He says quaintly, "Wherefore, to render our Discourse the lesse offensive, we have cast it into a *thetic* and *dogmatic* Method, rather than *agonistic* and *polemic*."[58]

He begins his treatment of divine predetermination with an introduction of anthropological terms, and it is these that we will focus on. He notes how the opponents of divine predetermination are keen to safeguard the majesty of God from the charge that a predetermining God must be the author of sin.[59] But this charge must also face divine concurrence, a commitment to which all parties have in common, Gale asserts, and certainly the Reformed theologian Strangius. This made Gale more prolix, as he wishes to "give the blessed God and his sinful Creatures both their dues."[60] We will concentrate attention on this phase of a larger argument because of the light it throws on anthropology, and so we will not follow him on the theological side of things, which is to show that his arguments, both his anthropological and theological commitments together, vindicate this position from the charge of making God the author of sin.[61]

---

56. Gale, *Court of the Gentiles*, IV.iii.2.

57. John Strang (Strangius) (1584–1654) was the author of *De Voluntate et Actionibus Dei circa Peccatum* (Amsterdam, 1657). Strang was, for a time, principal of the University of Glasgow.

58. Gale, *Court of the Gentiles*, IV.iii.1.

59. Gale, *Court of the Gentiles*, IV.iii.2.

60. Gale, *Court of the Gentiles*, IV.iii.3.

61. Gale, *Court of the Gentiles*, IV.iii.3–4.

On the anthropological side, Gale is basically concerned with human evil acts and their privation of the good. He holds that sin first came into the world from "the *Defectibilitie* of our first Parents, and has been ever since maintained and fomented by the *Vitiositie* [an Anglicization of *vitiositas*, viciousness] of human nature depraved by Adam's sin."[62] By these terms, Gale indicates that for him sinfulness is not a positive quality, but a deficiency. When a person becomes blind, he does not gain an additional power or set of powers, but he suffers a loss. The first sin was a loss in this way. Nevertheless, it had powerful and palpable effects, as blindness may have, as Gale indicates by using the terms "vitiositie," or viciousness. But these effects are also negative and destructive in their character. A sinful act is also the action of a person, and that person is the creature of God, and was and is a good. So moral evil, while not a good in and of itself, is parasitic on what is good, the goodness of the being of a person.[63] He notes, "The wise Creator and Gubernator [governer] of althings has by his Law so constituted all moral beings, both Virtues and Vices, as that they cannot subsist but in something *natural*: albeit sin be, according to its formal reason, a mere privation yet it required some positive, real natural being of its subject, according to the nature of all other privations."[64]

As creatures of God, the agents of evil are created by God and held in being by Him; but insofar as they are evil and so opposed to goodness they are, considered in their own right, not good. Yet they are permitted by God in order to serve His own good purposes, "who can extract the greatest good out of the greatest evils."[65]

Here Gale is not making a categorical difference between the soul and the body, the body being permitted to act immorally as God sees fit. He does not have the body principally in mind, but the soul. God upholds and governs it and all its faculties and (as an aspect of His governance) permits the occurrence of evil thoughts, intentions, and desires. And the body, until it is involved in acting wickedly, is morally indifferent, until utilized to further wicked intentions. There may be nature and no morality, as is the case with nonhuman animals, but where there is morality, good

---

62. Gale, *Court of the Gentiles*, IV.iii.4.

63. Among those who take this line are Andreas Rivet in the *Synopsis Purioris Theologiae*.

64. Gale, *Court of the Gentiles*, IV.iii.5.

65. Gale, *Court of the Gentiles*, IV.iii.5.

or evil, there is nature. "Al thoughts, words and actions considered physically and abstractly, without regard to their moral determination by the Wil and Law of God, are neither good or evil."[66] Though Gale might have added that they are good insofar as they are the work of the good Creator and Preserver. All morality and moral acts being good or bad depend on their relation to the moral divine law. In his emphasis on the divine will as establishing the standard of what is good and bad, Gale follows "*Scotus*, and other Scholemen."[67] Here, as against the Platonic notion that good and evil are eternally grounded in reason. (Gale also cites Voetius, Baxter, and Strangius in support.) Yet though neutral in this way, there is nevertheless a natural congruity on the part of human beings to obey, for human nature was fitted for obedience, which is the service and worship of the Creator. "Nature," as used by Gale and the scholastics more generally, is not an abstract, neutral term, as it frequently is in modern culture. It cannot be separated from the purposes of the original creation, even when that creation is spoiled by sin.

Sin formally consists in its being a transgression of the divine law, a falling short of perfect obedience. That is, sin in its form and nature is privative, not positive (like the Manicheans—among others—held). Gale supports this by his knowledge of the history of ideas. (The language gets difficult here, even in English. According to Gale, sin has a *nature*, which is to act contrary to the *nature* of things as intended in the creation.) In Gale's view, Pseudo-Dionysius, Simplicius, Gregory of Nyssa, and (especially) Augustine all held to the view of evil as a morally privative relation.[68] Or rather, as a relative privation insofar as being a transgression of the law, it may be said to have a relation to the moral law. So sin is not a mere nothing, a nonentity, for it has positive effects. But it is not a positive act or real being.

According to Gale, there are different kinds of sinful action. Such actions may be *modally* sinful or *intrinsically* so. So a pious person, being nonetheless in this present life morally imperfect, performs morally good actions that are mixed with sin and evil, even though he does not intend it so. "For such is the profound mysterious wisdom of God, that he permits a mixture of sin even with the best good works on this side Heaven, thereby

---

66. Gale, *Court of the Gentiles*, IV.iii.6.
67. Gale, *Court of the Gentiles*, IV.iii.7.
68. Cited in Gale, *Court of the Gentiles*, IV.iii.8.

to render the methods of his Grace to be more illustrious: so that the same Act, which is in evangelic estimation sincerely good, is also modally sinful and imperfect."[69]

Intrinsically evil actions are generally understood to be referred to and determined by such an object as causes them to be moved in an intrinsically vicious and malignant direction, so that they are irreparably evil. But, as Gale qualifies, it is "not that those acts are in their formal determination or reference to their object."[70] Taking up a knife and stabbing is not in itself an evil act, but it becomes evil when employed in an attack upon a neighbor. It may seem that the acknowledgment of such acts gives no room for God, who is the governor of them, not to be the author of their sinfulness. But Gale is adamant that God's concourse to the "material or substrate matter of sin" does not suppose a divine concourse in the formally sinful character of the act. This is the conclusion that he aims for. The act is the use of a good means to an evil end. The "material or substrate matter," which is good, is what is necessary to make possible an evil act, which is privative.

A word or two on the concourse of God is necessary to complete the outline of Gale's position. Sometimes it appears that Gale is concerned *only* with the concourse of God, with His upholding of His creation, His first creation and then the fallen creation. But Gale is concerned with both the concourse of God and the governance of God of all His creatures and their actions, where governance is concerned with God's intentions and ends and with the vexing question of how God's necessarily good intentions mesh with the evil intentions of those He governs.

However, Gale's answer to the problem of whether or not God is the author of sin is the same in each case. It is based on a further distinction, just referred to, between the material constitution of an evil act and its formal nature.[71] "For al sin being, as to its formal nature, but a *moral privation* or *relation*, it necessarily requires some natural good as its substrate mater or subject." The distinction between *form* and *matter* is a fundamental one in the medieval outlook and in its Aristotelian sources. It corresponds to two different kinds of cause. A formal cause is the essence of a thing, what

---

69. Gale, *Court of the Gentiles*, IV.iii.9.

70. Gale, *Court of the Gentiles*, IV.iii.9.

71. Gale, *Court of the Gentiles*, IV.iii.5.

the thing is to be. The formal cause of creating a donkey is different from the formal cause of creating a cat. The form is the realization of a set of properties, which is donkey-ness or cat-ness. The material cause is that "stuff" out of which the efficient cause produces the form of the thing. But in the case of human actions, we are concerned first and foremost with the activity of the soul. In scholastic thinking, however, the same fourfold causation applies, whether the soul is thought of in dualistic or hylomorphic terms. So the phrase "material cause" does not refer only to physical matter, but to "the substrate matter or subject" of sin, which is good on account of being created by God. The soul is an immaterial or spiritual essence; that is its "matter." That which performs evil actions is (for Gale) "matter," therefore, but spiritual rather than material matter; and it is good, because created and upheld and governed by God. (The terminology of form and matter is not helpful in such "spiritual" activities.)

To complete his survey of anthropological terms, Gale then considers the freedom of the will (which we will reserve for the next chapter) and the difference between natural and moral liberty, which we consider next in conjunction with the views of others.

Andreas Rivet on Natural and Moral Liberty

Andreas Rivet (1572–1651), a Huguenot who became professor of theology at Leiden, also takes a similar way in his work on providence in the Leiden *Synopsis Purioris*, characterizing the privative nature of evil:

> And so it is rightly said that He exercises providence regarding them [sins], since He disposes to do well regarding them.[72] But if one considers only that which is real and sin and "positive," as they say, what others call the "matter" of sin, namely as an entity or as an action, in this sense sins can be said even to be provided by God, but only in a relative sense and not in itself. That is because the formal structure of sin exists in the absence of being and of good, in a certain deformity and disorderliness, which does not come from God and so cannot have been provided for by Him.[73]

---

72. That is to say, to bring good out of their evil.
73. *Synopsis Purioris Theologiae*, 277 (*Disputatio XI, De Providentia Dei*).

If we think of an action, then God upholds it. But if it is evil, it is privative. Considered as a state of affairs, it is defective. God does not conserve such deficiencies, but only what is positive in them; and in the case of privative actions, this is the "substrate" of the action.

John Davenant on Sin as Disorder

In his *Animadversions*,[74] John Davenant makes the same general point as Gale on the question of God's relation to morally evil actions. He was writing in 1641, in the context of whether God's predetermination, His predestination of sinful acts, makes Him the "author of sin." He distinguishes between the formal and material elements, using much the same terminology as Gale. The crucial point in his argument is that God's attitude to the formal aspects differs from His attitude to the material aspects of a sinful act. The material element is the soul and its particular powers; the formal element is the motive or intention of the agent in doing this or avoiding that act. "This distinction is a sound and necessary distinction, and approved by all judicious divines, whether Papists or Protestants."[75]

Davenant grants "God to be the cause of the materiall part, as it denieth him to be any cause at all of the formal, which is the repugnancy or disconformity which the will of the Agent hath with the law or will of God."[76] Davenant does not hesitate to refer to these as two "parts" of the soul, even though he upholds at the same time the simplicity of the soul, that it is "without parts," a position held by most of his contemporaries. Yet a distinction between the formal and the material cause is a clear and sharp distinction for him and critical to his argument that there is a significant distinction between causes, since God has a causal relationship to the one that it is impossible for Him to have to the other.

---

74. John Davenant, *Animadversions Written by the Right Reverend Father in God, John, Lord Bishop of Salisbury, upon a Treatise intitled Gods Love to Mankind* (Cambridge: printed by Roger Daniel, Printer to the University, 1641).

75. Davenant, *Animadversions*, 174. Davenant quotes Diego Ruiz de Montoya (1562–1632), a Spanish Jesuit, and Gabriel Penottus with approval, despite the obvious theological differences. These are good examples that show Reformed theologians did not differ from Roman Catholics as a matter of principle, and where they shared an outlook with a Roman Catholic thinker they were prepared to say so.

76. Davenant, *Animadversions*, 174. But in the case of some "Papists," they disputed the application to sinful acts.

Davenant then considers an objection that this distinction does not apply to all sins. But if God is the creator and sustainer of human actions, then the following will apply. "Against this is excepted, *That all sinnes receive not this distinction*"—to which Davenant replies:

> If all sinnes subsist in some actual motion of the soul, body, or both, and this motion abstractively considered be the materiall part of every actuall sin, and hath God for the prime cause in whom we live, move, and have our being; then no sinne can be assigned wherein this material part may not be found. *In eating the forbidden fruit* the materiall part of the sinne in regard of the soul was the Appetition [an appetite, desire, or craving] thereof; in regard of the body, the Mastication and Manduction and other bodily acts: Separate these from the formall part, which is the *Modus appetendi*, and conteineth a repugnancy to Gods command, and God was the prime author thereof.[77]

So Davenant's reply is not to invoke God's relation to His law, but to God as the primary cause of all that occurs in His creation, the activity of secondary causes. The formal part of an action (its having the particular form that it has) is, in the case of sin, due to human disobedience of the divine law, his falling short of the divine glory. But the soul is the creature of God and as such is good and upheld by Him. So, like Gale, Davenant used the term "material" to refer both to the basis of intentions and volitions, which lie in the soul, and the movements of the body which have their basis in the body. These, the bodily movements, the material part of the act, are also caused by God as the primary cause, as the upholder of the creation. The way of willing these various spiritual and bodily parts and functions, what Davenant calls the *modus appetendi*, is the way that sinful desiring and believing work against the revealed will or law of God in this instance, the form or the formal part of the act.[78]

God brings about all the material side of things, but not the "disorderly Manner of desiring and eating contrary to the law of God."[79] This He upholds and governs but does not cause, "being a defect," as Davenant puts it.

---

77. Davenant, *Animadversions*, 175.

78. Davenant, *Animadversions*, 175.

79. Davenant, *Animadversions*, 175.

So there is a basic outlook that Davenant and Gale and the others we have mentioned have in common, though differences of detail. In answer to the objection, Davenant refers to God as the primary cause but stresses the privative nature of sin less than Gale, who is more overtly Augustinian on this point.

Moral Ability and Inability

In chapter 4, when we considered the place of the human will in the fall, we saw that according to Reformed theology the turning away from what God had commanded had a ratchet-like effect. The fateful choice permanently affected what mankind could do and fail to do thereafter. It had a *modal* effect, affecting and establishing what it was possible and impossible to do thereafter. These effects were not primarily the result of the decay of old habit and the growth of new habits. Rather, the choice had immediate consequences for what it was possible to do and not to do. It was hereafter impossible to be motivated to love and obey God out of love for Him, and possible to be motivated only to live selfishly. As the Westminster Confession put it, "And so [our first parents] became dead in sin and wholly defiled in all the faculties and parts of soul and body." As a result, we are "utterly indisposed, disabled, and made opposite to all good, and wholly inclined to all evil" (WCF 5.2, 4).

This is a sad deterioration in human nature. However, the doctrinal underpinnings of this view do not concern us here, only the view itself. In the course of considering those who make the distinction between natural and moral ability and inability as part of describing the consequences of the fall, we will find appreciable differences in outlook.

Francis Turretin and Freedom and Moral Inability

In his discussion of the way in which human nature may be said to possess free will despite being necessitated to sin in the sense that we have just been sketching, Turretin distinguished between various different senses of necessity—six in all. He notes that a necessity which he calls "physical necessity" is "repugnant to liberty." In physical necessity, things are done by force, and "the things done by force and compulsion cannot be done voluntarily."[80] Secondly, in the case of the moral necessity arising from

---

80. Turretin, *Institutes of Elenctic Theology*, 1:662.

habits, though the will is "slavish," such slavishness "by no means over-throws the true and essential nature of liberty."[81] "Although the sinner is so enslaved by evil that he cannot but sin, still he does not cease to sin most freely and with the highest liberty."[82]

The slavishness of sin brings impotence of a different kind than having a wooden leg or a glass eye do. Neither is it like what prison bars do. The sinner cannot but sin because he has not sufficient will. He lacks the moral ability not to sin. When Reformed divines referred to the "bondage" of the will to sin in mankind's fallen state, it is to such moral inability to which they are referring. Fallen men and women are naturally able to do certain things, but they are morally unable to do others—that is, they cannot will to do them.

Turretin goes on to claim that even in a state of a person's moral inability, the will of such a person is free in the sense that what he chooses is for him a good, the choice is *sub specie boni*. What he does of moral necessity he nevertheless wills and wants to do. "For all, by a universal and natural appetite, always seek good and happiness for themselves."[83] "Although the sinner is so enslaved to evil that he cannot but sin, still he does not cease to sin most freely and with the highest liberty."[84]

Theophilus Gale on Moral Liberty and the Fall

In Part IV of *The Court of the Gentiles*, Gale also considers the distinction between natural and moral ability.[85] This follows his discussion of the liberty of the will, a topic to be considered later. But though he distinguishes between natural and moral liberty, and therefore in a sense between natural and moral ability (and inability), he actually has a different emphasis from Turretin,

Gale considers moral liberty in the context of the fall and the degenerated character of the human will. Such liberty is generally understood as the moral potency or spiritual ability of the soul to do good. Gale thinks that the Pelagians and Arminians confound it with the natural liberty that

---

81. Turretin, *Institutes of Elenctic Theology*, 1:663.
82. Turretin, *Institutes of Elenctic Theology*, 1:663.
83. Turretin, *Institutes of Elenctic Theology*, 1:663.
84. Turretin, *Institutes of Elenctic Theology*, 1:663.
85. Gale, *Court of the Gentiles*, IV.iii.13.

we have been outlining. They take the denial of natural liberty in corrupt human nature to imply that the Reformed deny moral ability as such. So there is some untangling to be done, Gale thinks. He sets out his view in a number of propositions.

The first is that natural liberty[86] is essential to the will and all its acts, but moral liberty or free will to do good is only accidental and separable. Natural liberty is essential to free will. Whatever act is voluntary is for that reason free in this sense. He writes, "But now as for *Moral Liberty* and free-will to good, that is only *accidental* to the human Soul; it may come and go, be present and absent without the natural destruction of the soul, or violation to natural liberty. It's true that moral liberty, consisting in virtuous Habits, Inclinations and Exercises, is the Perfection of Man, yet so as the Essence of the soul is not diminished or destroyed by the loss thereof."[87]

The fall is "accidental" or "adventitious" (*adventitium*).[88] As a consequence, its loss did not result in the destruction of the soul, but in its perversion. It seems that Gale here makes precisely the same point.

As a result of the fall, certain modalities, necessities, became established in human nature, and correspondingly certain impossibilities. This impotence, impossibility, regarded what is morally and spiritually good. It is both a necessary and a voluntary impotence, for it arises in the will. It is thus an accidental necessity, since it came freely in the fall, but may be removed, only by regeneration. Gale notes that in this loss "the Soul, as a rational and voluntary subject, is *remotely, passively* and *naturally* capacitated for the reception of gratiose infusions."[89] Having lost the "accident" of original righteousness, human nature nevertheless remains fit for regeneration in a way that a sheep, for example, is not and never could be. It may be said in a parallel way that a light bulb is remotely, passively, and naturally capacitated to receive an electrical current and to shine, but that a blade of grass is not so capacitated.

Gale makes further distinctions regarding what is impossible for the soul. It is not a simple and absolute impossibility, but a limited and conditional

---

86. It has to be remembered that throughout this discussion "natural" has a reference to the creation, to what has a created nature, and not only to physical flora and fauna.

87. Gale, *Court of the Gentiles*, IV.iii.23–24.

88. As we saw in chapter 2, this is Calvin's word for the metaphysical status of original righteousness and of its loss. Calvin, *Institutes* II.i.11.

89. Gale, *Court of the Gentiles*, IV.iii.15.

impossibility. What is simply and absolutely impossible is a statement or statements the negation of which would imply a contradiction.[90] And what is not a contradiction may occur. It will occur under certain conditions. What are these conditions? Gale's answer is, the working of God's grace in the soul. "Albeit it be in a limited sense impossible [not to sin] to corrupt nature, yet it is possible to Grace." How is this? Because, Gale says, in a situation when the will is divinely predetermined to one act, being a creature with "an habitual indifference or radical flexibility to the opposite act," the opposite can occur.[91] This indifference is not that espoused by Jesuits, which is unconditional indifference, but it is a conditioned indifference. If the correct conditions occur, then the action can occur. *"That in free wil there is a simultie of [simultaneous] power to opposites, but not a power of simultie, i.e. a power of embracing opposites at one and the same time; whereof the reason is this, because a power to one act is not opposed to the power unto the negation of the same act, or to a contrary act, but two contraries or contradictories cannot be together in the same subject."*[92] Gale cites Alvarez[93] on the point. This discussion connects with that on free will to be discussed in chapter 7.

Stephen Charnock on the Soul and Regeneration

Stephen Charnock (1628–1680) is best known for his *Discourses upon the Existence and Attributes of God* (1682). He also had a great interest in the doctrine of regeneration and is clear on the soul and its faculties.[94] In setting forth the character of regeneration, he has things to say about the soul, its faculties, and its habits. The grace of regeneration is the result of the activity of the Spirit of God directly on the soul, and hence on every faculty. The union is between God and the whole soul, not with some part of it only.

---

90. Gale, *Court of the Gentiles*, IV.iii.15–6.

91. Gale, *Court of the Gentiles*, IV.iii.16.

92. Gale, *Court of the Gentiles*, IV.iii.16.

93. Diego Alvarez (1550–1635), a Spanish Dominican, author of *De auxiliis divinæ gratiæ et humani arbitrii viribus et libertate, ac legitimâ ejus cum efficaciâ eorumdem auxiliorum concordiâ libri XII* (Rome, 1610). This was critical of the middle knowledge of Luis de Molina.

94. E.g., *A Discourse of the Nature of Regeneration*, *A Discourse of the Efficient of Regeneration*, and *A Discourse of the Word, the Instrument of Regeneration*. These are found in volume 3 of *The Complete Works of Stephen Charnock* (Edinburgh: Banner of Truth, 1985).

The proper seat of grace is the substance of the soul, and therefore it influences every faculty. It is the form whence the perfection both of understanding and will do flow; it is not therefore placed in either of them, but in the essence of the soul. It is by this the union is made between God and the soul; but the union is not of one particular faculty, but of the whole soul. "He that is joined to the Lord is one spirit"; it is not one particular faculty that is perfected by grace, but the substance of the soul.[95]

If it dwelt only in one faculty there could be no spiritual motion of the other. The principles in the will would contradict those in the understanding; the will would act blindly if there were no spiritual light in the understanding to guide it. The light of the understanding would be useless if there were no inclination in the will to follow it, and grace in both those faculties would signify little if there remained an opposing perversity in the affections.[96]

And such grace is in the form of a set of habits. Charnock notes:

This habitual grace is the principle of all supernatural acts, as the soul concurs as an immanent principle to all works by this or that faculty. As Christ had a body prepared him to do the work of a mediator, so the soul has a habit prepared it to do the work of a new creature. To this purpose, there is a habit of truth or sincerity in the will, and a "hidden wisdom" in the understanding Ps. li. 6. As the corrupt nature is a habit of sin, so the new nature is a habit of grace; God does not only call us to believe, love, and obey, but brings in the grace of faith, and love, and obedience, bound up together, and plants it in the soil of the heart, to grow up there unto eternal life; he gives a willingness and readiness to believe, love, and obey.[97]

The Holy Spirit works on the soul not with force, like the throwing of a stone in the air, but by inclining the soul, changing its nature, making it productive of gracious aspirations and actions, new habits.

This habit is necessary. The acts of a Christian are supernatural, which cannot be done without a supernatural principle; we can no more do a gracious action without it, than the apostles could do the works of their office unless endued with power from above, which our Saviour

---

95. Charnock, *Works*, 3:96.
96. Charnock, *Works*, 3:96.
97. Charnock, *Works*, 3:106.

bids them tarry at Jerusalem for, Luke xxiv. 49. If there were not a gracious habit in the soul, no act could be gracious; or supposing it could, it could not be natural, it would be only a force. New creation is not from the Spirit compelling, but inclining; not like the throwing a stone contrary to its nature, but changing the nature, and planting other habits, whereby the actions become natural. As sin was habitual in a man by nature, so grace must be habitual in a new creature, otherwise a man is not brought into a contrary state (though the acts should be contrary) if there be not a contrary habit; for it is necessary the soul should be inclined in the same manner toward God as before it was toward sin; but the inclination to sin was habitual.[98]

Charnock stresses that this new principle is one, but imparts new habits to the faculties of the soul, like one shaft of light which produces a rainbow of colors. The regenerate person is (in this sense) a new man. "This habit," he notes, "is but one. For it is an entire rectitude in all the faculties, and an universal principle of working righteously. As the corrupt nature is called the 'old Adam,' and a 'body of death,' the gracious nature is called the 'new man,' Col. iii. 9, 10."[99] Despite its pronounced and supernatural power in changing a man's character, Charnock importantly adds that the soul and its faculties are not new, even though its regenerate habits are. "It is not a removal or taking away of the old substance or faculties of the soul. Some thought that the substance of Adam's soul was corrupted when he sinned, therefore suppose the substance of his soul to be altered when he is renewed. Sin took not away the essence, but the rectitude; the new creation therefore gives not a new faculty, but a new quality."[100]

Just as the fall did not affect the essence of the soul but its loss of holiness, so in regeneration there is no new essence. It is the character of a person which is restored. The Puritans in general respected the distinction between nature and grace. Here is another case where respect is paid to the words of Aquinas that "grace does not scrap nature but brings it to perfection."[101] The moral and spiritual character of a person is radically changed in regeneration, but he remains a human being throughout.

---

98. Charnock, *Works*, 3:106.
99. Charnock, *Works*, 3:107.
100. Charnock, *Works*, 3:91.
101. Aquinas, *Summa Theologiae*, Ia.1.8.2.

As he delineates the grace of regeneration, Charnock proves to have an expert grasp of the principles of faculty psychology, which provide the template for his discussion. He distinguishes senses in which regeneration is a new nature—nature as essence, and nature as character—and is situated in the soul and produces new life in each faculty, a new habit of the soul. We shall return to the topic of regeneration in the next chapter.

John Owen's Use of "Natural" and "Moral"

In his treatment of regeneration in *A Discourse Concerning the Holy Spirit* (1674), John Owen is someone else who has things to say about natural and moral ability. In unregeneracy, people will not and cannot receive "spiritual things." "Through the immediate depravation of the faculties of the mind or understanding, whereby a natural man is absolutely *unable*, without an especial renovation by the Holy Ghost, to discern spiritual things in a saving manner."[102]

Owen distinguishes between natural and moral impotency:

> There is in unregenerate men a *natural impotency*, through the immediate depravation of the faculties of the mind or understanding, whereby a natural man is absolutely *unable*, without an especial renovation by the Holy Ghost, to discern spiritual things in a saving manner. Neither is this impotency, although absolutely and naturally insuperable, and although it have in it also the nature of a punishment, any excuse or alleviation of the sin of men when they receive not spiritual things as proposed unto them.[103]

Such impotency is "absolutely and naturally insuperable." "This impotency is *natural* because it consists in the deprivation of the light and power that were originally in the faculties of our minds and understandings."[104] "Natural," because human nature; "the natural capacity of the human faculties of our minds" suffered loss, the loss of its "accidental perfections," as Owen states later,[105] in the fall. It is broken and needs repair. It cannot repair itself.

In this state there is "*moral impotency*, which is reflected on them greatly from the will and affections, whence the mind never *will receive*

---

102. Owen, *Discourse Concerning the Holy Spirit*, in *Works*, 3:266–67.
103. Owen, *Discourse Concerning the Holy Spirit*, in *Works*, 3:266–67.
104. Owen, *Discourse Concerning the Holy Spirit*, in *Works*, 3:267.
105. Owen, *Discourse Concerning the Holy Spirit*, in *Works*, 3:285.

spiritual things."[106] So "natural impotency" respects the understanding, fallen in Adam. And "moral impotency" respects the will and affections. So such impotence respecting the will and affections is "more corrupted than the understanding." It is interesting that Owen judges that some faculties are more depraved than others. As a result of this corruption, there is "no man doth *actually* apply his mind to receiving the things of the Spirit of God to the utmost of that ability which he hath…. There is not in any of them a due improvement of the capacity of their natural faculties, in the use of means, for the discharge of their duty toward God herein."[107]

Once again we must be wary regarding the way in which a writer is using "natural" and "nature." So in Owen's use of the "natural" and "moral" distinction, there is a difference in the scope of each. Natural inability has to do with the loss of understanding; moral inability has the consequence that the mind will never receive the things of the Spirit of God. It is not that human natural ability is intact and the moral ability is warped, but that both are warped and the natural inability of the understanding has the consequence that the will and affections are warped in turn. Here, in Owen's account, the will is in bondage to a fallen understanding, and (though Owen does not refer to them in these passages) what we have referred to as the Augustinian modalities are more apparent. It is made clearer in Owen's anthropology how it is that the will is in bondage. It is a result of the damage to the soul, not in its essence but in its accidents.

Joseph Truman on Inability, Pity, and Blame

Joseph Truman's essay *A Discourse of Natural and Moral Impotency*, which was referred to earlier, is a full treatment of the difference between natural and moral inability, which he is at pains to uphold against misunderstanding, partly by considering certain cases of conscience and then by responding to certain difficulties and misunderstandings of the doctrine of grace in its application.

The distinction between natural and moral power and impotency is not made *de origine*, on account of them having a different origin, for both are in that sense natural. But it is made "to denote the species or kinds, and

---

106. Owen, *Discourse Concerning the Holy Spirit*, in *Works*, 3:267.
107. Owen, *Discourse Concerning the Holy Spirit*, in *Works*, 3:268.

the essential difference of their Natures."[108] Truman sets out the distinction as follows:

> That is a Physical or Natural habit or action, that is neither…laudable or vituperable,[109] *In genere morum*, that a man can neither be counted good and honest, and bad or dishonest, for his agility or lameness, dullness, blockishness, or acuteness; but he may be (having such power, and doing accordingly) admired though not praised; and for the defect of such power may be pitied, but not blamed or punished, and this Impotency may be a punishment, but cannot be a sin.

A man may have only one leg but cannot be blamed for what he cannot do as a result, though he may be pitied. Truman continues:

> The Moral and Ethical act or habit is just contrary. It is that which is laudable or vituperable, and that which a man may be looked on as honest or dishonest for.
>
> Now Natural Impotency is always, in this sense, of something that a man cannot do if he would never so much; or hath not the very faculty of willing it.
>
> The *Moral Impotency* is of somthing that a man hath the natural faculty to will, or can do if he would; but is hindered only by moral vitious habits, from willing or doing it.[110]

Truman's distinction between natural and moral ability and inability construes "natural" as "bodily." A lame man, a drunk, someone with an allergy to a particular food, someone living in a place where the gospel is unknown—these have "natural inabilities," that is, a lack of a normal bodily or mental function or of an opportunity as a result of being in a particular place.

> The want of this natural power, their *Natural Impotency*, doth excuse, as is commonly granted; and they that deny it…. Total *Natural Impotency* doth excuse before God and Man: Yea all *Natural Impotency* doth excuse according to the measure and degree of it.[111]

---

108. Truman, *Discourse of Natural and Moral Impotency*, 4.
109. That is, deserving of blame.
110. Truman, *Discourse of Natural and Moral Impotency*, 4.
111. Truman, *Discourse of Natural and Moral Impotency*, 4.

> Moral Impotency is when a man hath the Natural power, can do the things in respect of his Natural powers, but will not, and not only so, but cannot obtain of himself to will it though yet he hath the Natural power of obtaining this by himself…. These expressions *a se impetrare non potest ac velit*, he cannot find it in his heart to chuse it, cannot obtain of himself to will it, seem the fittest to represent it to you by.
>
> And it is not from any Natural defect that he cannot find it in his heart, cannot obtain of himself to will it, but from his Wickedness, his Pride, Covetousness, Malice, Voluptuousness, and such things as prevail with his will in a Moral way, to keep it fast to them.[112]

Truman says that everyone has an awareness of the distinction between what a man may be pitied for and what he may be blamed for. If a man cannot stomach cheese, for example, he is to be pitied and not blamed. But if a man hates God and good men and cannot receive good instruction, he is to be blamed. (Note that Truman is particularly interested in these *in*abilities, but a parallel point can be made for abilities. A man with exceptionally good eyesight may be admired, while another who is born blind may be pitied for his disability.) So natural power may consist in factors such as having reasons to do an act that a person is required to do, if he were to pay attention. If he were to pay attention, he has power to perform what Truman calls *impetrate* acts.[113] These are acts that can be performed upon request.[114]

Truman holds to the moral impotency of the unregenerate. The unregenerate have an intellect and will, and these are warped such that there is always a prevailing motive to continue in their unregeneracy. Truman prefers to say that they *may not* will a godly way, not that they *cannot*. His emphasis is on willingly persisting in a course of action, not on being physically necessitated to that course.[115]

---

112. Truman, *Discourse of Natural and Moral Impotency*, 24–25.

113. Truman, *Discourse of Natural and Moral Impotency*, 24.

114. Truman makes use of the distinction between *imperate* and *licit* acts; e.g., Truman, *Discourse of Natural and Moral Impotency*, 21, 50. *Imperate* (or "elicit") means "commanded," in this case, commanded by the will; and *licit* means "desired" or "permitted." Truman says that imperate acts need, besides a willingness, the means to carry out what is willed. For this use, see also Owen, *Discourse Concerning the Holy Spirit*, in *Works*, 3:284; and Turretin, *Institutes of Elenctic Theology*, 1:664.

115. Truman, *Discourse of Natural and Moral Impotency*, 2. See also Richard Baxter, *Catholick Theology, Plain, Pre, Practical; for Pacification of the Dogmatical Word-Warriors*

The "cannot" of unbelief is not a natural impotency, like that which results from being paralyzed. It is a "cannot" of unwillingness. Not to will to believe is just what unbelief is. If I wanted to will and couldn't for some physical reason, that is different.[116] But a will not to do such and such, though a person has the natural power to will but cannot find it in his heart to choose to will that thing, cannot "obtain of himself" to will it. Due to wickedness, pride, and so forth, he cannot want to want to please God.[117] Truman distinguishes between a "will not" and a "can not."[118] He cites Genesis 37:4: "Joseph's brethren hated him and could not speak peaceably to him." This "cannot" is a "will not" for a reason, as Truman puts it.[119] It is a "cannot" that is of their own choice. God regenerates not by giving new faculties, but by causing us to will and do of His good pleasure.[120] It is impossible that there is anything but will in this impotency.[121]

On the casuistical side of things, Truman considers the objection that a drunk man may be physically incapacitated and not able to talk or stand up. If he cannot stand up, then he is not to blame for not standing up. But is he not to be blamed for his state and the inabilities that it entails? Truman thinks that "*Legislators* do wisely and justly in inflicting a penalty of men for doing the thing when drunk, that they would inflict if he had done when sober."[122] Truman is clearly quite versed in the law, as he discusses responsibility of being in debt and its limits, and its similarities and differences with drunkenness or with being in debt.[123] So drunkenness is a halfway house between moral inability and physical inability. And even if they lost the use of reason due to drink, they are capable of harming others. Nevertheless, they ought to be punished, otherwise they would be encouraged to "designedly drink to excess."[124] And Truman makes the point that though drunkenness may incapacitate, becoming drunk was a

---

(London: printed by Robert White, for Nevill Simmons at the Prince's Arms in St. Paul's Churchyard, 1675), I.10 ("Natural and Moral Power and Impotency; Their difference").

116. Truman, *Discourse of Natural and Moral Impotency*, 21.

117. Truman, *Discourse of Natural and Moral Impotency*, 24–25.

118. Truman, *Discourse of Natural and Moral Impotency*, 26.

119. Truman, *Discourse of Natural and Moral Impotency*, 26–27.

120. Truman, *Discourse of Natural and Moral Impotency*, 27.

121. Truman, *Discourse of Natural and Moral Impotency*, 28.

122. Truman, *Discourse of Natural and Moral Impotency*, 14.

123. Truman, *Discourse of Natural and Moral Impotency*, 8–18.

124. Truman, *Discourse of Natural and Moral Impotency*, 14.

voluntary act. He also deals with a parallel difficulty, whether or not one is responsible for debts that one cannot repay.

In his "uses" at the end of the book, Truman considers the case of a person who is persuaded of what is true, that he is morally unable to respond positively to the preaching of the gospel. "*But I cannot turn from sin to God, I cannot leave my sinful ways.*"[125] If this is genuinely intended and is not a mere excuse, then Truman replies: If the person means that he *cannot* turn to God, then that is false, because the faculties, the understanding and will, are intact. What he should say is not that he cannot turn to God, but that he won't. Such says to himself, "*I am resolved to please my Flesh and Senses, come what will of it. I have such a chosen Averesnesse to God and his Wayes, and such a Love to the wayes of sin, that though the Minister should lift up his Voyce like a Trumpet, and speak and sound as terribly as the Trumpet will as the last day, I will go on.*"[126] Truman has a number of other similar objections, with answers in the same plain way.

Truman's approach is in contrast to Gale's use of modal language. In doing so, Gale is following Augustine's contrasts between *posse* and *non posse* in his characterization of the fourfold state of mankind. For Truman, man is morally impotent only through the possession of vicious habits. He makes hardly any use of the language of the bondage of the will to sin.

Is Gale's a more modalized account than Truman's, who emphasizes the persistence of the will and not choices being made impossible by the fall? Is this a difference of presentation or of substance? Truman's emphasis is not on the impossibilities of fallen humanity, but on a consequence of this. He seems to hold that if people come to believe that certain things are impossible for them to do, then the obvious response is not to try to do them and to adopt a kind of fatalism with respect to them. But the situation is different if such people are told that they do not come to Christ because they are unwilling to do so, the implication being that if they were willing they could come to Him.

In his discussion, Truman shows little interest in the fall and its consequences, its loss of "accidental perfections," as Owen calls them, which leads Owen to a different sense of "natural inability" than Truman, a sense in which natural inability encompasses the loss of spiritual integrity as a

---

125. Truman, *Discourse of Natural and Moral Impotency*, 190.
126. Truman, *Discourse of Natural and Moral Impotency*, 190.

consequence of the fall. The natural state of man as created is changed. Hence "natural inability" takes in the consequences of this loss. Indeed, it is the chief feature of such an inability for Owen, who pays little attention to natural inabilities such as lameness.

In his answer to the question, "But whence came this Moral Impotency?," Truman does refer to the fall and its consequences, but in different terms than Owen. Truman writes:

> There is much of Natural Impotency to many desireable things, yea, in the best in this life, as a punishment, or product of Adams Fall, and much as a punishment, or effect of our (in the stricter sense) own sins e.g. many ignorances, and natural roving extravagancies of the mind, melancholly, yea, and natural desires or inclinations in the sensitive part of the affections, which are not at all subject to the Will and understanding…. I do believe, that not only the rational part of the affections, and that part which is now subject to the Will, but [except] the most sensitive part of them, was subject to the Will in *Adam*, before his Fall, and that he could not say, as we, *I would not be troubled, or afraid, or put into a trembling, but cannot help it; I would have the more affecting most sensible part of joy, but cannot.*[127]

For Owen, the fall resulted in loss, a sort of withering or shrinking of the soul's accidental perfections. For Truman, on the other hand, it resulted in mental rearrangement. Their different understandings of "natural inability" is no doubt symptomatic of wider theological differences. There is a significant terminological difference between Owen and Truman. As we have seen, for Owen a "natural impotency" is a depravation of the faculties of the mind, particularly the will and affections.[128] For Truman, a natural inability is a physical loss, a loss of the totality of our physical abilities, that in some way incapacitates us. For Owen, this loss includes the mind. It is a defect of our *phusis*, or nature. He restricts a moral inability to the deformity of the will and affections. But for Truman, a natural inability is a bodily defect, which physically disables us, and a moral inability is unwillingness. Whether clearing up this terminological difference would bring their minds any closer is difficult to say.

---

127. Truman, *Discourse of Natural and Moral Impotency*, 143–44. This is one of the few references to Adam's fall in the book.

128. Owen, *Discourse Concerning the Holy Spirit*, in *Works*, 3:267.

Francis Turretin on the Ambiguity of "Natural" and "Moral"

Turretin cuts through the verbal ambiguity of "natural" and "moral" with the following clarification:

> Nor do they make a better escape who pretend this impotence to be moral, not natural, and thus a thing not absolutely and simply impossible to man, but[129] that man can do it if he wishes. We answer that whether this impotence be called natural or moral…. it is certainly inextricable to man. In vain is it said that man can do this or that if he will, since it is evident that he is not able to will; not because he is destitute of natural power to will (because thus he differs from brutes), but because he is without the disposition to will what is good.[130]

John Gill on Ought and Can

The Puritan theologian John Howe (1630–1705),[131] who was more influenced by Platonism than by scholasticism, did not adopt a scholastic style, though nonetheless he may be said to be among the Reformed orthodox. And there were others. John Gill (1697–1771), not a Platonist, is included in surveys of Reformed orthodoxy because he owes much to it, even though he was a Baptist. He was self-educated, and thus his style did not owe much, if anything, to the tradition of the scholastic disputation. Nevertheless, many of the authors he quotes are Reformed orthodox, and the distinctions he makes and the concepts he uses are drawn from such sources.

In Gill's early work, *The Cause of God and Truth*,[132] he defends the "Five Points of Calvinism" against its eighteenth-century detractors, in particular Daniel Whitby (1638–1726), an Anglican clergyman with outspoken Arminian views.

The question Gill poses is, Does "ought" entail "can"? This takes us back to Truman's distinction between natural and moral inability. That is, does the obligation that one has to do something or to refrain from doing

---

129. For an appraisal, see R. A. Muller, "John Gill and the Reformed Tradition: A Study in the Reception of Protestant Orthodoxy in the Eighteenth Century," in *The Life and Thought of John Gill (1697–1771), A Tercentennial Appreciation*, ed. Michael A. G. Haykin (Leiden: Brill, 1997), 51–68.

130. Turretin, *Institutes of Elenctic Theology*, 1:675.

131. See the discussion of David Field, *Rigide Calvinism in a Softer Dresse, The Moderate Presbyterianism of John Howe 1630–1705* (Edinburgh: Rutherford Studies in Historical Theology, 2004).

132. John Gill, *The Cause of God and Truth* (London: Thomas Tegg & Son, 1838).

something entail that one has the ability to do it? Or is it possible to be obliged to do something while not having the ability to do it? How one answers that question is something of a theological criterion, like a blood test is for the state of the body. If one answers no, then this generally is a sign of Augustinianism.[133] The denial of "ought implies can" is presupposed by the Reformed teaching on the role of the moral law to bring about conviction of sin. On this account, it is the very realization of one's inability to observe the law that may and should drive a person into the arms of Jesus. If one replies that ought does entail can, then this is generally a sign of Pelagianism or Arminianism or of a moralistic liberalism. For instance, that ought implies can is critical for Immanuel Kant's view of "pure moral religion" as developed in his *Religion within the Limits of Reason Alone*.[134]

In a number of places, Gill clearly says that obligation does not imply ability. But he does not distinguish between moral and natural ability. In his *The Cause of God and Truth*, discussing the biblical teaching about reprobation, Gill considers the following argument: "This decree is said to be 'contrary to the justice of God' because by it God is made to require faith and obedience of persons from whom he has either taken away strength to perform, or to whom he has absolutely decreed not to give it; which makes it impossible for them to believe and obey: and no man is bound to do that which is impossible."[135] His response: "I reply, that the rule, which is so frequent in the mouths and writings of our opponents, *Nemo obligatur ad impossibile*, no man is bound to that which is impossible, in many cases will not hold good."[136]

Gill cites the case of a debtor who cannot pay his debts and yet does still have the obligation to do so. The fact that a person may become habituated to evil does not entail that he does not have an obligation to live uprightly. More generally, it is "man's duty to believe the word of the Lord, and obey

---

133. It is a pervasive theme in Augustine's Anti-Pelagian writings. See, for example, *On the Grace of Christ*, ch. 20. Also Calvin, *Institutes*, I.ii.3.

134. This is the English translation. Immanuel Kant, *Religion within the Limits of Reason Alone*, ed. T. M. Green and H. H. Hudson (New York: Harper and Row, 1960).

135. Gill, *Cause of God and Truth*, 292. He references Stephanus Curcellaeus (1586–1659) or Philipp van Limborch (1633–1712), Arminian divines. The quotations in the text are an amalgamation from the writings of each, who both appeal to the principle *nemo obligatur ad impossibile*. I am grateful to Richard Muller for this information.

136. Gill, *Cause of God and Truth*, 291.

his will, though he has not a power, yea, even though God has decreed to withhold that grace, without which he cannot believe and obey."[137]

So far this looks like a fairly standard Augustinian position. But then Gill goes on to say,

> However there are many things which may be believed and done by the reprobates, and therefore they may be justly required to believe and obey; it is true, they are not able to believe in Christ to the saving of their souls, or to perform spiritual and evangelical obedience, but then it will be difficult to prove that God requires these things of them, and should that appear, yet the impossibility of doing them, arises from the corruption of their hearts, being destitute of the grace of God, and not from the decree of reprobation, which, though it denies them that grace and strength, without which they cannot believe and obey in this sense, yet it takes none from them, and therefore does them no injustice.[138]

It is evident that in this passage as a whole Gill makes a significant distinction between obedience to the law and the performing of spiritual and evangelical obedience. This seems a curious difference, however, because Gill appears unnaturally to restrict spiritual obedience to a person's relation to the gospel. But Reformed theologians generally held that the obedience of the law required of us all is a purely motivated and perfect obedience: "with all your heart, with all your soul, and with all your strength" (Deut. 6:5; see also Matt. 22:37). Of this obedience, fallen people are incapable. This appears to be a clear case of spiritual obedience. (To confuse things further, in one place Gill grants, "God requires all men, and it is their indispensable duty, to love Him with all their heart, soul, and strength, to fear Him always, and keep His commandments."[139]) The preaching of the law involves the call on people to keep the law perfectly, not merely to keep it in an outward, self-righteous, or hypocritical manner, but at the same time making them aware that they do not and cannot do so, but have an obligation to obey it nonetheless. So it would seem that unless Gill is going to restrict obedience to the law in an implausible and unsatisfactory fashion, not characteristic of Reformed theology more generally, then the inability

---

137. Gill, *Cause of God and Truth*, 292.

138. Gill, *Cause of God and Truth*, 292–93.

139. Gill, *Cause of God and Truth*, 278.

fully to keep the law does nevertheless entail an ability to keep it fully. And, by parity of reasoning, the inability to exercise true faith in Christ ought not to remove the obligation to believe in Him.

"Ought" may not imply "can," but there are different grades of ability, and so different grades of obligation—or so Gill seems to say. Yet it also seems that he has not quite made up his mind on this issue. On the one hand, since the reprobates can believe and do certain things, they are required to believe and do them. They cannot, however, believe in Christ to the saving of their souls, but—and here Gill appears to hesitate—it is "difficult to prove" that these are required by God. But "should that appear" that they (the reprobate) are required to do such things, the impossibility of doing so arises from their hearts, not from the decree.[140]

So there may be some hesitancy or inconsistency in Gill's attitude to the principle that ought implies can. In some instances not covered by straightforward cases of physical impossibility, Gill seems to imply that ought does imply can; in other cases, the distinction between moral inability and spiritual ability appears to apply. But Gill does not use the phrase "moral ability." This inconsistency is unfortunate. Nevertheless, it makes it harder to pin the label of "hyper-Calvinist" on Gill. Certainly some of his high Calvinist views suggest hyper-Calvinism, but not the view insofar as it reflects the usual Reformed theologian's position on *nemo obligatur ad impossibile*.

---

140. Gill, *Cause of God and Truth*, 292.

The Intertwining Self

In discussing the unity, spirituality, and simplicity of the human soul in its various states, Christian faculty psychologists must make numerous distinctions, as we have been seeing. They base these distinctions on what they find in Scripture and what they observe in themselves and others, regimented by the scholastic terminology of Aquinas and Aristotle, adapted where necessary to their Augustinianism. Yet to be a faculty psychologist is not to think that each faculty can be defined and understood without reference to the others—that the full description of the intellect or understanding or reason is wholly separable from that of the will, for example. Nor does it imply that separate psychological operations imply separate souls, or the operation of separate substances within the soul. To underline the unitary nature of the soul, it is necessary to note the interdependence of each operation of each faculty with other operations of other faculties.

We saw earlier that the will has the role of discharging what is proffered to it by the understanding, the practical intellect, and so is subordinate to it in the hierarchy of soulish powers. But in performing this role, the will must be able to discern what the understanding's preference is from all other possible outcomes considered by the intellect and held in the mind at that time in order to know what is that outcome that the understanding prefers. Only then can the will execute what the reason wants, and not execute something else or remain idle. Conversely, if the reason is to exercise its appetite, to draw one appetite from the set of such, and so to draw a conclusion or to make a preference, then for this to happen the will must be involved in such a process. For how otherwise is the intellect to be a lively operation and not wholly passive or inert? If John chooses his yellow tie to wear in preference to all the others, what energizes the consideration of these possibilities and then the selecting of the yellow tie? The only candidate for a positive answer appears to be the will. And what makes him voluntarily take the tie to wear it? Presumably the understanding must inform the will to do so. The reason must form a practical decision or judgment, and in this the will must be involved. So it seems that the operating of the will is a necessary condition of the operating of the understanding, and that the understanding is a necessary condition of the operating of the will. So if the will is "blind," as we saw earlier was Reynolds's view, then it must need to be informed by the reason. A person's reason cannot convey its desire for a particular end without an exercise of the will. It is inert until in alliance with the will. For only then can it make a choice. This is the sort of area that we occupy in this chapter, the cooperation—or its absence—of the faculties.

William Pemble on the Union of the Faculties

We have already noted Pemble's concern about reifying the faculties, treating them as if they are parts, like body parts. In the course of discussing the place of assent in justifying faith, Pemble provides an excursus on the relation between the mind and the will. We looked earlier at some of his views in his book *Vindiciae Gratiae*. In that book, Pemble also has a discussion on the faculties of the soul.

In the Roman Catholic view of justification, the assent that is faith was said to be purely intellectual. Some formulations of the Reformed view may also agree with this, setting out their view of faith as consisting of *notitia*, *assensus*, and *fiducia*, and reserving the role of the will for *fiducia*, trust. Pemble dissents from this view. *Assensus*, as well as being an act of the intellect, is also an act of the will. This leads him to outline a view of the soul that was less hierarchical than other views.

So before we consider how the faculties cooperate according to representative theologians, we will consider more of Pemble's radical attitude to the various faculties. Pemble makes the usual distinction between the understanding, the object of which is the truth, and the will, which has its object, the good. Then, having distinguished them, he brings them together. For in the topic under view (justification), the object of assent is what God has revealed respecting human need and the receiving of the grace of Christ as the truth. And this truth is a good, as justification is a good. So in believing it, *assensus* embraces both truth and goodness and hence engages both the understanding and the will. He concludes that assent cannot be purely intellectual. It is also volitional, for it includes the will, which embraces the good. So we do not have to wait until the exercise of trust, *fiducia*, for the will to be engaged.

As we saw in our earlier extract from Pemble in chapter 4, he observes generally, in Ockhamist fashion, that within faculty psychology distinctions have been multiplied unnecessarily. This may be a criticism of Roman Catholic "subtilty," but Pemble is obviously aware of Protestant acceptance of various distinctions as well. He is certainly charging that some speculations have taken the various powers of the body to have a parallel in the various powers of the mind. However, he is not proposing a root-and-branch dismantling of faculty psychology. Reading the entire work on grace and faith reveals that scholasticism is in the warp and woof of his prose. The various faculties are upheld, the understanding is not the will, and so on. But he proposes that each does not operate independently and exclusively of the other. Each has powers that involve the other. How determined he was in this view is not clear. It is worth noting that in his *Summe of Moral Philosophy* (1630), published five years later than *Vindiciae Gratiae*, the project of the work lies in making the more conventional claim that the passions typically rule the reason and that morality thus consists in an endeavor to weaken the effect of the passions and to assert or reassert the primacy of the reason. Here at least it seems that the will, of which the passions are a consequence, is a separate faculty from the reason.

But in *Vindiciae Gratiae*, Pemble is adamant:

First, the Understanding essentially includes the Wil. For the Understanding hath a natural inclination to Truth, as the Will hath to Goodnesse: It abhors Falsehood, as that doth Evil. This desire and love of Truth in *volitio*, this refusal and hatred of Falsehood is *Nolitio*: and so *Velle* and *Nolle* are actions even of the Understanding too, and this proposition [*intellectus vult verum, non vult falsem* (the intellect wills the truth, not falsehood)] is most true and proper.

Secondly, The Will essentially includes the Understanding. For to will or nil any thing good or evil, is an action either of knowledge, or of ignorance. If of ignorance, then the Will in reasonable nature shall be an unreasonable Faculty, which is blindely carried to the embracing or refusing of that, which it self knowes not at all, but onely it is knowne to another faculty, the Understanding. But this were an absurd imagination to make the Will *facultatem non intelligentem*, and to appropriate unto it such a motion as is destitute of knowledge, like a blinde man that is led by thee seeing, he knows not whither. So should the Doctrine of Free-will in any kinde whatsoever, fall to the ground: for how is the Wil free, but because it may choose this or that? How can it make choice, unless it do also understand, compare, advise, and deliberate about the nature and consequences of things offered unto its choice? Wherefore it is manifest, that *Intelligere* and *Judicare* are actions belonging unto the Will also, and that this proposition [*Voluntas intelligit bonum aut malum*] is true and proper. Thus in regard of the actions *Volendi,* and *Intelligendi,* we have no reason to make a distinction of Faculties, where the actions are common, and indifferently agree to each of them. If one faculty can do both, what reason is therein to make two? And if the Philosopher [Aristotle] be in the right, denying a distinct faculty for the Memorie in the reasonable soul, because the Understanding sufficeth to that, forasmuch as *eiusdem est servare Habitus & iis uti,* we have the same reason to hold the Understanding and Will to be no distinct Faculties seeing, *eiusdem est intelligere & velle.*[1]

So Pemble is arguing that the understanding has a natural inclination to what is true, and this inclination is an instance of willing. And if the will is required to be an understanding will, what reason remains for positing here the operation of two distinct faculties, rather than only one combined operation? Pemble is also saying here that whatever view one has of free will—whether it be the liberty of indifference or the liberty of coaction—if that freedom involves making a choice, then this involves the combining together of the will and understanding.

The root of this is a Platonic thesis, that truth and goodness are identical, or at least that they are necessarily connected, and that this being so it is unnecessary to multiply faculties. Where the actions of understanding and will are "common," having the same object at the same time, there is no need to employ the conceptuality of the operation of two faculties. For a similar reason, memory is to be considered an aspect of the understanding, not as a separate faculty:

Thirdly, the Object of the Understanding and Will are one and the same. For Truth and Goodness are essentially the same thing. In natural things it is most plaine, that their Truth and Goodness is all one. Their goodness is nothing but the Truth of their being in their

---

1. Pemble, *Vindiciae,* 112.

perfect conformity to Gods Understanding and Will, when their Essence and Qualities are perfectly the same which they had by their creation. When the Creature is as it was made, then it is both true and Good; so farre as any part of truth is lost, so much of goodness is gone. And this appears by the contrary; *Malum* and *Falsum* in the creature, opposed to this natural goodness and truth of it, are both but one thing; namely any Defect or Excess in the parts or degree of their Essence and Qualities, otherwise than according to the Truth of their Creator. Such defects and excesses we call Errors, Untruths and Evils in nature. So that if we consider Truth and Goodness in the nature of things themselves, it is not possible to make any real distinction between them.[2]

So there is a two-way connection between the understanding and the will. Each needs the other. They have a common objective, bringing about what the agent regards as true/good.

Pemble applies all this to the act of assent, *assensus*, in saving faith. Assent cannot be merely an intellectual act:

For conclusion of this point touching the subject of Faith, we do not appropriate Faith either to the Understanding, or the Will, nor yet referre it to both, as unto two distinct faculties; but we place it immediately in the whole intellectual Nature; whether of mans soul, or of Angels. In which we follow the sentence of the Scriptures, that seat faith in the whole heart as Rom.10.10 [With the heart man believeth unto righteousness] and Acts 8.37 [If thou believest with all they heart]. Now it is [a] thing manifest, that in the Scripture the heart is taken for the whole soule with all its powers and operations.[3]

So Pemble's outlook is not strictly a case of the intertwining of the faculties, but of the union of their operations in cases where it is a matter of the heart, "the whole soule with all its powers and operations."[4]

We come now to distinct cases of intertwining.

---

2. Pemble, *Vindiciae*, 112.

3. Pemble, *Vindiciae*, 114.

4. Pemble, *Vindiciae*, 114.

John Owen on the Intertwining of the Faculties

As far as I know, the Puritan Owen never wrote about human nature in a textbookish way, but only rather incidentally, as the need to do so arose. In his writings on experiential divinity, Owen discusses the mind's renewal by the Holy Spirit in the following way. Owen is commenting on Paul's words "be renewed in the spirit of your mind" (Eph. 4:23). There is the faculty itself, which Owen takes Paul's words to be a reference to "the rational principle in us of apprehension, of thinking, discoursing and assenting." Further, Owen claims that the understanding is "the *directive, discerning, judging faculty* of the soul, that leads it unto practice. It guides the soul in the choice of the notions which it receives by the mind. And this is more corrupt than the mind itself; for the nearer things come to practice, the more prevalent in them is the power of sin."[5]

The understanding makes choices between the "notions" which it receives in the mind. Finally, Owen understands that besides all this there is "the heart," which is closely allied to the "heart" in the New Testament as the practical principle of operation and so includes the will.[6] Owen adheres more closely than is usual to the wording of Scripture. He takes the phrase "the spirit of the mind" to refer to the manner in which the mind works, taking the "mind" here as equivalent to the "heart."[7] He writes,

---

5. John Owen, *Discourse Concerning the Holy Spirit*, in *The Works of John Owen*, ed. W. H. Goold (Edinburgh: Banner of Truth, 1966), 3:252.

6. Owen, *Discourse Concerning the Holy Spirit*, in *Works*, 3:252.

7. Opinions of the meaning of the "heart" in the New Testament varied among the Puritans. John Arrowsmith (1602–1659) has this interesting passage:

> This word *Heart* is of various acceptions in the Scripture. Sometime it signifieth the understanding, as when it is said, *"God gave Solomon largeness of heart, as the sand,"* that is, He had an understanding full of notions, as the sea-shore is full of grains of sand. Sometimes put off the will, as when *Barnabas* exhorteth the Christians of *Antioch to cleave to the Lord with purpose of heart*, that is, with the full bent and inclination of their wills. For as to know is an act of the understanding, so to cleave is an act of the understanding. Sometimes for the memory, as when the blessed Virgin is said *to have laid up all our Saviours sayings in her heart*, that is, kept them under lock and key, like a choice treasure in her remembrance. Sometimes for conscience. So the Apostle speaketh of a *condemning and not condemning heart*, Now Gods deputy in point of judicature is conscience, which *Nazianzen* therefore calleth a domesticall tribunal, or a judge within doors. Lastly, Sometimes for the affections, So the Prophet *Ezekiel* saith of people, that when they sate hearing the word, *their heart went after their covetousness*, that is, their fears, and hopes, their desires, love and other affections were upon shops, ships, land and other commodities even

"It is the actual compliance of the will and affections with the mind and understanding, with respect unto the objects proposed by them. Light is *received* by the mind, *applied* by the understanding, used by the heart."[8]

The darkness (of the understanding) referred to by Paul is "not a mere ignorance or incomprehensiveness of the notions of truth that is intended, but a stubborn resistance of light and conviction," the work of the depraved will upon the mind. The darkened mind resists the light. So here the understanding and the will are intertwined prior to any executive role the will then plays.[9] Similarly, in his work *On the Dominion of Sin and Grace* (1688), in writing of the dominion of sin, Owen states that sin gives evidence of its dominion in the distinct faculties of the soul and in the course of the life.[10] So the mind, fancy, and imagination are each affected, as well as the affections themselves.

It is not being suggested that a preacher-theologian such as Flavel, with his tendency to characterize the faculties separately, would doubt or deny any of this. It could be said that Owen's approach is more Augustinian than Flavel's, in that the *voluntas*, understood here as the heart, plays a more fundamental role. The effects of the *voluntas* are distributed across the various roles of the understanding, and so it may be said to be more basic to the orientation of the understanding than when the understanding is considered in isolation. Separating these powers and identifying them is a purely intellectual matter discerned by the inquirer who wishes to think clearly about the make-up of the soul; but these powers do not in fact work in isolation. Owen's observations do greater justice to the unity if not to the simplicity of the soul than do some others.

So there is not a strict separation of the roles of the various faculties that, for example, Flavel and others emphasize in their descriptions and places of the faculties of the soul. Owen is more in the line of Pemble. When Owen characterizes the understanding, it is not simply as the recipient and manipulation of data, nor is it merely passive in receiving and

---

while they were busied in the worship of God. Each of these faculties called Heart in the book of God is liable to its peculiar disposition and distemper.

John Arrowsmith, *Armilla Catechetica or A Chain of Principles* (Cambridge: John Field, 1659), 438–40.

8. Owen, *Discourse Concerning the Holy Spirit*, in *Works*, 3:252.

9. Owen, *Discourse Concerning the Holy Spirit*, in *Works*, 3:252.

10. John Owen, *On the Dominion of Sin and Grace*, in *Works*, 7:519.

conveying that data. Rather, it is engaged in the activities of discerning and judging, activities themselves characteristic of the will or which involve the will. Owen says that in the heart the understanding, will, and affections are included, and there is an actual compliance of the will and affections with the mind and understanding. But more than this, the will is active in the working of the understanding itself.

So while Owen by no means denies the propriety of distinguishing the faculties, he stresses that there is a cooperation between them or an intertwining of them. For he wants to make clear, for example, that the darkness of the soul is not mere ignorance, but a resistance to the light, just as in regeneration the understanding is not only enlightened, a purely cognitive change, but it welcomes the light. A true understanding of the separate roles of the faculties in the various stages and elements of such faith is not denied. Nevertheless, such an understanding requires them to be set in a context involving a person's conviction of sin, sincerity in faith, and a positive estimation of the way of salvation by Jesus Christ.

While works of experiential divinity like Owen's stress the intertwining of the faculties, where the author attempts to delineate the character and motions of the soul, the same intertwining emphasis can also be found at the level of generalized doctrinal description.

Francis Turretin on the Opposing of the Faculties

In a discussion of free will, Turretin says:

> The subject of free will is neither the intellect, nor the will separately, but both faculties conjointly. As it belongs to the intellect with regard to the discussion of choice; so it belongs to the will with regard to freedom. Hence you may rightly call it a mixed faculty or a wedlock and meeting of both—the intellect as well as the will. Nevertheless you would not properly say it consists in each faculty; for as the decision of the intellect is terminated in the will, so the liberty of the will has its roots in the intellect. Hence the philosopher, leaving this undetermined, says that it is either the "appetitive intellect" or the "intelligent appetite."

Turretin goes on to say that this should not be thought unusual since the intellect and will are mutually and necessarily connected so that their actions are inseparable. He writes, "Nor does there seem to be a real and intrinsic distinction here, but only an extrinsic with regard to the objects (as one and the same faculty of the soul both judges by understanding and by willing embraces what it judged to be good and it is called 'intellect' when it is occupied in the knowledge and judgment of things but 'will' when it is carried to hatred or love of the same)."[11]

But what about Medea's "I see the right, and approve it too, and still the worse pursue"?[12] And Paul's "For what I would, that do I not; but what I hate, that do I"?[13] Of the sort of twofoldness that Paul invokes, Turretin distinguishes between a theoretical judgment, which the will can oppose, and the "decided and last judgment," which "it can never oppose."[14]

So faculty psychologists make legitimate distinctions in the soul and its operations; but when they are considering the soul in its fallenness or in its regeneration (in *phases* of the life of the soul, as we might say), they connect up these distinctions, bringing out the various conditions of the soul. This does not mean that the will may perform the operations of the understanding, or vice versa. One must always bear in mind that the distinctions between the faculties is not a real—that is, objective—distinction, as an arm is an objectively distinct part of the body from a leg. Rather, these are distinctions formed by observation of the various activities of the soul. The "real" object is the soul and its powers. When these powers are occupied with knowledge and judgment, we refer to them as "intellectual" and the product of the "intellect." And when the powers are of hating or loving these objects of knowledge, the powers are referred to as those of the will and the affections. This stance, that the structure of the soul is constructed out of the observation of its powers in operation, is fundamental to the use of faculty psychology in theology and in casuistry.

Turretin rounds off this discussion with some general observations about the soul, distinguishing it not in terms of the kind of faculty it possesses, but in terms of levels of goings-on in the soul. If we approach the soul at the level of the faculty, we speak of different faculties in an unqualified way and of different kinds of activity possessed by each faculty. If we approach it in terms of level, there are three levels. The understanding is

---

11. Turretin, *Institutes of Elenctic Theology*, 1:660.

12. Cited by Turretin, *Institutes of Elenctic Theology*, 1:664. This is an example of the "divided self" frequently cited by the Reformed orthodox.

13. For a discussion on the theme of weakness of will, see Risto Saarinen, *Weakness of Will in Renaissance and Reformation Thought* (Oxford: Oxford University Press, 2011).

14. Turretin, *Institutes of Elenctic Theology*, 1:664.

the rational *faculty* and is good or evil as seen by its *acts* and *habits*. The habits of the soul in its various faculties are not further faculties, but they are properties of the faculties of the soul. Habits have already been briefly discussed in chapter 4.

Perhaps Turretin's and Owen's approaches are reminders that despite the distinctions among faculties, the soul nevertheless remains simple, without divisions, the character of which is recognized by the range and variety of its powers and their effects.

The Developments in the Understanding of Faith

The discussions of justifying faith provide instructive instances of the ways in which the Reformed orthodox and Puritans discussed the anthropological side of things—both their differences and what unites them. We have already discussed Pemble's concern with the unwarranted separation of the understanding and will in connection with the nature of justifying faith. In the case of Turretin, we have the more rigid separation of the soul's powers that Pemble took exception to. Turretin writes,

> As to the acts [of justifiying faith], they are explained by theologians in different ways—some making more, others fewer. Some make only one, namely assent or persuasion. Others acknowledge only two—knowledge and assent. Others add a third (to wit, trust). Others a fourth also (to wit, confidence or the acquiescence of the will). These different opinions do not so much change the nature of faith as unfold it in different ways. And hence it is that some place faith equally in the intellect and the will; others only in the intellect formally and in the will only energetically or effectively and consequently (or even principally) in the will. And thus certain ones include all these acts formally in faith; others, however, suppose or infer some of them.
>
> III. The more common and truer opinion recognizes three acts in faith: knowledge, assent, trust (*notitiam, assensum, fiduciam*). Although all the others can be referred to these, still that we may understand the whole subject more easily, we must treat distinctly of them.[15]

That is, the nature of justifying faith is best explained by explicitly distinguishing its elements rather than by leaving such elements implicit. Knowledge is referred to the understanding, while assent and trust involve

---

15. Turretin, *Institutes of Elenctic Theology*, 2:560–61.

the will. Turretin's attitude here is a good example of a way of a topic, the act of justifying faith in this case, recognizing different emphases—some preferring a full account, others without denying these emphases preferring a more terse approach.

As the sixteenth century wore on, the view of faith in justification as essentially involving *fiducia*, understood as assured trust, lost ground. Earlier the *Consensus Helviticus* (1566) asserted in chapter 16, "Of Faith and Good Works: and of Their Reward, and of Man's Merit": "Christian faith is not an opinion or human conviction, but a most firm trust and a clear and steadfast assent of the mind…a most certain comprehension of the truth of God set forth in the Scriptures and in the Apostles' Creed; yes and of God himself, the chief blessedness, and of Christ, who is the consummation of all the promises."[16]

By the middle of the seventeenth century, the idea that assurance was not an essential feature of saving faith was openly recognized. Petrus van Mastricht asserted that "on the actual application of trust our theologians too hold diverse views. (1) The older men in accordance with our catechism make this act of faith essential, but not to be conceived of apart from a previous embracing of it and the repentance involved in that. (2) Several of the more recent men will rather have it that it is the result of faith itself and of justification which may be absent from faith and abiding salvation."[17]

Van Mastricht's view is that faith is an "act of a reasonable soul, which consists in receiving God as the supreme end and Christ as the sole Mediator. This requires in the reason (1) knowledge of the evangelical promises, and (2) explicit assent; consent in the will by which we receive…God and mediator; in the emotions, (1) love to God, and the mediator, (2) longing for them, (3) joy, (4) hatred and detestation of the things that are contrary to them."[18] That is, there is a reflex element to the assurance of faith, that a person by self-examination, involving various tests or marks of that person's faith, involving the soul's acts and the effects of faith on the virtues and emotions, gives grounds to that person to conclude that he indeed has this faith, and so is assured of it. The distinction of faith from the assurance of

---

16. *Reformed Confessions of the 16th and 17th Centuries in English Translation*, compiled and intro. James. T. Dennison Jr. (Grand Rapids: Reformation Heritage Books, 2010), 2:841.

17. Cited in Heppe, *Reformed Dogmatics*, 533.

18. Cited in Heppe, *Reformed Dogmatics*, 533.

faith is not meant to denote distinct temporal stages, for the reflex may be an instantaneous one, but only the various elements of faith.

In the middle of the seventeenth century, the Westminster Confession (1647) asserted that saving faith "is different on degrees, weak or strong, may be often and many ways assailed and weakened but gets the victory; growing up in many to the attainment of a full assurance through Christ, who is both the author and finisher of our faith" (14.3).

So the combination of three essential acts of saving faith—knowledge, assent, and assured trust—were reduced to knowledge, assent, and trust.[19]

John Owen on the Limitations of Scholastic Distinctions

Once again, Owen takes a rather different line. He affirms the character of the exercise of faith, but he does not altogether rely on that alone to give the sense of faith. Moreover, he is scathing of the attempt to distinguish true faith from false by making yet further distinctions in its activity. He writes, "When men are once advanced into that field of disputation, which is all overgrown with thorns of subtleties, perplexed notions, and futilous [futile] terms of art, they consider principally how they may entangle others in it, scarce at all how they might get out of it themselves."[20] Owen says that there are in circulation "twenty several opinions" among Protestants as to the definition of justifying faith:[21]

Owen's work on justification is one of his later works of experiential divinity (1677), and his concern in it (as regards the nature and place of faith) is not to be dissatisfied with this or that definition of faith, but rather to contextualize faith in terms of what other elements are in play in the life of a believer. So his approach is scholastic, but not simply scholastic. As he puts it, he is concerned not simply with *definitions* but with *descriptions* of the state of the soul and its relation to God:

> I know of no man that hath labored in this argument about the nature of faith more than Dr Jackson; yet, when he hath done all, he gives us a definition of justifying faith which I know few that will subscribe to: yet is it, in the main scope of it, both pious and sound. For he tells us

---

19. There is a nuanced and detailed discussion of these changes in Beeke, *Assurance of Faith*.

20. Owen, *Faith and Its Evidences*, in *Works*, 5:11.

21. Owen, *Faith and Its Evidences*, in *Works*, 5:11.

"Here, at length, we may define the faith by which the just do live, to be a firm and constant adherence unto the mercies and loving-kindness of the Lord; or, generally, unto the spiritual food exhibited in his sacred word, as much better than life itself, and all the contentments it is capable of; grounded on a taste or relish of their sweetness, wrought in the soul or heart of a man by the Spirit of Christ."[22]

Owen continues,

For the lively expressions of faith, by receiving of Christ, leaning on him, rolling ourselves or our burden on him, tasting how gracious the Lord is, and the like, which have been reproached, yea, blasphemed… convey a better understanding of the nature, work and object of justifying faith, unto the minds of men spiritually enlightened, than the most accurate definitions that many pretend thereto; some whereof are destructive and exclusive of them all.[23]

So, as he had written earlier:

Wherefore I cannot but judge it best (others may think of it as they please), for those who would teach or learn this doctrine of justification in a due manner, to place their consciences in the presence of God, and their persons before his tribunal, and then, upon a due consideration of his greatness, power, majesty, righteousness, holiness—of the terror of his glory and sovereign authority, to inquire what the Scripture and a sense of their own condition direct them unto as their relief and refuge, and what plea it becomes them to make for themselves.[24]

So for Owen the doctrine can only be appreciated in the context of conviction of sin before God. It is not primarily an argumentative matter, or one of conceptual tidiness. Owen says that he will come to that. But first he is "declaring the experience of faith in the expressions of the Scriptures, or such as are analogous to them."[25] And so granting that faith includes assent to the revelation of God, it is an act of the understanding

---

22. Owen, *Faith and Its Evidences*, in *Works*, 5:107. The reference is to Thomas Jackson (1579–1640), who was originally a Calvinist but later became an Arminian. His works were published in 1673.

23. Owen, *Faith and Its Evidences*, in *Works*, 5:107.

24. Owen, *Faith and Its Evidences*, in *Works*, 5:19–20.

25. Owen, *Faith and Its Evidences*, in *Works*, 5:41.

only, though assenting to a truth involves the judgment. "It is distinguished from opinion and moral certainty on the one hand, or science and demonstration on the other."

The distinctions of the schools take us only so far. More important is to recognize that faith "compriseth all the faculties of the soul as one entire principle of moral and spiritual duties."[26] "It is not what notions men may have hereof, nor how they express their conceptions, how defensible they are against objections by accuracy of expressions and subtile distinctions; but only what we ourselves do, if we truly believe."[27] Owen makes the point that, after all, assent is necessary for the belief of any proposition of Scripture, such as that Judas was a traitor. So justifying faith is *the heart's approbation of the way of justification and salvation of sinners by Jesus Christ proposed in the gospel and proceeding from the grace, wisdom and love of God, with its acquiescency therein as unto its own concernment and condition.*"[28] Less scholastic, perhaps, and more descriptive. It is not clear that Owen could not have achieved the same result by emphasizing the operation of characteristic emotions, such as sorrow for sin and penitence, and an approval of the way of salvation of Jesus Christ. But that was not his way of doing things.

So the tools of scholastic analysis will only take the Christian theologian so far, Owen thinks. To repeat the *cognitio-assensus-fiducia* formula of saving faith or one of its variants only provides raw conceptuality. Such an analysis is only at best a necessary precondition. Owen's position requires that due regard be had to the context in which the formula has a place, the epistemological framework, and also what we might refer to nowadays as its phenomenological character. If this context is appreciated, then the differences over justification that were touted in Owen's day will be seen to be of secondary importance and may even be a distraction from the proper treatment of faith.

---

26. Owen, *Faith and Its Evidences*, in *Works*, 5:81–82.

27. Owen, *Faith and Its Evidences*, in *Works*, 5:83.

28. Owen, *Faith and Its Evidences*, in *Works*, 5:93. This is followed by trust in Christ. Owen, *Faith and Its Evidences*, in *Works*, 5:101. For the distinction between definition and description, see Owen, *Faith and Its Evidences*, in *Works*, 5:106–7.

John Weemes on Willing and Understanding

We move from justification to inner conflicts in the saints. As we have seen, Weemes was a theologian who was overtly dependent on Aquinas for his scholastic outlook. In his *Portraiture of the Image of God in Man* (1632), he raises the question, What is the reason that the will does not always follow the last judgment of the understanding? He observes that often the will goes in a contrary way to that which the understanding has discerned. Weemes has in mind Paul's language of inner conflict in Romans 7.

Weemes claims that the understanding has a mutual dependence on the will and is set going by the will. By this he means, I think, that an act of the understanding is willed. The understanding is energized by the will. But the understanding is also affected by the affections, and they may influence it in a way that, strictly speaking, is not willed. He does not indicate where the source of the strength of the affections springs from.

The mind wills to deliberate a particular issue, and so the will and understanding are intertwined, the will then deliberating what is true or false:

> There is a reciprocall dependence then betwixt these two, the Will dependeth upon the deliberation of the *Minde*; both particularly setting downe the object [of the understanding]; and how it should exercise it selfe about the object, but the mind dependeth upon the will…. For when the mind hath given out her last determination concerning any particular object, the will must chuse that particular and not another, and neither refuse it nor suspend it; and it must chuse it in that measure of earnestness, as it is known to be good.[29]

So it seems the will must have powers of choice and discernment.

Weemes discusses other questions, including whether we first will or first understand a thing. He answers that we will a thing, in the sense of identify it, by an inbred desire and blind appetite, but that we cannot will a thing in respect of the means, until the understanding has identified it as a good to be sought. Weemes notes, "In all our actions there concurre foure things. First, the *Object* which is the thing wee apprehend. Secondly, the *apprehending power* of the *understanding*, judging this to bee good or evil. Thirdly, the *Will* which is mooved by the *understanding*. Fourthly,

---

29. Weemes, *Portraiture of the Image of God in Man*, 98–99.

the *members* mooved by the *Will*; here the *understanding* considering the object giveth light to the *Will*."[30]

So it would seem that Weemes attributes at least two roles to the will. There is its energizing of the understanding, in which the will is an aspect of an appetite, and then the more familiar scholastic sense in which the will is necessitated by the understanding.

Bernardinus de Moor on the Modes of the Intellect

Next we look in this chapter at an attempt to consider the unity and interdependence of the faculties of the soul more formally than we have done so far. We have seen Pemble's caution against reifying the powers of the soul and his insistence that the understanding and will are not distinct when the soul has regard to truth and goodness together. Bernardinus de Moor (1709–1780), who lived and worked during the last phase of Reformed orthodoxy, has a similar outlook. But his treatment is more formal than Pemble's. De Moor argued against the presence of Cartesian influences in Reformed theology, though his own work bore some signs of Descartes's positive influence. This discussion is concerned with his starting point in his treatment of faculty psychology.[31]

Earlier we considered Reynolds's view that the will is blind. De Moor discusses this point and objects to the description. It suggests to him that the will is not aware of or does not perceive whatever it wills. To call something blind is to suppose that it could have been sighted. But to call the will blind is to forget that both intellect and will are powers of one and the same mind, but insofar as we can use the language of the "sight" of the mind, this must be attributed to the intellect alone. It alone perceives: "But the spiritual sight of the mind belongs to the intellect—whose task it is to see spiritually, that is, to understand and perceive—not to the will. Also for this reason we are not correct, if we ascribe spiritual blindness to the will. But without absurdity it can be said about the will that it does not see, that is, perceive,

---

30. Weemes, *Portraiture of the Image of God in Man*, 100.

31. For references to faculty psychology at Leiden after the time of de Moor, see appendix A, "Herman Bavinck's Psychology."

as well as of the intellect that it does not will."[32] So the will cannot be blind because it is incoherent to suppose that it could ever be sighted.

This introduces the idea of "modes" of the intellect. The intellect and the will are each modes of the self or soul. It is not that the will is a mode of the intellect, but that both intellect and will are modes of the self, or perhaps of the "heart." De Moor stresses that intellect and will are not subjects or substances in their own right, but powers of a subject. This view is contrasted with a view of the faculties which treats them as parts of an organic whole, and these parts are "really" distinct, that is distinct *realiter*, and not simply distinct to the human mind. It may be that there is some influence here from the prevailing Cartesianism which de Moor worked against. De Moor espoused a duality of soul and body.[33] In hylomorphism, it is easier to think of the faculties as really distinct because there are sharply diverse effects flowing from them, vegetative and sensitive appetites as well as the rational appetites, for example. Whereas in Cartesianism, the body is self-perpetuating clockwork guided and affected by the soul and also guiding and affecting the soul, the *res cogitans*, but the body is not animated by the soul, which has no vegetative appetites.[34]

Understanding the soul as consisting in various modalities allows de Moor to raise another question about the relation between the faculties, the familiar question of whether or not the will is determined by the final judgment of the intellect. As we have seen, this is the routine way in which earlier Reformed orthodox theologians such as Turretin characterized the work of the practical intellect. Turretin says that the intellect *necessitates* the will.[35] But—and this is the heart of the distinctiveness of de Moor's view

---

32. The extracts from and references to de Moor's *A Continuous Commentary on à Marck's* Compendium of Christian Theology, Leiden, 1761–71, are taken from the extracts of de Moor in chapter 7 of van Asselt et al., *Reformed Thought on Freedom*, 204.

33. Cited in van Asselt et al., *Reformed Thought on Freedom*, 212n37.

34. In later work discussing the consequences of Descartes's dualism, Herman Bavinck remarked that in order to be able to distinguish the natural sciences from the humanities, Descartes put the essence of the body in largeness (*extensio, spatium*) and the essence of the soul in mind (*mens, cogitatio*). Consequently, the soul ceased to exist as the life principle; it came to stand dualistically over against the body, and the body became an object of the natural sciences, whose task it was to mechanically explain everything physical. Herman Bavinck, "The Unconscious," in *Essays on Religion, Science and Society*, trans. Harry Boonstra and Gerrit Sheeres, ed. John Bolt (Grand Rapids: Baker, 2008), 181.

35. Turretin, *Institutes of Elenctic Theology*, 1:663.

of the faculties—de Moor argues that this would have been a correct view if the understanding and will were genuine faculties, were really distinct from each other and from the mind, which on his view they are not, but only modalities of the mind. J. Martin Bac suggests[36] that this wider understanding of the intellect was prompted by the influence of Cartesianism, since for Descartes the intellect is passive in perception, whereas on the Reformed view of judgment, it involves the will. De Moor takes the view that errors are due to the prejudices of the will and not to ignorance and argues that judgment belongs to the will.[37] But, to take one example, Anthony Kenny understands Descartes more along the lines of what is the Reformed view. Or at least he claims that Descartes's views on perception and judgment were less straightforward.[38] So the influence may be less direct.

Thus, holding this modal view of the faculties, it is possible also to ask whether it is correct that the will is determined by the final judgment of the intellect. But this question in turn would have been more important if intellect and judgment had been faculties, really distinct from each other and from the mind, and not only modally so:

> Yet, it is one and the same rational mind which, when it judges something to be willed this determines itself to will that thing. The mind judges freely that this or that is to be sought, and because it judged thus, it freely determines itself to will that thing. But if the faculty of both intellect and will are here considered as mutually distinct, the will cannot be said to be *determined* by the intellect, but to *follow* the intellect, in such a way that the previous judgment of the intellect is followed by the inclination of the will.[39]

A further question is, what consequences does the modal view of the faculties have for the issue of the freedom of the will? The answer is that for

---

36. Cited in van Asselt et al., *Reformed Thought on Freedom*, 210.

37. Cited in van Asselt et al., *Reformed Thought on Freedom*, 214.

38. "There seem to be separate elements in Descartes' account: the pain, the perception of the pain, and the judgment about the pain. The perception of the pain seems to be something distinct from pain, for there are properties such as clarity and distinctness that belong to the perception, but not to the pain. The perception seems to be something distinct from the judgment; judgment is an act of the will that is in our power to make or withhold, and we are enjoined to restrict our judgment to what we clearly and distinctly perceive. But it is not at all easy to work out what Descartes considers to be the relationships between these three." Anthony Kenny, *Descartes, A Study of His Philosophy* (New York: Random House, 1968), 122–23.

39. Cited in van Asselt et al., *Reformed Thought on Freedom*, 204–5.

de Moor it strengthens the necessary connection between the goal of the intellect and the willing achievement of that goal. This becomes clear when he notes this consequence of his modal view, since "the faculties of intellect and will are not really separated from each other, nor from the mind itself, and the actions of both are connected to each other by a tight necessity, such that the mind is acting upon the same things in understanding, when it is occupied in cognition and judgment of these things; and in willing, when it is drawn to love or hate toward them."[40] So if anything, the modal view of the faculties ties the strings of necessity more tightly between intellect and will than does the nonmodal view.

In one place (*Epimetron,* a supplement to his *Commentary*), de Moor refers to Jonathan Edwards's *Freedom of the Will*,[41] which had been translated into Dutch in 1774. It appears to have been a comment on Edwards's distinction between natural and moral ability and inability. De Moor and Edwards (1703–1758) were born within a year or two of each other, but Edwards died twenty years before de Moor. In de Moor's *Supplementum* to his *Commentary*, a further supplement after *Epimetron,* he also cites some antischolastic remarks which tended in a unitary direction, as we have seen.[42] (Perhaps we could conclude from this circumstantial evidence that de Moor had sympathy with the views of his slightly older contemporary on the self and the will, seeing the human soul in a unitary way rather than possessing distinctly operating sets of powers, as in faculty psychology.)[43] We shall give further attention to this in chapter 8.

Treating the faculties as modalities of the self or mind may also suggest a symmetry in the behavior of one modality and the behavior of the other. But de Moor makes it clear that this is not a consequence of his view: "If you inquire nevertheless, which of these faculties is said to be the first *in order,* it has to be answered that these two faculties are indeed *temporally* simultaneous, because they do not really differ; they are also naturally

---

40. Cited in van Asselt et al., *Reformed Thought on Freedom,* 205.

41. Cited in van Asselt et al., *Reformed Thought on Freedom,* 209. Edwards is referred to in *Epimetron.*

42. The translation of Edwards on the will in Dutch was published as *Een Bepaald en Nauwkeurig Onderzoek van de Thans Heerschende Denkbeelden over de Vryheid van den Wil* (Utrecht: Gisbert Timon van Paddenburg, 1774).

43. The Lockean view. See van Asselt et al., *Reformed Thought on Freedom,* 205n20. This is also cited in Franciscus Buddeus, *Institutiones Theologiae Moralis* (Lipsiae: Thomae Fritsch, 1727), 94–95.

simultaneous, because they are the soul itself which has the power to extend itself in these two ways: in *structural* order, however, the intellect is first, if you consider the actions to those faculties, because the intellect is the guide of the will."[44] One can see how finely drawn the distinction between them is intended to be, yet if the intellect is "guide" of the will, guiding is itself an act of the will. In a parallel way, the modality of the will must understand what is going on in the modality of the intellect. It seems increasingly difficult to retain the distinctness of the faculties in what is a unitary view of the self.

It must not be thought that faculty theology led to psychological naiveté, to "one-dimensionality." It is in their detection of the capacity of the soul to deceive itself that the Reformed are at their most skillful as physicians of the soul. Despite their concern to think clearly about the structure of the self, this structure can be disordered, for sin has the capacity to disorder the self. The faculties do not metaphysically necessarily retain an order, nor are their workings transparent. Their pastoral writings reveal their ability to detect these weaknesses.

John Owen on Self-Deceit

A good instance of this is to be found in Owen's several writings on temptation and indwelling sin. The Puritans produced a number of books on sin,[45] considering it both dogmatically and pastorally. I have chosen Owen to discuss the effects of sin on the faculties. Although this book on anthropology is purposely not dealing with soteriology, yet (as we have been seeing) there are places where a treatment of the soul soteriologically is anthropologically illuminating, as is the case in regeneration. Owen's treatment of the deceitfulness of sin is another case, and it is worth highlighting his writing on this theme as he deals explicitly with the faculties and with sin's power to disorder them.

---

44. This is from his *Commentary* XIII.13, 1042. See van Asselt et al., *Reformed Thought on Freedom*, 216n55.

45. For example, Anthony Burgess, *The Doctrine of Original Sin Asserted & Vindicated against the Old and New Adversaries Thereof* (London, 1658); Ralph Venning, *Sin, the Plague of Plagues* (London: John Hancock, 1669); and Thomas Goodwin, *An Unregenerate Man's Guiltiness before God in respect of Sin and Punishment* (London, 1692).

We have seen earlier that the biblical "heart" can connote various different aspects of the soul. In his writings on this theme, Owen takes the term to refer to the whole soul.

In his work on indwelling sin, *The Nature, Power, Deceit and Prevalency of the Remainders of Indwelling Sin in Believers* (1668),[46] Owen maintains that sin indwells the soul as such and not in a particular faculty exclusively. Sin indwells the heart, the soul. He takes his cue from Matthew 15:19, "For out of the heart proceed evil thoughts, murders, adulteries, fornications, thefts, false witness, blasphemies." Owen emphasizes that the manifestation of sin is outward from its residence in the inner self. So the heart is not a featureless *substratum*, but comprises the understanding, will, and the affections, memory, and conscience, taken together.

According to Owen, in fallen people sin is seated in the heart in this comprehensive sense, that the sinner has a hearty attachment to the goals of sin, as well as a resolve to follow the means to sin. So the heart "is the entire principle of moral operations, of doing good or evil."[47]

In fallen man the heart is unsearchable and deceitful. This introduces another dimension, or dimensions, of the soul, to which we have not so far paid much attention. Reformed scholasticism does not of course have a theory of the unconscious in the modern sense, the sources of irrational weaknesses, bizarre behavior, and so forth, which a modern professional analyst may counsel his patient over and attempt to uncover and so help to free him or her from the effects of the unconscious goings-on. Nonetheless, the Reformed have an understanding of the depths or layers of the human personality. So Owen, who, as we have noted, is something of a master of experiential divinity, stresses that a person is not fully known to himself nor to others. God alone is the "searcher of hearts":

> Hath any one the perfect measure of his own light and darkness? Can any one know what actings of choosing or aversation his will will bring forth, upon the proposal of that endless variety of objects that it is to be exercised with? Can anyone traverse the various mutability

---

46. Besides *Indwelling Sin*, Owen wrote *Of the Mortification of Sin in Believers* (1656), and *Of Temptation, The Nature and Power of It* (1658). All are together in volume 6 of Goold's edition.

47. John Owen, *The Nature, Power, Deceit and Prevalency of the Remainders of Indwelling Sin in Believers*, in *The Works of John Owen*, ed. W. H. Goold (Edinburgh: Banner of Truth, 1966), 6:171.

of his affections? Do the secret springs of acting and refusing in the soul lie before the eyes of any man? Doth any one know what will be the motions of the mind or will in such and such conjunctions of things, such a suiting of object? Such a pretension of reasonings, such an appearance of things desirable? All in heaven and earth, but the infinite, all-seeing God, are utterly ignorant of these things.[48]

In addition, the sinful heart is deceitful. Nothing is so deceitful as it is. Owen notes, "There is great deceit in the dealings of men in the world; great deceit in their courses and contrivancies in reference to their affairs, private and public; great deceit in their words and actings: the world is full of deceit and fraud. But all this is nothing to the deceit that is in man's own heart toward himself."[49]

Owen stresses the deceit of others, but especially self-deception. The heart's deceitfulness is seen in the contradictoriness of the human character: "In general, in respect of moral good and evil, duty or sin, it is so with the heart of every man,—flaming hot, and key cold; weak, and yet stubborn; obstinate, and facile. The frame of the heart is ready to contradict itself every moment…. None know what to expect from it. The rise of this is the disorder that is brought upon all its faculties by sin."[50] And so Owen proceeds to outline these disorders.

The mind was at first subject to God, and all was orderly and harmonious. But once the mind is disturbed by sin, it and the other faculties are at odds with each other.

> The will chooseth not the good which the mind discovers; the affections delight not in that which the will chooseth; but all jar and interfere, cross and rebel against each other. This we have got by our falling from God. Hence sometimes the will leads, the judgment follows. Yea, commonly the affections, that should attend upon all [i.e., be subordinate to the understanding] get the sovereignty, and draw the whole soul captive after them…. Sometimes the mind retains its sovereignty, and the affections are in subjection, and the will ready for its duty. This puts a good face upon things. Immediately the rebellion of the affections or the obstinacy of the will takes place and prevails,

---

48. John Owen, *Indwelling Sin*, in *The Works of John Owen*, ed. W. H. Goold (Edinburgh: Banner of Truth, 1966), 6:171–72.

49. Owen, *Indwelling Sin*, in *Works*, 6:172.

50. Owen, *Indwelling Sin*, in *Works*, 6:173.

> and the whole scene is changed. This, I say, makes the heart deceitful above all things. It agrees not at all in itself, is not constant to itself, hath no order that it is constant unto, is under no certain conduct that is stable; but, if I may so say, hath a rotation in itself, where oftimes the feet lead and guide the whole.[51]

This sort of interplay between disorderly faculties may be thought to be the effect of the unconscious upon the conscious, and vice versa. Or maybe it is the familiar phenomenon of weakness of will. Owen does not say. Instead, he writes in general terms.

Here it seems that due to the disordering, the metaphysical principles of the mind are shown to be difficult to apply. The self behaves irrationally. Such an account is to be contrasted, for example, with Turretin's more principled understanding of the primacy of the intellect over the will, which we noted earlier, and the will's necessarily choosing only what the understanding judges good. For Owen, the original relationship of the understanding, will, and affections has to be understood in terms of orderliness rather than of metaphysical necessity. The fall itself was disorderly, and further instances of disorderliness occurred after the fall. So the orderliness was not essential to the soul as such; and as the fall was "adventitious," as we have noted, so presumably are its consequences. Moreover, the soul could not reorder itself. It is not like someone who may with difficulty get up after slipping on the ice. Rather, it is more like slipping further as one unsuccessfully strives to regain one's feet. This ratchet-like action of the fall on the soul was both the effect of disorder and the cause of further disorderliness.

This untidiness is not easy for textbook treatments of faculty psychology to handle. In Turretin, for example, we find a stress in the fall on its strength and disabling character. Turretin gives full place to the metaphors of deadness and hardness, and of the inextricableness of the plight of the fall, against Jesuit and Arminian semi-Pelagianism.[52] The faculties are uniformly weakened. And therefore there is need of an effectual call from God, who gives light to the blind and life to the dead.

Owen's dominant notes are rather different and more complex. They stress the waywardness and willfulness, disorderliness and sheer irrationality of the faculties. But this is not a topic or a common anthropological

---

51. Owen, *Indwelling Sin,* in *Works,* 6:173.
52. Turretin, *Institutes of Elenctic Theology,* 1:673.

theme in its own right, as far as I can see. With Owen, the fall produced chaos, and there is in addition the operation of self-deception and the influence of the subconscious, of what currently would be called the onset of moods and the persistence of drives, yet with a readiness to give way to contrary moods and drives. Following the work of Perkins and Ames on conscience and the practical reason (discussed in chapter 5), many Puritans developed an experiential emphasis. They pursued the practice of self-examination using the examples of Scripture for the reality of spiritual life in the soul: assurance, motivation, obedience, and so on. Owen, along with many other Puritans, endorsed this emphasis in many of his later works. It is compounded by Owen's suspicion that pursuing scholastic theology had itself become a display in personal cleverness, as we saw earlier in the chapter, in Owen's remarks on the character of justifying faith.

CHAPTER 7

Faculty Psychology and Reformed Polemics

For the student of Reformed anthropology, certain theological debates are enlightening and reveal how anthropology works as a theological resource. When we enter the seventeenth century, the context is shifting. Not only is Reformed thought in both anthropology and theology being elaborated in its own right, but the Reformed positions required elaboration and rebuttal against Counter-Reformation and Remonstrant positions, and later against Socinianism.

So Theophilus Gale says,

> Neither do I as yet see any reason to repent thereof; for I have found those Controversies about Divine Concourse and Efficacious Grace, no where more accurately examined and demonstratively determined, than among the Scholemen, specially Bradwardine and Alvarez, neither can I conceive how any one can distinctly and perfectly dis- cusse these Controversies, specially as now miserably perplexed with ambiguous obscure termes, without some inspection into and knowl- ege of Scholastic Theologie.[1]

Scholastic philosophy provided theology with a set of tools that promoted exactness in theological debate; these tools were essential in controversy if only because one's controversial opponents were also versed in such philosophy.

In this chapter, we will look at theological disputes which have an anthropological aspect. We will first consider a perennial issue—free will— that figured in debates with Remonstrants and Jesuits, and then turn to

---

1. Gale, preface to *Court of the Gentiles*, pt. IV, bk. III. Thomas Bradwardine (1290–1349) was archbishop of Canterbury and the author of *Causa Dei Contra Pelagium*. Diego Alvarez, a Spanish Dominican, died in 1635.

intra-Reformed debates between those who are the same or similar in theological outlook but who have or may have theological differences that are anthropological in character. We will look at the intrusion into the Reformed world of a non-Reformed figure, the renowned philosopher René Descartes. This is of interest because his presence in Holland and the impact of some of his disciples exerted a positive influence on some Reformed theologians in Holland. And one of these was Francis Burman. When Burman was a student, he had an interview with Descartes, who was in the closing years of his life, and the results were published as *Descartes' Conversation with Burman.*[2]

Francis Turretin on Indifference

As we have seen, the topic of free will in Reformed anthropology became quite complex, having to do with mankind in its fourfold state as well as theological matters such as the divine decree. Here we will confine discussion to a central anthropological theme, the nature of the human will itself, and in particular its indifference. Here, metaphysical differences about the nature of the will occur between Augustinians and the semi-Pelagianism of the Jesuits and, as we shall later see, the Arminians.

According to the Reformed orthodox position, the will could not be coerced. Coercion, psychological or physical force, disables the will. Not even God can coerce the will. The will also chooses what the mind regards as the good. And more importantly for this discussion, the will exercises choice between alternatives. Indeed, the Reformed held to its essential indifference. However, upon the will's choice having been made, its indifference is "spent" on this occasion so that the will is "not always so indifferent and unaltered that it can act or not act."[3] The crucial point is that in choice the will is "tied" to the intellect. It becomes indifferent until confronted with the next choice. For the opponents of the Reformed orthodox, the will is always indifferently free and so could have acted alternatively had the intellect been different.

To understand this debate, we need to be clear on the scholastic distinction between the compound sense of "indifference" and the divided

---

2. *Descartes' Conversation with Burman*, trans. John Cottingham (Oxford: Clarendon Press, 1976).

3. Spent or "removed" (as Voetius expresses it).

sense of the power to do A or B, or A and not-A. Suppose we ask, "Is John in a state of indifference with respect to some matter?" The question can be understood in two ways. We can ask this of his will *considered in itself* (the divided sense), or we can ask it of his will *acting in certain circumstances* (the compound sense). This distinction is crucial for understanding Turretin's position and others of the Reformed orthodox.[4] Their opponents held that the will retains indifference in the compound sense, which the Reformed orthodox denied.

The Reformed orthodox were faced with the Jesuit claim that human beings possess "a free potency by which all things requisite for acting being posited, someone can act or not act."[5] This is indifference in the compound sense, a potency of choice persisting even in the circumstances in which "all the requisites to acting [are] posited."[6] This the Reformed orthodox denied. In this sense, indifference cannot be of the essence of freedom; hence, they denied that given all the requisites for choosing A, at one and the same moment t_1 John can choose either A or not-A.

The Reformed orthodox deny indifference in this compound sense but affirm it in the divided sense, in a sense according to which the will is indifferent prior to a completed choice. The divided sense may be expressed as the following: John has a will which in itself can choose A or not-A. For illustration of the distinction, let us imagine a nonhuman example, one not involving the will. We might ask, Can the weather vane *as such* point to all points of the compass? Or we might ask, in this strong southerly wind, can the weather vane point to all points of the compass? To the first question, the divided sense, the answer is yes, while to the second question, the compound sense, the answer is no.

Turning to a case involving a human being, suppose we ask, Can John speak? That is, is he, *as a person*, able to speak? Or we might be asking, *in a state where John is bound and gagged*, can he speak? To the first question,

---

4. On the evidence provided by the texts examined in van Asselt et al., *Reformed Thought on Freedom*, the position of Turretin was also held by Voetius and others.

5. Taken from Voetius in van Asselt et al., *Reformed Thought on Freedom*, 148. The sentence has its source in Jesuit writings.

6. Turretin, *Institutes of Elenctic Theology*, 1:666.

where the question is taken in the divided sense, the answer is yes, while to the second question, the compound sense, the answer is obviously no.[7]

So according to the Jesuits, a person possesses a free potency or power if, as Voetius puts it, "all things requisite for acting being posited someone can act or not act."[8] Or, as Turretin expressed it, the Jesuits believed that the essence of free will is indifference, defined as "the faculty by which all requisites for acting being posited, the will can act or not act."[9] This language follows word for word the well-known definition of the Jesuit Molina according to which the will of a person "with all the prerequisites for acting posited, is able to act and able not to act, or is able to do one thing in such a way that it is able to do some contrary thing."[10] That is, the will possesses the freedom of contradiction and the freedom of contrariety so that power is retained *even when the decision on an occasion has been taken.*

For the Jesuits, being in possession of the power of indifference, one is able to will in accordance with the requisites, and at the very same time, retaining the power to have done the opposite, one could have willed a contrary end. The Reformed orthodox rejected indifference in that sense—that is, indifference in the compound sense—and held that placing the essential structure or formal reason (*ratio formalis*) of the free choice in such indifference is an error.[11]

This is how Turretin makes the discrimination:

> III We contend here again the Jesuits, Socinians and Remonstrants, who (following Pelagius) place the essence of free will in indifference (*adiaphora*) and are wont to define it as "the faculty by which all things being requisite for acting being posited, the will can act or not act." Now those are called requisites to action without which the action cannot be performed (such as the decree of God and his

---

7. Incidentally, such examples show that it is inaccurate for the contributors to *Reformed Thought on Freedom* to assert that the distinction between the divided and the compound sense of itself presupposes a contingency of simultaneous logical alternatives. See van Asselt et al., *Reformed Thought on Freedom*, 47. See also Muller, *Divine Will and Human Choice*, pt. 3.

8. Quotations from Voetius are taken from van Asselt et al., *Reformed Thought on Freedom*, 148.

9. Turretin, *Institutes of Elenctic Theology*, 1:665.

10. Quoted by Alfred J. Freddoso in the introduction to *On Divine Foreknowledge* (Ithaca: Cornell University Press, 1988), 24–25, which is his translation of part IV of Luis Molina's *Concordia*.

11. Turretin, *Institutes of Elenctic Theology*, 1:667.

concourse; the judgment of the mind; and other circumstances which belong here).

IV Hence it is evident that it is not inquired here concerning indifference in the first act or the divided sense, as to simultaneity of power which is called passive and objective (to wit, whether the will considered from its natural constitutions, the requisites to action being withdrawn, is determinable to various objects and holds itself indifferent toward them). We do not deny that the will of itself is so prepared that it can either elicit or suspend the act (which is the liberty of exercise and of contradiction) or be carried to both of opposite things (which is the liberty of contrariety and of specification). We also confess that the will is indifferent as long as the intellect remains doubtful and uncertain whither to turn itself. But as concerning indifference in the second act and in a compound sense (as to simultaneity of power called active and subjective)—whether the will (all requisites to acting being posited, for example, the decree of God and his concourse; the judgment of the practical intellect, etc.) is always so indifferent and undetermined that it can act or not act. This our opponents pretend in order that its own liberty may be left to the will. We deny it.[12]

This is about as difficult as it gets in Reformed orthodoxy. To help, let us consider some examples. Suppose you are offered to choose an orange and an apple. You choose the orange. On another occasion, you are offered a banana but decline it. The first example is what Turretin refers to as a case of the liberty of contrariety, and the second case, the liberty of contradiction. Both are exercises of the liberty of indifference, as is the case where you cannot make up your mind which to choose. But he objects to the idea that the will is always indifferent in the compound sense—that is, having chosen the orange it is true that the will acting could have chosen the apple, indifferently and undeterminedly, by an act of unconditional choice. This is the Jesuit and Remonstrant idea of freedom, which the Reformed reject.

Voetius's expression "free necessity"[13] is not a deliberately paradoxical term. It is simply his way of pointing to the fixity of the choice once the ultimate practical judgment of the intellect has been made. The faculty of choice chooses "out of itself" according to its "natural mode of acting."

---

12. Turretin, *Institutes of Elenctic Theology*, 1:665–66.
13. Cited in van Asselt et al., *Reformed Thought on Freedom*, 149.

So even God must "respect" the natures of His creatures.[14] "It is in vain if it is claimed here that our will could be forced, since 'being forced' and 'will' are contradictories."[15] It is a free choice (an uncoerced choice between alternatives, not a case of natural necessity, and so on), which has an irrevocably determined outcome. This is because indifference at this point is "removed" or spent for that occasion by the choice, while the will retains its indifference in the divided sense, to be exercised in making the next choice to occur.

In the discussions of indifference, one aim of the Reformed orthodox is to put clear blue water between their use of the term and that of the Jesuits. The word "indifference" may be the same for the Jesuit and Reformed, but the conceptuality is quite different. On the Reformed view, in human choice there is the reality of choosing between alternatives, but it is a different kind from the synchronic contingency proposed by the Jesuits. On this matter the two parties are not members of the same family, each with synchronic contingency running through their veins. The Reformed were out to show that the Jesuit sense of indifference is a mere figment of the mind.[16]

Consistently with this, when Turretin turns to the issue of human accountability or responsibility, he again stresses that human choice, that for which a person is accountable, is not the result of blind impulse or other coercive factors.[17] The action of the will is said to be free, spontaneous, and without compulsion. He cites Aristotle,[18] as Calvin had done before him.[19] Such actions cannot be performed by natural brutes.[20] A free human action is a "mode of acting of the free potency that fits its nature." "Given these indifferences, no external agent, not even God, can overturn

---

14. Something very similar to this can be found in John Calvin. See Helm, *John Calvin's Ideas*, 122; and Paul Helm, *Calvin at the Centre* (Oxford: Oxford University Press, 2010), 227–32.

15. Cited in van Asselt et al., *Reformed Thought on Freedom*, 151.

16. "Synchronic contingency" is said to be a development of Duns Scotus, who certainly uses it. See, for example, Richard Cross, *Duns Scotus on God* (Aldershot: Ashgate, 2005), 57. But the idea may be earlier, in the work of Jean Olivi. See for example, Robert Pasnau, "Olivi on Human Freedom," in *Pierre De Jean Olivi (1248–1298)*, ed. Alain Boureau and Sylvain Piron (Paris: Librairie Philosophique, J.Vrin, 1999).

17. Turretin, *Institutes of Elenctic Theology*, 1:667.

18. Turretin, *Institutes of Elenctic Theology*, 1:667.

19. See, for example, Calvin's brief excursus "Coercion versus Necessity," in *The Bondage and Liberation of the Will (1543)*, ed. A. N. S. Lane, trans. G. I. Davies (Grand Rapids: Baker, 1996), 146–50. Cf. Turretin, *Institutes of Elenctic Theology*, 1:2.7.

20. Turretin, *Institutes of Elenctic Theology*, 1:667.

freedom in its natural mode of acting. Thus the ownership of the will's own acts is permanently left to it."[21]

There are further features having to do with freedom and responsibility. For example, regarding eligibility for punishment, Turretin states that "a place may be granted for reward and punishment, it is not necessary that there should be indifference in the will to either of two opposites. It suffices that there be a spontaneity and willingness depending upon a judgment of the reason (such as there is in all men)."[22] So freedom for Turretin is what he calls "rational spontaneity." The understanding prompts the will to choose to act uncoercedly in pursuit of the understanding's goal.

Benedict Pictet on Rational Spontaneity

Benedict Pictet (1655–1724), who followed Turretin as professor of theology at Geneva, straightforwardly denied that freedom consisted in indifference:

> In order that any *agent* may be said to be free, it is enough that he act *voluntarily*, and with *judgment*, which evidently appears in the case of God himself who is a very free and independent Being, and yet is necessarily determined to what is good: and the same in the case with the angels and glorified spirits. *Liberty* therefore does not consist in *indifference*, for otherwise God himself would not be free, and the more man was determined to good, i.e. the more perfect he became, the less free would he be, which is absurd.[23]

So freedom is a matter of what Turretin (along with others) referred to as "rational spontaneity." The context in which Pictet makes these statements is the condition of Adam before the fall, a state of mutability. This state is not to be confused with one of indifference, "as though his will were equally balanced between an inclination to good, and an inclination to evil. For such an indifference would have been sin."[24] And Pictet goes on to suggest that Adam's mutability "was a kind of appendage to Adam's liberty, which so peculiarly belonged to *him* that it has never again been found in any man."[25] There is a matter-of-factness to Pictet's account of the first fall

---

21. Cited in van Asselt et al., *Reformed Thought on Freedom*, 149.
22. Turretin, *Institutes of Elenctic Theology*, 1:668.
23. Pictet, *Christian Theology*, 138.
24. Pictet, *Christian Theology*, 138.
25. Pictet, *Christian Theology*, 139.

into sin, something that others regarded as something problematic, how it came about that a human being created upright and pronounced "very good" could succumb to sin.

John Owen on the Will

Owen's first book, *A Display of Arminianism* (1642), written when he was twenty-six, was perhaps devised to make public his decidedly Reformed convictions. He set out his views on the will in chapter 12, "Of free-will, the nature and power thereof." Though the rather florid style is quite a contrast to Turretin's measured scholasticism, the outlook is very similar. Owen indicates in the footnotes a firsthand knowledge of Arminius and other Arminian theologians such as J. A. Corvinus (d. 1650), a signatory to the Remonstrance. Owen tells his reader that he does not quibble about the phrase "free will,"[26] even though two very different understandings of free will are at the heart of deep theological differences. He writes, "We grant man, in the substance of all his actions, as much power, liberty, and freedom as a mere created nature is capable of. We grant him to be free in his choice from all outward coaction, or inward natural necessity, to work according to election and deliberation, spontaneously embracing what seemeth good unto him. Now, call this power free will, or what you please, so you make it not supreme; independent, and boundless, and we are not at all troubled."[27]

He quotes from Arminius's Articles: "Herein consisteth the liberty of the will, that all things being required to enable it to will any thing being accomplished, it still remains indifferent to will or not."[28] This formulation has a history, as we saw when discussing Turretin. The phrase "the faculty by which all things requisite for acting being posited the will can act or not act" is almost identical to that used by Molina: "But freedom can be understood in another way, insofar as it is opposed to *necessity*. In this sense that agent is called free which, with all the requisites for acting posited, is able to act and able not to act, or is able to do one thing in such a way that it

---

26. John Owen, *A Display of Arminianism*, in *The Works of John Owen*, ed. W. H. Goold (Edinburgh: Banner of Truth, 1966), 10:116.

27. Owen, *Display of Arminianism*, in *Works*, 10:116.

28. Jacobus Arminius, *Opera theologica* (Leiden, 1629), 948–66.

is also able to do some contrary thing."[29] And as we have seen, Turretin presents a Reformed version of this, in which the requisites include the divine decree.

As Owen puts it, this is the assertion of the power of indifference *in actu secundo*—not the power of indifference considered in itself, *in actu primo*, but that power which has already made a choice. It is in that situation, Arminius claims, according to Owen, that the will retains the power of alternativity for a choice that is contradictory or contrary to the one it has already made in exactly the same circumstances. Owen denied this.

Owen applies this to the matter of Christian conversion. He quotes the Arminians further, "All unregenerate men have, by virtue of their free-will, a power of resisting the Holy Spirit, of rejecting the offered grace of God, of contemning the counsel of God concerning themselves, of refusing the gospel of grace, of not opening the heart to him that knocketh."[30] Here we get a glimpse of the knock-on effects for soteriology of this debate, which itself may seem abstruse and overtechnical—effects relating particularly to the effectual call.

Owen judged that such a view undermined God's effectual calling as maintained by Augustine, making that call always resistible. "What a stout idol is this, whom neither the Holy Spirit, the grace and counsel of God, the calling of the gospel, the knocking at the door of the heart, can move at all, or in the least measure prevail against him!"[31]

In Owen's estimate, what this view of the will of man comes down to, in the broadest theological terms, is one that is absolutely (that is, unqualifiedly) indifferent in doing what we will, indifference *in actu secundo*—that is, in the compound sense. Arminianism has a fundamental disregard for our creaturely dependence on God:

---

29. Quoted in Freddoso, introduction to *On Divine Foreknowledge*, 24–25.

30. Quoted by Owen, *Display of Arminianism*, in *Works*, 10:117. Owen refers to Molinism only once, to dismiss it: "Of that late figment of *middle science* in God, arising neither from *infinite perfection* of his own being, as that of simple intelligence, nor yet attending his *free purpose* and decree, as that of vision, but from a consideration of the second causes that are to produce the things foreknown, in their kind, order, and dependence, I am not now to treat." *Vindiciae Evangelicae; or, The Mystery of The Gospel Vindicated and Socinianism Examined*, in *The Works of John Owen*, ed. W. H. Goold (Edinburgh: Banner of Truth, 1966), 12:128.

31. Owen, *Display of Arminianism*, in *Works*, 10:117.

> Most free it is in all its acts, both in regard of the object it chooseth and in regard of that vital power and faculty whereby it worketh, infallibly complying with God's providence, and working by the motion thereof; but surely to assert such a supreme independency and every way unbounded indifference as the Arminians claim, whereby, all other things requisite being pre-supposed, it should remain absolutely in our own power to will or not to will, to do anything or not to do it, is plainly to deny that our wills are subject to the rule of the Most High.[32]

This seems to be a clear endorsement of freedom as rational spontaneity and a rejection of indifference *in actu secundo*, what Owen calls "unbounded indifferency" or "plenary indifference."

Owen then proceeds to the allied topic of the bondage of the will to sin,[33] coming to themes which he develops at large throughout his life in productions such as those on the Holy Spirit, the mortification of sin, and perseverance. Over a decade after *A Display of Arminianism*, in his work on Socinianisn, *Vindiciae Evangelicae* (mentioned above), Owen discusses indifference and freedom in connection with the Socinian views which limited God's foreknowledge. He refers to the sense of free will which he views critically in similar terms to what he had referred to as Arminian liberty, as "that latitude and absoluteness as none before him had once aimed at."[34] By now, he seems to have developed the habit to use the term "absolute" to qualify the strong sense of free will as the Arminians and now the Socinians used. It has "that latitude and absoluteness."[35]

But Owen also uses "indifference" in what he takes to be the orthodox view, as here: "It is true, in respect of their immediate causes, as the wills of men, they are contingent, and may be or not; but that they have such a cause as before spoken of is evident from the light of this consideration: in their own time and order they are."[36] What Owen means, I take it, is that if the choice is for A then the will can carry it out, and if it is for B, then also. Until such a choice is made irrevocably a person does not know which way he will go. He has freedom of indifference in the sense that if he has

---

32. Owen, *Display of Arminianism*, in *Works*, 10:119.

33. Owen, *Display of Arminianism*, in *Works*, 10:120–21.

34. Owen, *Vindiciae Evangelicae*, in *Works*, 12:116.

35. Owen, *Vindiciae Evangelicae*, in *Works*, 12:116.

36. Owen, *Vindiciae Evangelicae*, in *Works*, 12:129.

a sufficient reason for A, then A will occur, or if he has such a reason for B, then B will occur. Such indifference is not absolute, unconditioned, but contingent on the reason for which the action is chosen:

> That which is so contingent as to be also *free*, is contingent both in respect of the *effect* and of its *causes* also. Such was the soldier's piercing of the side of Christ. The effect was contingent—such a thing might have been done or not; and the cause also, for they chose to do it who did it, and in respect of their own elective faculty might not have chosen to. That a man shall write, or ride, or speak to another person tomorrow, the agent being free, is contingent both as to the cause and the effect.[37]

A man might read or write, and which he does is up to him, up to his desires or purposes. He chooses, exercising his "elective faculty" to read instead of to write, or the reverse, for a prevailing reason. The man can read or write—he is not under constraint to one or the other, and which he chooses he has a preponderating reason for.[38]

So for Owen, as for Turretin, there are two kinds of indifference and, correspondingly, two kinds of contingency. There is the absolute indifference of the Arminians, expressed in various of their articles. Owen's chief concern here is with the compatibility of this with the divine decree, with the Creator-creature relation insofar as this involves divine concurrence with them—what Turretin refers to as indifference *in sensu composito*. Owen accepts a weaker use of indifference (understood *in sensu diviso*). He rarely uses these terms, however, preferring to use more paraphrastic language conveying rational spontaneity. As far as contingency is concerned, Turretin also disallows the stronger, unconditional sense found in Arminian and Jesuit formulations, but sees contingency in the normal procedure of deliberating and deciding what to do. However, it seems that Turretin is less concerned with the workings of the human intellect and will and more concerned with their bearing on divine action on and in the creation. He is rather unconcerned here with the charge that his view makes God the author of sin, a matter that very much concerned Theophilus Gale, whose views we will shortly discuss.

---

37. Owen, *Vindiciae Evangelicae*, in *Works*, 12:128–29.

38. This reading of contingency is somewhat different from that of Muller, *Divine Will and Human Choice*, 235.

Arminian Anthropology

The Arminians emerged from Reformed orthodoxy toward the end of the sixteenth century, and they very naturally utilized the basic categories of faculty psychology: the intellect, the will, and the affections. The disputes over the will which Owen and numerous others identified was a consequence of the Remonstrant view that the fall had scarcely touched the human will. This led to them imputing to the will a stronger power of choice than the orthodox, for whom the will was in need of regeneration in order to be "freed."

On the basis of documents giving their views on the five disputed articles and other matters which the Remonstrants submitted to the Synod of Dort (1618–1619), it is possible to note a variety of anthropological positions taken by the Arminians and at variance with Reformed orthodoxy.[39] Thinking of the three powers of the soul—the intellect, will, and emotions—this was accepted by both parties: intellect, heart, and emotions, ordered hierarchically as intellect-will-affections. So both parties were intellectualist. The area of disagreement concerned the fallen human nature. In particular, while as we have seen for the Reformed orthodox the fall led to the loss of original righteousness, a loss that is restored in part by regeneration, for the Arminians the intellect remained intact in its unfallen powers. This was expressed in a positive view of the light of nature, as seen in the good use of natural ability, leading to a virtuous consequence, which led to reception of the divine gift of "supernatural grace." The Arminian Corvinus stated that "Arminius prefers saying that God gives further grace to him who makes the right use of the first [grace], but denies further [grace] to him who does not make the right use of it."[40]

In a somewhat parallel fashion, the assumption was made that fallen humans have the ability to correctly read and understand Scripture, including what it says about divine matters, whereas the Reformed orthodox held that for such understanding the enlightening of the Holy Spirit is necessary. Finally, in the case of the will, which as we have seen exercised Owen, this presents the most marked contrast between the two parties. So for

---

39. What follows is indebted to Aza Goudriaan, "The Synod of Dordt and Arminian Anthropology," in *Revisiting the Synod of Dordt (1618–1619)*, ed. Aza Goudriaan and Fred Lieberg (Leiden: Brill, 2011).

40. Quoted by Goudriaan, "Synod of Dordt and Arminian Anthropology," 92.

the Reformed, concerning spiritual things the fallen will is in "bondage," though able to choose in the case of "civil" matters. For the Arminians, the will has the innate power to choose between good and evil, to will or not to will. In the case of the will, Aza Goudriaan concludes that the difference between the two parties was "profound." There is less difference in the case of the affections, perhaps. And although similarities are discernible between the Jesuit Molina and Arminians, as we have noted, while Molina held that the fall had weakened the will, the Arminians, being more optimistic, denied this.[41]

Theophilus Gale on "New Methodism"

The position of Turretin on free will against the Jesuits and by implication against the Arminians is borne out by other writers in England besides Owen—for example, by Theophilus Gale. Throughout 1669–1678, he worked on his great project *The Court of the Gentiles*. It appeared in parts in 1669 (part 1), 1671 (part 2), 1677 (part 3), and 1678 (part 4). Besides providing a fund of philosophical and theological learning, Gale's idea was to provide evidence that the foundation of European Christian philosophy is a distorted reproduction of biblical truths, an idea Augustine first suggested but later abandoned. In the latter parts of the *Court*, Gale became preoccupied with questions to do with the divine decree and the will of man, in which his view of natural liberty, presented earlier in the book, was taken up in connection with conflicting ideas in Roman Catholicism and in Protestantism. Another of the themes of the wider debate that Gale is concerned with, in connection with the consistency of the predetermination of God and human freedom, is what is meant by human freedom, "the hinge on which our whole controversie turns, as our more intelligent Opponents confess."[42] There are two short discussions of this in Part IV.[43]

In controversies over free will, Gale saw his position assailed from two sides. He quotes Cornelius Jansen: "The principal fraud and cheat of the Pelagians lay in their philosophic hallucination about natural free will,

---

41. Goudriaan, "Synod of Dordt and Arminian Anthropology," 100–101.
42. Gale, *Court of the Gentiles*, IV.iii.10.
43. Gale, *Court of the Gentiles*, IV.iii.10–13, 16–17.

which they place in Indifference, but Augustine in a rational spontaneitie."[44]
The Pelagians are followed in this by the Jesuits and Arminians. On this
side, Gale also cites Durandus of Saint Pourçain (1274–1332), who objected
to God's immediate concourse to human acts in that he held that it destroys
or is incompatible with the freedom of indifference. This is the view that is
standardly objected to by Reformed writers such as Turretin and Owen, as
we have seen. That is one kind of opponent to those who, like Gale, along
with such as Turretin and Owen, uphold the position that free will consists in rational spontaneity, which they argue is consistent with the divine
immediate concourse of even evil acts.

In addition to these "mainstream" opponents, there are others from
within the Reformed community (and so not Arminians), such as the Scot
John Strang (or Strangius) and Louis Le Blanc,[45] who "generally placed
Natural Libertie in a *Rational Spontaneity, and so presumed, that voluntary
necessity is very wel consistent therewith.*"[46] Besides them, Gale cites another
Scot, John Baron (or Baronius).[47] Gale refers to them and others as "New
Methodists." "But other of our Antagonists, Strangius, Le Blanc &c, perceiving that our Reformed Divines have generally placed Natural Libertie in a
Rational Spontaneity, and so presumed, *that voluntary necessitie is very well
consistent therewith,* hence they have found out an artificial distinction for
the reconciling the *Calvinists* with the *Jesuits, Pelagians and Arminians.*"[48]

Gale states that these "Antagonists" make a distinction between types
of liberty as follows: "(1) That Libertie taken *largely,* as it is a perfection of
the Soule, so it has one and the same notion with *Rational Spontaneitie;* and
such is the liberty of glorified Souls. This Libertie they make essential to
the wil…But, adde they, (2) There is also a *liberty strictly* so termed, which

---

44. Gale, *Court of the Gentiles,* IV.iii.11. Cornelius Jansen (1585–1638) was the author of
Augustinus, which was completed shortly before his death. The Jansenists opposed what they
regarded as the semi-Pelagianism of the Jesuits.

45. Louis Le Blanc de Beaulieu (1614–1675) was professor of theology, Academy of Sedan,
and wrote *Theses Theologiae Varii Temporiblus in Academia Sedanensi* (London, 1675).

46. Gale, *Court of the Gentiles,* IV.iii.11.

47. Robert Baron (1596–1639), who evidently was influenced by Cameron. Gale noted
that according to Samuel Rutherford, Baronius was an Arminian. Gale, *Court of the Gentiles,*
IV.iii.11.

48. Gale, *Court of the Gentiles,* IV.iii.11.

consists in the Indifference of the wil to this or that object, also to act or not to act: and this Libertie is most proper to this our imperfect state."[49]

So they seek to harmonize these two seemingly incompatible notions of natural liberty, rational spontaneity and liberty of indifference, a "habitual indifference" to act or not to act. Gale goes on, "There were some first lines of this distinction drawn by *Camero, who makes libertie* strictly so termed to be about the *means*, not the *end.*... But the first creator of this distinction touching a *two-fold Libertie*, among those who owned the *Synod of Dort*, was *Strangius*, who asserts a two-fold Libertie, one considered in *its own Nature*, which is essential to the wil, and the other as *limited to lapsed man*, which includes *Indifference*, &c."[50] "Or," he continues, "the will has at that very time, when it is predetermined by God to this or that act, an habitual power or radical indifference to the negation of that act, or to the putting forth a contrary act."[51]

So on Gale's view, Strangius, Baronius, Le Blanc, and others have a twofold liberty, one corresponding to the original natural liberty, rational spontaneity. They distinguish "into *that which is largely, or strictly taken*: and they confess, (1) That Libertie taken *largely*, as it is a perfection of the Soul so it has one and the same notion with *Rational Spontaneity*; and such is the Liberty of glorified Souls. This Libertie they make essential to the will."[52]

So Strangius commits himself to the view that liberty is both rational spontaneity and indifference. The first is free will in the unfallen pair, and the second "is most proper to this our imperfect state."[53] Likewise with Le Blanc. Gale says that these views originate with "Camero,"[54] who allegedly

---

49. Gale, *Court of the Gentiles*, IV.iii.11.

50. "Camero" is John Cameron (1579–1625), a Scottish Reformed theologian most of whose career was spent in France, teaching at the Academy of Saumur. He was influential on Huguenot theologians such as Moise Amyraut (1596–1664) and Claude Pajon (1628–1685) and, it seems, Louis Le Blanc, and also perhaps the Scots Baron and Strange. It is this group that Gale refers to as "new Methodists." Gale does not provide a reference to "Camero" in Gale, *Court of the Gentiles*, IV.iii.11. For further information on Cameron, see Richard A. Muller, "Divine Covenants, Absolute and Conditional: John Cameron and the Early Orthodox Development of Reformed Covenant Theology," *Mid-America Journal of Theology* 17 (2006): 11–56.

51. Gale, *Court of the Gentiles*, IV.iii.11, 17.

52. Gale, *Court of the Gentiles*, IV.iii.11.

53. Gale, *Court of the Gentiles*, IV.iii.11.

54. Gale, *Court of the Gentiles*, IV.iii.11–12.

first had the notion of a two-stage liberty. Such a liberty is very much a minority view on any account of what free will is.

At first sight this is a curious twofoldness. It appears to be a case of mankind created *ab initio* with the freedom of spontaneity, and so expressing the obedience and service of God from the heart and being settled on that one course of action, but "mutably." This original situation was metaphysically *accidental*, adventitious, a perfection that was not essential for humanness, only essential for the *imago Dei* in its fullness. Gale gives little more detail, unfortunately. Perhaps the fall occurred through the exercise of an act of "indifference," an expression of willfulness or deception or weakness, or some combination of factors. However this is, the fall issued in the liberty of indifference.

Gale is perplexed by this proposal. He regards this "mixed" view of liberty as a novelty, not to be found before in the history of the church, as much opposed by the Jesuits as by the Reformed. To his mind it does not provide "a clear Explication and Demonstration of the wils natural Libertie."[55] Presumably this is because the two ideas, rational spontaneity and indifference, are at odds. And Gale is naturally puzzled by this:

> What these new Methodists mean by this new coined distinction of *Libertie*, unless it be a gratification to the Pelagians, I cannot conjecture: Certain I am, that I never could find it among the Ancient Philosophers, Primitive Fathers, Scholastic Theologues, or any other but these new Methodists or their Sectatators [followers or partisans]. Do any of the Greek Philosophers make mention of any libertie but what is essential to the will and al human acts? Can one find among the Greek Theologues any notices of this two-fold Libertie? Yes do not the very Jesuits herein concur with us, that Liberty is essential to al moral acts, both in the future, as well as the present state of the Soul? Is not Libertie constituted by them and the Arminians as the foundation of al Moralitie?[56]

To say that human beings are sometimes free in any sense of possessing "Libertie" and sometimes not is of no use to Jesuits and Arminians, nor will it help the Calvinists in their conflicts with them.[57]

---

55. Gale, *Court of the Gentiles*, IV.iii.13.

56. Gale, *Court of the Gentiles*, IV.iii.12.

57. Gale, *Court of the Gentiles*, IV.iii.13.

Of what use then can this distinction of a two-fold Libertie be? Wil it satisfie the Pelagians, Jesuits or Arminians? No; because they al make Libertie strictly taken essential to al Moral Acts. Or, wil it any way relieve the Calvinists in their conflicts both with Jesuits and Arminians, to say the wil is sometimes free and sometimes not? If it be supposed, that Indifference be essential to libertie in this imperfect state, wil it not then be replied by Pelagians and Arminians, that the wil is not, according to these new Methodists, free in Conversion, because not indifferent? It were not difficult to demonstrate, how invalid this new-coined distinction of Libertie is, and unapt to reach those ends for which it was designed by the authors thereof.[58]

Each party in their turn holds that either indifference or rational spontaneity are essential to moral acts, fallen and unfallen.

I am not ignorant, that some new Methodists, together with the Arminians, stiffly contend, *that this impotence is not natural but only moral*; but either they intend under that ambiguity of the termes to concele some Pelagian Infusions of natural seeds of virtue and Free-wil to Moral good, or else they must wrest these terms Moral and Natural from their native sense, and what is intended by those that defend a natural impotence.[59]

This Impotence is not less voluntary than necessary, yea the more necessary it is, the more voluntary. The necessitie of this Impotence is seated in and ariseth from the Wil.... *That albeit the avoiding of sin and the observation of Divine commands be legally impossible to corrupt nature, yet both are Evangelically possible through the habitual and actual assistances of the Spirit of Grace.*[60]

According to Gale, "free will" can only possess one sense, that of rational spontaneity, and all free acts have it, whether occurring in a prelapsarian or postlapsarian condition. This liberty is not absolute or unconditional, as is the liberty of indifference, copied from the Jesuits by the Arminians, but limited by and conditionally dependent on God's creation and concourse. To take away such liberty, violence must be done to it. The will must be constrained or coerced in some fashion, its spontaneity compromised.

---

58. Gale, *Court of the Gentiles*, IV.iii.12.
59. Gale, *Court of the Gentiles*, IV.iii.14.
60. Gale, *Court of the Gentiles*, IV.iii.15.

God's predetermination of A does not make it absolutely impossible to have done not-A. It is not logically impossible that X does not-A.[61] "The will predeterminated to one act has an habitual indifference or radical flexibilitie to the opposite act; and therefore the impossibility is only 'conditionate' and limited."[62] What Gale means by a habitual indifference or radical flexibility is a dispositional indifference such that having chosen A, the agent could have chosen not-A had there been a good reason for him to have done so. Indifference *in actu primo.* This is the view expressed earlier by Turretin and Owen.

In light of this unsatisfactory and, for Gale, rather exasperating discussion of the ideas of the New Methodists, he sets out what he takes "Natural Libertie" to be in six propositions:

> (1) Natural libertie, as it denotes a power, has one and the same idea of nature with the Wil…. (2) All acts of the Wil have libertie in the strictest notion essentially appendent to them. (3) The Dominion which a free Agent has over his own Acts is not absolute, but limited and conditionate…. (4) The necessitie which ariseth from the concurse of God the first cause, no way diminisheth, but establisheth the Natural libertie of the Will…. (5) Actual Indifference to varieties of Objects or Acts, is no way essential to Natural Libertie, but only an Accident arising from its imperfection. (6) The formal, native and genuine Idea or notion of natural libertie, both as to state and exercice, includes no more than a rational spontaneitie.[63]

Peter Martyr Vermigli on Regeneration and Conversion

In discussing regeneration, Peter Martyr Vermigli made a conceptual distinction between *regeneration,* the implanting of new life by God the Spirit, and *conversion,* the response of the one regenerated to this secret, divine energizing. In regeneration, "the intellect is actively predisposed" to assent to the words and promises of God, but it is passive in respect of the empowering of God, which inclines the mind, causing the incapable to be willing pupils of God's will.[64] The believer may pray for more of such understanding and a strengthening of the will. Such prayers are themselves

---

61. Gale, *Court of the Gentiles,* IV.iii.16.
62. Gale, *Court of the Gentiles,* IV.iii.17.
63. Gale, *Court of the Gentiles,* IV.iii.12–13.
64. Vermigli, "Free Will," in *Philosophical Works,* 288.

the product of regenerating grace. Still, there is no cooperation by humans to the commands of God *ab initio*, but only after regenerating grace is received.[65] Vermigli refers to the "outward and inward word," meaning the communicated word through preaching, reading, and the like, and the Spirit's enlightening work in the mind, which is acquainted with the outward word. Imparting the inward word is not a violent act of coercion or such. "For we are created rational, in the image and likeness of God. A passive power of this kind may be rightly called, in the scholastic manner, a power of obedience because we are to undergo such a divine change when God wills to effect it."[66] Such power is a potentiality to receive something at the behest of another, "a previous conversion that may be called a kind of disposition."[67] People have been given a nature that is changeable by God, and such divine activity is pure grace.

In the case of acts proceeding from regeneration, Vermigli shows how God works on the mind and will in a fully Augustinian sense, not by cooperating with grace already present, grace of a general kind, but in efficacious grace, the provision of new powers and appetites.[68]

Such a discussion shows that Vermigli, due to his use of Aristotelian conceptuality, is able to make distinctions that Calvin, who thinks of regeneration as the first step in conversion, cannot do or does not choose to do. In this way, Vermigli is able to take new steps in the analysis of regeneration. In particular, he is able to make a clear distinction between the divine imparting of a new habit and its growth and flourishing at the level of consciousness in penitence and faith and other aspects of sanctification. These distinctions proved to be not all gain, for they led in turn to sharp differences of view among the Reformed.

We now move to a more radical development in Reformed anthropology, the development of a more naturalistic conception of regeneration, the Congruistic account of Claude Pajon.

---

65. Vermigli, "Free Will," in *Philosophical Works*, 291.

66. Vermigli, "Free Will," in *Philosophical Works*, 306.

67. Vermigli, "Free Will," in *Philosophical Works*, 288.

68. Vermigli, "Free Will," in *Philosophical Works*, 281.

John Cameron and Claude Pajon on Congruism

Claude Pajon's anthropology and its roots were largely passed over before Albert Gootjes's work *Claude Pajon (1626–1685) and the Academy of Saumur* was published in 2014.[69] This neglect is perhaps because it had little or no influence in the Anglophone Reformed world and few publications. This section is indebted to Gootjes's pioneering work.

The French Reformed confessional position was founded on the Canons of the Synod of Dort and the Second Helvetic Confession approved by the Synods of Alès (1620) and Charenton (1623). This is part of the third and fourth heads of doctrine of the Canons: "By the efficacy of the same regenerating Spirit He pervades the innermost recesses of man; He opens the closed and softens the hardened heart, and circumcises that which is uncircumcised; infuses new qualities in the will, which heretofore dead, he quickens; from being evil, disobedient, and refractory, He renders it good, obedient and pliable; actuates and strengthens it, that like a good tree, it may bring forth the fruits of good actions."[70]

Among the convictions confessed was a clear commitment to the fallenness of human nature in all its powers, to its hardening. As a consequence, through the effect of the fall the intellect was biased in its deliberations and in other powers and likewise the fallen will's desiring and willing. They are each depraved, though naturally each was depraved differently, in accordance with the powers of each. The depravity of the will lay in its weakness, its sluggishness in regard to the commands of its Creator and Lord, and its instability, the way in which it is easily diverted and unable to will what is good. This is the bondage of the will.

John Cameron was a teacher of Pajon, and he developed a view of regeneration that I call "semi-Congruism" in contrast to "full Congruism," which we will eventually encounter. According to Cameron, while in regeneration the Holy Spirit imparted His influences by immediately and directly acting on the intellect, He did not do so in connection with the parallel work on the will. Rather, being under the direct influence of the

---

69. There is a brief reference to it in B. B. Warfield's *The Plan of Salvation* (Grand Rapids: Eerdmans, n.d.), 90.

70. "The Canons of Dort (1618–1619).Third and Fourth Heads of Doctrine. The Corruption of Man, His Conversion to God, and the Manner Thereof," in Dennison, *Reformed Confessions of the 16th and 17th Centuries in English Translation* (Grand Rapids: Reformation Heritage Books, 2014), 4:137.

intellect, the will was favorably altered only by the influence of the directly regenerated intellect upon it. This halfway position is that in regeneration the will is not directly and immediately affected by the Holy Spirit, but only mediately via the Holy Spirit's direct influence on the intellect. It is the intellect's influence on the will that affects the will. The will is thus congruent with the work of the renewed intellect. As a consequence, for Cameron faith is an act solely of the intellect.[71] He writes, "Of course, that force by which the heart of man is moved is not *physical*, although it is a force; but it is, as it were an ethical force. Indeed, that force is a *demonstration*, yet no human mind can reject a demonstration."[72]

Here, Cameron makes reference to the distinction between a moral force and a physical force, or moral and natural ability and inability, in one of its senses as discussed in the last chapter. As we saw there, "physical" is a reference to the Greek word *phusis*, meaning a nature. So a "physical" change in modern usage is narrower in scope than references to physical changes in this seventeenth-century context. A change in the nature of the human soul may be described as a "physical" change, meaning an accidental change to its spiritual nature. According to Cameron and Pajon, the *phusis* of the soul was *not* corrupted by the fall, and could not be. It remained intact. But its powers, its moral force, was spoiled through ignorance.[73]

So an effectual call does not involve a change that repairs the mind's *phusis*, but a purely moral change, a change or changes in the habits and dispositions of the soul. The activity of the Spirit in effectual calling consists in presenting the soul with the word of God in a set of circumstances the total effect of which is certainly effectively persuasive, and this in turn means that these circumstances were demonstrative[74]—demonstrative, that is, from the self-evident data of special revelation and valid logical inferences therefrom. Hence, faith is purely intellectual and epistemological. Regeneration is primarily educative, dispelling the ignorance due to the fall.

Later, Pajon would argue that the Spirit's role in conversion was not to be described as an "acting on" the soul and claimed that this was Cameron's

---

71. Albert Gootjes, *Claude Pajon (1626–1685) and the Academy of Saumur* (Leiden: Brill, 2014), 40.

72. Cited by Gootjes, *Claude Pajon (1626–1685)*, 41.

73. Gootjes, *Claude Pajon (1626–1685)*, 129–30.

74. Perhaps this claim provides justification for the accusations of rationalism against Pajon. See the later remarks on the approach of Walter Rex.

view too. So Cameron's position was, or was taken by Pajon to be, semi-Congruent, in the sense that the persuaded intellect brings about, by virtue of its primacy, changes to the strength and direction of the will. (For this to happen, the will must be thought of as possessing the power of "intellect-reception," or teachableness.) This is another instance of the intertwining of the faculties. Pajon writes, "For, we are speaking about a faculty against which no external force can be applied; we are speaking about someone whose mind has not been removed, and whose organs are most excellently constituted; we are speaking about someone to whom the object has been revealed and to whom objective grace has been given."[75]

The study of Pajon's Congruism, what I have called "full Congruism," is somewhat hampered by the fact that he published little if anything on his views. According to Gootjes, most of Pajon's writings remain unpublished. The chief of these is a manuscript, *De Natura efficasis ad amicum dissertatio*,[76] whose contents Gootjes summarizes.[77]

What motivated Pajon's move toward full Congruism, besides a devotion to his teacher Cameron? One influence was sensitivity to the Roman Catholic charge that an appeal to the immediate influence of the Spirit on the soul was "enthusiastic."[78] The French Reformed in general took this objection very seriously. Regeneration was such that an immediate divine influence was needed to "repair" a breakdown in the *phusis* of the soul. But for Cameron, and then for Pajon, there was no such breakdown. Once the Congruist view was fully developed, it was expressed in terms of the denial of the need of any immediate influence of the Spirit in regeneration, thus doing its best to avoid the charge of enthusiasm but as a consequence fostering a naturalist or providentialist account of regeneration.

Pajon no doubt also had in mind the upholding activity of God and the governing of the created order through secondary causes. So as we have seen, his way was to maintain that the fall had not resulted in a *physical*

---

75. Gootjes, *Claude Pajon (1626–1685)*, 99.

76. This manuscript of thirty thousand words was completed by Pajon in the early 1660s for his friend Paul de la Fonsa, a fellow student from his Saumur days. Its importance is testified to by the fact that at least six separate manuscript copies circulated in the course of the controversy. These have been rediscovered by Gootjes, *Claude Pajon (1626–1685)*, 83n72.

77. Gootjes, *Claude Pajon (1626–1685)*, 129–30.

78. Gootjes, *Claude Pajon (1626–1685)*, 45–46. This charge was evidently made against the Reformed appeal to the internal witness of the Holy Spirit as the grounding of the Bible's inspiration as God's word.

weakening of the intellect or will, but only in their *moral* weakness, the possession of moral inabilities and habits through a willful ignorance. So, correspondingly, the "renewing" work of the Spirit is not a physical restoration of the nature of the understanding and will, but only their moral restoration. Central to this account is the idea of the Spirit's effective persuasion first of the intellect, and then the effect of the operations of that restored intellect in straightening the skewed operation of the will. This concourse retains a certain kind of immediacy beyond the semi-Congruism that Pajon seems initially to have taken from Cameron, one energized by a moral influence but not at any point by an immediate physical (*phusis*) influence of the Spirit.

This full-fledged position is reached when the work of the Spirit on the intellect (and thus on the will) is understood in exclusively moral terms and generated and mediated through a concatenation of providential influences such as education, temperament, the personal example of others, and personal experiences such as being struck by a particular text or expression in Scripture. Thus, the work of regeneration was a combination of traits of an individual person and a unique set of providentially arranged circumstances, working effectually in accordance with the divinely predestined purposes for that person, and so it falls within broad Augustinian parameters, and is a case of the combination of word and Spirit. Gootjes points out that the view that sin was a matter of moral inability was not denied by anyone in Reformed orthodoxy, although the phrase meant different things to different people.[79] But it is generally understood as a consequence of sin, not the matter of sin, what sin is.

Pajon sought advantage for his Congruism by connecting the opposition to it with the views of the Lutheran theologian Flacius Illyricus (1520–1575), who held that sin had effects on the substance of the soul and was not metaphysically accidental, and that in regenerating the Spirit provides new faculties and in regeneration "re-souls" an individual.[80] Pajon sought to distance himself from this extreme view of regeneration. Implied in this distancing is a consistent critique of "immediate" grace, the view that regeneration is conveyed by an immediate act of the Holy Spirit. For this is, or potentially is, "enthusiastic," in Pajon's view. But as we will see,

---

79. Gootjes, *Claude Pajon (1626–1685)*, 106.
80. Gootjes, *Claude Pajon (1626–1685)*, 104.

Turretin and other non-Congruentists also distance their own position from that of Illyricus.

Pajon also maintained that the operation of word and Spirit in regeneration was more intelligible when taken in Congruist terms. For he believed that the Spirit's work was not immediate (as we have seen), but mediate, mediated by the effect of the word, on the mind together with other providential circumstances, in the life of a person. The word, together with a unique mix of circumstances, ensures that the Spirit will intellectually persuade—demonstrate—the truth of the gospel, ensuring regeneration. For how otherwise can the fact that many spurn the word they hear be accounted for?

> When you hear that the Word is the proximate and sufficient cause of our conversion, understand the Word together with all those circumstances and aids that accompany it according to the providence of God, which ordains in this way. For only in this way is it an efficient instrument of the Holy Spirit.[81]
>
> The economy of the Holy Spirit in our conversion consists in awakening the sentiment of these common notions and in presenting in our souls at the same time the doctrines of the gospel and the arguments that prove them, which he does by the idea he forms of it in our intellects—with the intervention of his most wise dispensation of both the Word and of the other objects accompanying the Word—in such a way that the link and connection which the Christian truths have with the common notions is made to be seen by us necessarily, such that we cannot reject the Christian truth without at the same time rejecting these common notions.[82]

So in Congruism, there is a network of ideas. There is the central idea of moral inability, and with it the denial of physical (*phusis*) inability, and the view that faith is an act of the intellect alone. At the root of this intellectualistically inclined view of regeneration—for God's grace is never immediate—there is the anthropological view that the will must follow the

---

81. Gootjes, *Claude Pajon (1626–1685)*, 112.

82. Gootjes, *Claude Pajon (1626–1685)*, 112. By "common notions" is included rudimentary beliefs of the intellect and the senses.

last dictate of understanding. But this view is not held by Congruists alone but also by opponents of Congruism such as Turretin.[83]

In his full-fledged Congruism, Pajon held a pebble in his hand that, once thrown into the water, expanded its influence throughout the method of grace to embrace the character of divine providence and its relation to saving grace. What may seem, to begin with, to be a highly theoretical anthropological issue had ramified effects: on saving faith, on the nature of providence, on theological certainty, and no doubt on pastoral care and preaching.

Francis Turretin on Roman Catholic Congruism

It has to be remembered that Reformed theologians were already aware of Congruism as an established feature of some Roman Catholic views of grace. With this in mind, Turretin treats the issues of Congruism and Synergism together in his *Institutes*.[84] As far as I can see, he never alludes to or mentions Reformed Congruism, which as we have seen concerns the issue of natural and supernatural features of the instruments of reception of divine grace, involving the passivity and activity of the soul in receiving grace, and therefore perhaps leaving open the question of whether the soul might initiate that reception. As far as general anthropological matters are concerned, we have already seen that Turretin concurs with the general Reformed outlook of assigning primacy to the intellect in the soul and its necessitating of, without the compelling of, the will.[85]

Gootjes takes Turretin to have Pajonism in mind (without his referring to its proponents by name) in his critical discussion of the topic in his *Institutes*, and Gootjes may be correct. But Turretin may in fact be showing his opposition to Congruism not by discussing the views of Cameron and Pajon, but in connection with the Roman Catholic writers and with Arminianism.[86] If so, perhaps this was with a twofold intent: not to polarize

---

83. Whether Cameron and Pajon were accurate in claiming that upholders of the need for an infusion of grace in the soul imply the soul's physical inability will be considered below.

84. Turretin, *Institutes of Elenctic Theology*, 2:526. Synergism is the view that the reception of grace is a cooperative endeavor between God the giver and the needy soul. The issues of synergy and Congruism are closely connected, but not the same.

85. See, for example, Turretin, *Institutes of Elenctic Theology*, 1:663.

86. Turretin, *Institutes of Elenctic Theology*, 2:517.

the issue within the Reformed camp but also to make clear his view that Congruism represented an Arminianizing tendency.

Turretin keenly protects effectual calling from being understood as a cooperation between divine grace and human freedom. He mentions Congruism, that God's call is a resistible "moral suasion," only in the context of the Roman Catholic view, citing Robert Bellarmine.[87] Such persuasion may be regarded as effectual, according to Bellarmine, when the persuasion is with those who have a disposition to be persuaded, who are foreknown by God. This involves middle knowledge, as Turretin notes, and is thus doubly unacceptable to the orthodox.[88] Rather, for Turretin, regeneration consists in "the infusion of supernatural habits by the Holy Spirit," understood as the reception of certain dispositions, which at once spring to life.[89] Such an infusion unfailingly brings about conversion, of which God is thus the sole immediate cause. The will is renewed by grace, but not coercively.[90] And so "liberty in this affair conspires with necessity."[91] The final element in conversion is that the work of the Spirit acts both mediately through the word and also "acts immediately with the word on the soul."[92]

Clearly, this doctrine is a fine balance between immediate and mediate factors that Turretin says is mysterious and so not fully explicable. But because regeneration involves the mediation of the word, it is not enthusiasm, nor is it like it. "But the operation of the Spirit does not exclude, but draws with itself reasoning, and the grateful consent of the will…[while] enthusiasm does not produce a change of heart but affects the mind while the will remains unchanged," and thus enthusiasm is quite distinct from regeneration and conversion.[93] Turretin's idea of the immediacy of the Spirit in regeneration is strong. He writes, "Though the impotence of man were purely moral, it would not follow that it could be healed by moral reason alone through objective grace solely. Nay, since it is inexpugnable in the sphere of morals, it demands some power stronger than a moral power (i.e., a hyperphysical and divine) to conquer it. Nor can a remedy be

---

87. Turretin, *Institutes of Elenctic Theology*, 2:541.
88. Turretin, *Institutes of Elenctic Theology*, 2:518.
89. Turretin, *Institutes of Elenctic Theology*, 2:527.
90. Turretin, *Institutes of Elenctic Theology*, 2:514.
91. Turretin, *Institutes of Elenctic Theology*, 2:525.
92. Turretin, *Institutes of Elenctic Theology*, 2:616.
93. Turretin, *Institutes of Elenctic Theology*, 2:541.

brought to it by moral reasons more than to one naturally dead by natural means."[94] Strong as this may be, Turretin makes the point that it nevertheless is to be disassociated from the views of Illyricus.

While Turretin refers both to the intellect and will, he does not appear to treat them distinctly. Thus, he does not discuss the particulars of the semi-Congruism of Cameron. But insofar as he rejects a Congruistic approach, by implication Turretin rejects the full Congruism of Pajon. One place where his objection to Pajonism and, by implication, to Cameron's semi-Congruism is made clear (whether or not he had either or both in mind) in his brief expository comments on the "new heart" referred to in Ezekiel 36:26–27:

> Here the arguments are as weighty as the words are many. "I will give," he says, not only offer and prepare, a "heart," not only a mind, but the very sanctuary of the soul; "a new heart," not, I will patch up the old and change it into a better; but I will give an entirely new and another; not uniting mine with your heart, but removing wholly the hard, dry, and totally senseless stony heart; "I will put in you an heart of flesh" (i.e. flexible, soft, and obedient, endowed with active feeling); and that this grace may be more powerful and efficacious, "I will put my Spirit," not I will make it to pass like a stranger, but will put it as a Lord and ruler, not in your nostrils, but "within you" to exercise a governing power in you.[95]

This is a statement that appears to cover all human powers: heart, mind, and will.

As far as the Anglophone Reformed world is concerned, few, if any, were attracted to such Congruism, nor to combating Pajonism. This was not likely in any case, if only because Pajon published so little. But some British theologians nevertheless warned against Congruism.[96] For example, Owen is particularly decided against regeneration and conversion being understood as "moral persuasion." And he derides the idea that it proceeds

---

94. Turretin, *Institutes of Elenctic Theology*, 2:541.

95. Turretin, *Institutes of Elenctic Theology*, 2:551.

96. E.g., Stephen Charnock, "The Necessity of Regeneration," in vol. 3 of *The Complete Works of Stephen Charnock*; Samuel Willard, *A Compleat Body of Divinity* (Boston: B. Green and S. Kneeland for B. Eliot and D. N. Henchman, 1726), 441.

from "certain notions…demonstrable by the light of reason,"[97] coming close here to condemning the saving efficacy of the "common notions" to which Pajon appealed, and conversions as *inter alia* "rational."[98] But "rational" does not mean "clear and distinct" or similar, but suited to the needs and conditions of fallen humanity. In this sense, if there is a fire destroying the house, dowsing it with water is "rational." Or a doctor who prescribes a drug that will be effective in recovery from a certain disease may be said to be acting rationally. So it is in the grace of regeneration. And a purely moral persuasion is not rational in this sense. Such persuasions, involving the preaching of the law and the gospel, are necessary. But they are not sufficient. So conceivably Owen could have had Pajonist ideas in mind as a target, but it is not likely. He emphasizes that "there is not only a *moral* but a *physical* immediate operation of the Spirit, by his power and grace, or his powerful grace, upon the minds or souls of men in their regeneration. This is that which we must cleave to, or all the glory of God's grace is lost, and the grace administered by Christ neglected."[99]

Bear in mind that by "physical" Owen means an operation on the *physis* of the soul. He cites Ephesians 1:18–20 in support. He does not refer to moral inability but to "a *moral impotency*, which is reflected on them [i.e., the unregenerate] greatly from the will and affections, whence the mind never *will receive* spiritual things,—that is, it will always and unchangeably reject and refuse them."[100] Like Turretin, Owen distinguishes his view from enthusiasm and stresses that the work of the Spirit on the soul is not coercive:

> He therefore offers no violence or compulsion unto the will. This that faculty is not naturally capable to give admission unto. If it be compelled, it is destroyed…. [But] it will be inquired how this can any otherwise be done but by a kind of violence and compulsion, seeing we have evinced already that moral persuasion and objective allurement is not sufficient thereunto? *Ans.* It is acknowledged that in the work of conversion unto God, though not in the very act of it, there is a reaction between grace and the will, their acts being contrary, and

---

97. John Owen, *Pneumataologia*, in *The Works of John Owen*, ed. W. H. Goold (Edinburgh: Banner of Truth, 1966), 3:314.

98. Owen, *Pneumataologia*, in *Works*, 3:314.

99. Owen, *Pneumataologia*, in *Works*, 3:316.

100. Owen, *Pneumataologia*, in *Works*, 3:267.

that grace is therein victorious, and yet no violence or compulsion is offered unto the will.… [2] The will, in the first *act* of conversion (as even sundry of the schoolmen acknowledge), *acts* not but as it is *acted*, moves not but as it is moved; and therefore is *passive* therein, in the sense immediately to be explained.… Wherefore it must be granted… the same instant of time wherein the will is moved it moves, and when it is acted it acts itself, and preserves its own liberty in its exercise. There is, therefore, herein an inward almighty *secret act* of the power of the Holy Ghost, producing or effecting in us the will of conversion unto God, so acting our wills as that they also act themselves, and that freely.[101]

Effectual calling reaches its most developed form in the Westminster Confession. Its chapter "Of Effectual Calling" in prominently referring to the passivity of the soul in regeneration not only placed a barrier preventing synergism but also rejected any account of regeneration which "naturalizes" it in the Pajonian manner. As the Confession notes, "This effectual call is of God's free and special grace alone, not from anything at all foreseen in man, who is altogether passive therein, until, being quickened and renewed by the Holy Spirit, he is thereby enabled to answer this call, and to embrace the grace offered and conveyed in it" (10.2). This wording, with its emphatic stress on passivity and coupled with references to the renewal by the Holy Spirit, while not formally excluding Pajonism, makes upholding it very difficult. Owen's views, which were mentioned in chapter 5 in connection with moral and physical ability, are very similar. But he is silent on Reformed Congruism, not explicitly referring to it but nonetheless excluding it.

William Pemble on Mistreating the Faculties

There is something else as well. As we have noted earlier, the Puritan Pemble makes some salutary cautions on the academic treatment of the faculties.

If Pemble's view, which we have noted earlier, is borne in mind, the discussion we have noted involving the distinctness of and relations between intellect and will and the regenerating influence on each sometimes has the

---

101. Owen, *Pneumataologia*, in *Works*, 3:319–20. Owen cites Augustine: "Therefore he is drawn in wondrous ways to will, by Him who knows how to work within the very hearts of men. Not that men who are unwilling should believe, which cannot be, but that they should be made willing from being unwilling."

unfortunate tendency to treat these faculties as we might think of organs of the body. Pemble cautions that there are limits to this kind of theorizing. If we allow ourselves to think that the understanding and will are distinct faculties with distinct actions, then we are jeopardizing the unity and simplicity of the soul. Faculty psychology is not an *a priori* construct, nor is it found as such in Scripture as a revealed doctrine. Its appropriateness is demonstrated *a posteriori* from observation of the self and others, including the teaching of others. So the character of the faculties of the soul must be shaped by the phenomena, and not vice versa.

Pemble's strictures are of general application. Sometimes they may help a conservative defense, as they would help to respond to Pajonism or at least to semi-Congruism, arguments for which rely on the distinctness of the faculties. But they tend not to help arguments that rely on the working of the practical reason, which need the distinction between the intellect and the will to make sense.

The Influence of René Descartes

René Descartes's (1596–1650) influence in the seventeenth-century Reformed community was felt in a number of places: in Saumur, in the Academy of Geneva through the influence of Robert Chouet, and, most publicly, in Holland. This section concentrates on Descartes's influence on Holland.

Descartes arrived in Holland in 1628 and stayed there until 1649, at which point he moved to Sweden and died shortly thereafter in 1650. His presence in Holland at this time was an important factor in Dutch Reformed university life. Apart from his doctrine of God, which was markedly voluntaristic and considered in isolation may have been not uncongenial to the Reformed, his philosophy was chiefly anthropological, reinforced by the fact that as a lifelong lay Roman Catholic, he left the mysteries of the faith to the church.[102]

The impact of Descartes on the Reformed church initially was due to the suspicion and animosity of its leaders, notably Voetius in Utrecht. Their reaction centered on the methods of Cartesianism, which were regarded as disruptive of the status quo, not only in theology but also in law and medicine, in which scholastic methods ruled supreme. The substantive point at

---

102. While this is in general true, in his *Conversation with Burman* he expresses a series of theological opinions.

issue was that Descartes started philosophy from a position of skepticism; the existence of God was not taken for granted *ab initio* in his philosophy. Voetius, who was a scholastic to his fingertips, personally tangled with Descartes, with whom he corresponded, and with his followers, as can be gathered from such statements as these:

> As for the lies and crass calumnies with which a man skilled in mathematics but clearly no theologian, René Descartes, who is altogether ignorant of our affairs both in general and in particular, but abetted by others and covered by the old name and shadow of Jesuit-papist religion, sought to dishonour the theology which we have taught, not without success, thanks to God's grace, in church and school for many years; I do not know what to use against them except the decision and testimony of this church, by which the much discussed works of Descartes have been formally condemned.[103]

However, despite such opposition, some Utrecht professors became sympathetic to Cartesianism, notably Henricus Regius, professor of botany. In Leiden later on, several members of the theology faculty there became recognizably Cartesian. And as already mentioned, there was an interview between a Reformed student Burman and Descartes, a version of which was published. In his later career as a Reformed theology professor, Burman also became somewhat Cartesian. Others were more relaxed about Descartes's influence. So Andreas Rivet, the French Reformed theologian who spent most of his career in Holland, laconically asserted that "Philosophizing in this [Cartesian] way, one cannot go dangerously astray."[104]

Descartes's Dualism

What is of interest as far as Reformed anthropology is concerned is whether Cartesian dualism made inroads into the Reformed scholastic anthropology, and if so with what consequences. Descartes's philosophy was heavily anthropological, dominated by the skeptical procedure he outlines in the *Meditations* and elsewhere, as well as his answer to that skepticism, which

---

103. Voetius, "Concerning Practical Theology," 286–87.

104. Willem J. van Asselt, "Andreas Rivetus (1572–1651) International Theologian and Diplomat," in *The Theology of the French Reformed Church from Henry IV to the Revocation of the Edict of Nantes*, ed. Martin J. Klauber (Grand Rapids: Reformation Heritage Books, 2014), 268.

lay in relying on an appeal to the consciousness of such a skeptic, for such a consciousness was indubitable. "Even when I am doubting there is something that does the doubting." This led Descartes to affirm that the soul is a *res cogitans*, a thinking thing. And though he had received an education at the Jesuit College of La Flèche, the contents of this thinking thing were not determined by the Aristotelian and Thomist view that the soul was the form of the body. This could not be, since given his skeptical starting point Descartes did not know that he had a body. Thus, having a body could not be part of the answer to the question of who he was. "Soul" in Cartesanism was short for "human soul," a purely spiritual substance. The body, characterized by its spatial extension, was contingently connected to the soul.

The metaphysics of the position of the scholastics, certainly of Voetius, is that the human being is a substantial unity (following Aquinas). This is central to the debate provoked by Regius's Cartesianism in Utrecht. For Regius, it is an accident of the soul that it has a body, which was another substance than the *res cogitans*. The body is not a *res cogitans*, but a *res extensa*. The Socinians held such a view also, though not on Cartesian grounds; and for this reason (even if there were no other) scholastic theologians such as Voetius were strongly disposed not to favor it. For Voetius had what he regarded as good evidence for a hylomorphic view. According to Cartesianism, a human being is an accidental composite, while in hylomorphism the human being is a substantial unity of two essential components. So the human soul considered in isolation is an incomplete substance, and the human body likewise an incomplete substance. Together they form one human being. But how could this be, if death involves the loss of the body? The soul then suffers substantial loss. As was noted earlier, the Aristotelian notion of substance gets modified at this point.[105] There is an intrinsic substance, the soul, and it is the form of an extrinsic substance, the body, a unit temporarily lost at the death of the body. So this hylomorphism is tailored to fit the biblical teaching. With its affinities to Platonic dualism, one might think that Cartesian dualism would be a simpler option. But in general the price of the contingency of the body was a price too high for the Reformed to pay.

---

105. For a short but informative account of Voetius's appropriation of substantial unity, see Goudriaan, *Reformed Orthodoxy and Philosophy*, 238.

While protecting the moral character of the body as being in no respect morally inferior to the soul (both being essential), and not only differing from Cartesianism, scholasticism also provided an argument against Plato, for whom the body was the "prison house" of the soul. But does this modified hylomorphism entail the view that the human body, despite its gap between death and resurrection, is as immortal as the soul? The resurrection seems to be a metaphysical necessity, not dependent on the will of God.

On Regius's Cartesian view, the soul was considerably reduced in the range of its powers. No longer the form of the body, it is annexed to a body. It does not have vegetative or sensitive appetites, since these are the exclusive province of the body. Though stressing the metaphysical contingency of its connection to the soul, at certain places in his writings Descartes took pains to stress the linkedness of the soul to the body.[106] He observed that the sensations of pain, from a wound, for example, are *my* sensations, involving changes in my consciousness, and not a purely externally observed state of affairs. He draws some conclusions from these facts:

> Nature also teaches me by these sensations of pain, hunger, thirst etc., that I am not only lodged in my body as a pilot in a vessel, but that I am very closely united to it, and so to speak so intermingled with it that I seem to compose with it one whole. For if that were not the case, when my body is hurt, I, who am merely a thinking thing, should not feel pain, for I should perceive this wound by the understanding only, just as the sailor perceives by sight when something is damaged in his vessel.[107]

On the other hand, Descartes's speculations as to how the soul was able to interact with the body were not required by the scholastics, for whom the soul was more expansive than Descartes, who was content to describe the character of the body that the soul is annexed to in autonomous, mechanical terms.

In *Meditation* IV, Descartes considers error. Its source does not lie in the intellect, but in the will. God would never deceive him, but he is

---

106. E.g., *Meditations*, VI.

107. René Descartes, *Meditations on First Philosophy*, in *Philosophical Works of Descartes*, ed. G. R. T. Ross and Elizabeth Haldane (Cambridge: Cambridge University Press, 1911), I, 192. The *Meditations* was published in 1641, during Descartes's time in Holland.

nonetheless "subject to an infinitude of errors."[108] An error has about it something both positive and negative. There are some Augustinian themes here: evil as a privation, and that the entire universe with its imperfections is better than if there were no imperfections.[109] Descartes settles on the view that the cause of evil is free will, of which he is conscious that it has no limits. He uses familiar scholastic terms. This will is a faculty, and its power does not consist in the liberty of indifference, which is in fact the lowest grade of liberty, a negation rather than a perfection. "If I always recognized clearly what was true and good, I should never have trouble in deliberating as to what judgment or choice I should make, and then I should be entirely free without ever being indifferent."[110] So here the liberty of indifference is rather second-rate as compared with the liberty of spontaneity. And Descartes implies that the exercise of such indifference is a source of errors and is due to the fact that "since the will is much wider in its range and compass than the understanding, I do not restrain it within the same bounds, but extend it also to things which I do not understand: and as the will is of itself indifferent to these, it easily falls into error and sin, and chooses the evil for the good, or the false for the true."[111]

Even given Descartes's avowal to leave theology to the theologians, one cannot but be struck by the thought that his account of the source of error has similarities to Christian accounts of the fall. It is likely that his Reformed scholastic readers, critical though in the main they were, took it that way. His terminology is what they were accustomed to: "free will," "the liberty of indifference," "spontaneity," and so on. Descartes had no reason not to use the language of faculties. There are, however, significant differences. For example, Descartes's is an ahistorical narrative, and he is more concerned with error than with sin.

But what is Descartes saying? He stresses that error is due to the "ambition" of the liberty of indifference, with which God had endowed humankind. Given this, it is not surprising that some of his Reformed readers should cry "Pelagianism!"[112] This ambition reveals itself in the will (having the power of

---

108. Descartes, *Meditations*, IV, 172.

109. Descartes, *Meditations*, IV, 174.

110. Descartes, *Meditations*, IV, 175.

111. Descartes, *Meditations*, IV, 175–76.

112. See, for example, Theo Verbeek, *Descartes and the Dutch: Early Reactions to Cartesian Philosophy, 1637–1650* (Carbondale: Southern Illinois University Press, 1992), 14–15, 44.

indifference) to have made choices which go beyond the boundaries set by the deliverances of the reason, clear and distinct ideas.

What is faith's relation to the will, according to Descartes? The intellectual judgment of the senses is not purely deductive.[113] Error is due to the abuse of the liberty of indifference, whereas the relation between the understanding and the will is that of a metaphysical necessity, and there is no prospect of indifference, not at least *in sensu secundo*, for theologians such as Voetius and Turretin. The closest a Reformed theologian comes to the contours of Descartes in *Meditation* V who I have encountered is Louis Le Blanc, who, as we saw earlier in the chapter, seems to have had the idea, according to Theophilus Gale, that mankind unfallen acted with rational spontaneity, but the fall brought about the "disorder" of the freedom of indifference.

Later in the century, the theologian Anthonius Driessen (1684–1748) provides an example of a Reformed theologian who had absorbed important aspects of Cartesianism. According to Goudriaan,[114] Driessen was a Cartesian from the start of his career. For him, the mind is a thinking thing, a spiritual substance; and the body is a different thing. So what does the human being's unity consist in? The answer has to be in a sort of union, the mind being in the body, the one substance interacting with the other. But that still leaves the problem of resurrection. Driessen appears to be more concerned with the moral consequences of the acts of the soul. Responsibility in the social sense seems to have had particular importance for him. The question of the soul's responsibility for thoughts, intentions, or desires slips into the background. And he maintains interaction as against the doctrine of preestablished harmony or of occasionalism. But how the body affects the soul remains mysterious for him.[115] The soul is the source of the force of nature which gives life to the body and animates it. The idea of an autonomous clock, in the Cartesian sense, is sidestepped. So any interaction between body and soul is caused by the animation of the soul. The soul's freedom is expressed in the actions of the body.

---

113. Walter Rex, *Pierre Bayle and Religious Controversy* (The Hague: Martinus Nijhoff, 1965), 135.

114. Goudriaan, *Reformed Orthodoxy and Philosophy*, 249.

115. Goudriaan, *Reformed Orthodoxy and Philosophy*, 254.

The soul's immortality is not inherent in its spirituality and simplicity, even including the work of conscience. It is due to God's will alone. Driessen has a place for memory, but it is not what personal identity is due to, as it was for John Locke. So even theologians such as Driessen modified Cartesian anthropology in the interests of his theological and especially of his moral program.

Among other Reformed theologians positively influenced by Cartesian ideas were Franz Burman (1632–1679), Adrian Heerebord (1614–1661), and Abraham Heidanus (1597–1678). All seemed to have resorted to what Driessen had: a selective attitude to Descartes's anthropology and methodology.

There is a somewhat different account to be given of Descartes's reception in France, one that involves Jean-Robert Chouet, who displayed Cartesian allegiances first as a professor of philosophy at Saumur. Chouet seems to have adopted Cartesianism on first meeting it,[116] and then (via the beseeching of his uncle, Lionel Tronchin, who was a professor of theology there), he moved to the Academy at Geneva. Rex suggests that Cartesianism fortified the rationalist side of Calvinism. Chouet's interests in Descartes seem to have been more scientific than theological, but his other contributions seem more theological than philosophical. Chouet was a cheerleader to Pajon and others. It is not clear that Pajon's Congruism owes anything to Descartes. Chouet is an example of someone who used Descartes to form a modest methodological rationalism, as did Tronchin, the teacher of Pierre Bayle.[117] This is considered by Rex in his account of what he refers to as Reformed "rationalism" in France.

So there are two separate stories of Cartesianism and the Reformed: one Dutch and one French. The French story certainly had (if Rex is to be followed) an anthropological and theological focus, though it is not clear that this is so in the case of Chouet.

---

116. Rex, *Pierre Bayle and Religious Controversy*, 124.

117. Rex, *Pierre Bayle and Religious Controversy*, 128, 140. According to Rex, Bayle corresponded with both Tronchin and Chouet for many years after he left Geneva.

CHAPTER 8

Beyond Faculty Psychology?
John Locke and Jonathan Edwards

This chapter will be primarily devoted to the anthropology of Jonathan Edwards (1703–1758), the New England pastor and theologian. In the background will be the question of Edwards's continuity and discontinuity with the tradition of Reformed orthodoxy and of the scholastic theology in which (as we have been seeing) it was by and large expressed. No attempt will be made at a direct answer, though the intention is to provide some of the materials relevant to formulating an answer to this question.

Prima facie Edwards has a place in the Reformed orthodox tradition. He was educated in it, and writers such as Turretin and van Mastricht were among his favorite theologians. He also appeals to the Reformed scholastic theologian Johann Friedrich Stapfer, a Zurich theologian, in his *Great Christian Doctrine of Original Sin*, which we will briefly consider later on.[1] He regularly looks for support from such as Owen and Flavel, as well as from his New England forebears such as Thomas Shepard. The New England Congregational (or Independent) churches in which he was a minister had the Cambridge Platform of 1648 as their confessional position.

It is also worth reminding ourselves that there was life in Reformed orthodoxy in Europe and in New England throughout Edwards's time. As we noted earlier, Edwards was born around the same time as the theologian de Moor and died before him. And Samuel Willard's (1640–1707) *Compleat Body of Divinity* was published posthumously in 1726 when Edwards was twenty-three. Willard had been the pastor of the Third Church, Boston, from 1676 until his death. Willard's theology is a product of Reformed scholastic theology that Edwards met with. So Reformed orthodoxy was

---

1. Johann Friedrich Stapfer (1708–1755) was the author of *Institutiones Theologiae Polemicae Universae*, 4th ed. (Zurich, 1746–1753).

a live option—perhaps it would be fair to say that it was the default style in theologizing—for the occupiers of the pulpits of New England in Edwards's day.

Yet there were other influences at work in Edwards's formation. A main theme of the chapter will be the way in which he took on and interacted with John Locke, the English philosopher, a lay theologian of Anglican and Arminian persuasion, who was interested in the foundations of human understanding in the senses and also very much concerned with theology from a political angle, such as the limits of toleration. Other philosophers, Descartes and Malebranche, and Newtonianism were also influential on the youthful Edwards. But we will concentrate on the influence of Locke.

When Edwards was a teenage student at Yale College, he came across a copy of Locke's *Essay Concerning Human Understanding*. Some have thought that Edwards's reaction was a mere adolescent infatuation on his part. But Edwards's first biographer, Samuel Hopkins, famously captured Jonathan's lifelong attitude to that book:

> Taking that book [Locke's *Human Understanding*] in his Hand upon some Occasion, not long before his death, he said to some of his select Friends who were there with him, That he was beyond Expression entertain'd and pleas'd with it, when he read it in his Youth at College; that he was as much engaged, and had more Satisfaction and Pleasure in studying it, than the most greedy Miser in gathering up handfuls of Silver and Gold from some new discovered Treasure.[2]

Later on, Edwards formed part of the New England culture that had a great interest in the latest thought in England. He lived at the time in which the mainly scholastic curriculum of Harvard and Yale was being modified to incorporate the new natural philosophy. Students at Yale benefited from the recently acquired library of Jeremiah Dummer, Massachusetts's agent in London, which contained the edition of Locke that Edwards took such a delight in, as well as Isaac Newton.[3]

---

2. Samuel Hopkins, *The Life and Character of the Late reverend, learned and pious Mr Jonathan Edwards* (Boston: S. Kneeland, 1765), 3–4.

3. There is a short, interesting account of Yale and the young Edwards, as well as the cultural outlook of New England, in George Marsden's *Jonathan Edwards, a Life* (New Haven, Conn.: Yale University Press, 2009), ch. 4.

Edwards did not offer a blanket endorsement of Locke's philosophy, however. While appropriating significant elements of it, there are equally features that Edwards was silent on. For example, Locke is known as a skeptic over innate ideas. His *Essay* commences with an attack on them.[4] But Edwards is silent on this matter, and what he elsewhere writes about mankind's creation in the image of God or about conscience, for example, strongly suggests that he retained innateness in some form.

But a glance at Edwards's writings reveals that he was not scholastic in character. Gone is most of the characteristic conceptual apparatus that we have examined in previous chapters—the use of the fourfold Aristotelian causation, for example, and a disputational style. In his formation, he did not benefit from the scholastic organization of ministerial education, a course of philosophy, including natural theology, and then a course in (revealed) theology. Edwards's talents from the start were both philosophical and theological. His *Freedom of the Will* is almost wholly philosophical, largely free of scholastic divisions and distinctions.

Edwards was not conscious of being the product of a distinct tradition, as some of the European Reformed orthodox were. His literary style is more direct than that of his predecessors and relatively uncluttered. Note that he took on some scholastic distinctions, such as that between natural and moral ability, and other scholastic anthropological terms such as "indifference" and "habit." But we will see that some of these terms have a rather marginal role for him. To a degree, Edwards appeals to the language of common sense and writes in the manner of contemporary writers. He gives importance to definition. He shows great care in his use of language but also notes what he regards as its limitations. Although he read Latin, there is no evidence that he ever wrote it. Edwards was working in the midst of cultural change, and he had a good deal of the self-confidence of a new era about him, the era of Newton and Locke.

We will first consider the relation between body and soul; then Edwards's view of the faculties (a scholastic word he continued to use,

---

4. In this chapter references to the *Essay* are by book, chapter, and section. References in parentheses are to the fifth edition, in two volumes, edited by John Yolton (London: Dent and Co., 1961). On innate ideas, see Stephen Gaukroger, *The Emergence of a Scientific Culture: Science and the Shaping of Modernity 1210–1695* (Oxford: Oxford University Press, 2006); and Paul Schuurman, *Ideas, Mental Faculties, and Method; The Logic of the Ideas of Descartes and Locke and Its Reception in the Dutch Republic (1630–1750)* (Leiden: Brill 2004).

though with a distinct connotation); after that, the affections; and lastly, Edwards's fairly brief but significant remarks on personal identity.

Body and Soul

Edwards gives no time to discussing hylomorphism but adopts a pronounced dualism, as is seen from this passage from the *Freedom of the Will*:

> Man is entirely, perfectly, and unspeakably different from a mere machine, in that he has reason and understanding, and has a faculty of will, and so is capable of volition and choice; and in that his will is guided by the dictates or views of his understanding, in that his actions and behavior, and in many respects also his thoughts, and the exercises of his mind, are subject to his will; so that he has liberty to act according to his choice, and do what he pleases; and, by means of these things, is capable of moral habits and moral acts, such as inclinations and actions, as, according to the common sense of mankind, are worthy of praise, esteem, love, and regard; or, on the contrary, of disesteem, detestation, indignation, and punishment.[5]

This comes from his answer to the objection that his compatibilistic determinism was as mechanistic and materialistic as was Hobbes's determinism. There is here a nice blend of influences. Here is another such passage, on the possible disruptive effects of choice, countering a monocausal, mechanistic reading of his position:

> But the dependence and connection between acts of volition or choice, and their causes, according to established laws, is not so sensible and obvious. And we observe that choice is as it were a new principle of motion and action, different from that established law and order in things which is most obvious, that is seen especially in both corporeal and sensible things; and also that choice often interposes, interrupts and alters the chain of events in these external objects, and causes 'em to proceed otherwise than they would do, if left alone, and left to go on according to the laws of motion among themselves.[6]

At places, Edwards's dualism seems to be interactionistic, as was Descartes's. But he probably did not take it from Descartes, but from Locke.

---

5. Jonathan Edwards, *Freedom of the Will*, ed. Paul Ramsey, vol. 1, *The Works of Jonathan Edwards* (New Haven, Conn.: Yale University Press, 1957), 370.

6. Edwards, *Freedom of the Will*, 158–59.

Here is a sample of his interactionism from the *Religious Affections*: "Such seems to be our nature, and such the laws of the union of soul and body, that there never is any case whatsoever, any lively and vigorous exercise of the will or inclination of the soul, in some alteration of the motion of its fluids, and especially of the animal spirits. And on the other hand, from the same laws of the union of soul and body, the constitution of the body, and the motions of its fluids, may promote the exercise of the affections."[7] This is a clear statement of interaction between soul and body. Here also is exceptionless law, the laws established by God, but not exceptionless chains. Rather, we experience in our choices the power to interrupt and alter such chains. Such interactionism needs to be qualified by Edwards's avowal of occasionalism, which we will touch on later, though in our examination of Edwards's anthropology we will not go into his view of the relation of God to His creation.

We have seen a number of times the distinction that the Reformed orthodox make between indifference in the divided sense and in the combined sense.[8] If we understand indifference as a reference to the power of choice, then Edwards would have nothing to do with the second sense because he has strong exceptions to contingency as a categorical alternativity, a choice which, in a given situation, may be equally a choice of A or B. Such a two-way choice would be causeless[9] and irrational.[10] But then the Reformed orthodox also reject indifference *in actu secundo*, but allow choice *in sensu diviso*. No synchronicity, therefore, a term which in any case, as we have seen, the Reformed orthodox did not use except when describing the Jesuit use of freedom, which they regarded as unbiblical. For Edwards, the will is a reasoned or reason-informed power (*potestas*), the power to choose, which is exercised on sufficient reasons or grounds.[11] This appears to be the only way there seems of bringing together the rational spontaneity

---

7. Jonathan Edwards, *Religious Affections*, ed. John E. Smith, vol. 2, *The Works of Jonathan Edwards* (New Haven, Conn.: Yale University Press, 1959), 98.

8. See, for example, Turretin on indifference in chapter 7.

9. Edwards, *Freedom of the Will*, 174, 316.

10. Edwards, *Freedom of the Will*, 183–85.

11. Edwards, *Freedom of the Will*, 139, 175–76.

of the Reformed orthodox and Edwards's compatibilism. Whether or not the two views can be brought together I will leave to one side.[12]

Moral and Natural Ability

We noticed in an earlier chapter that there are stronger and weaker ways of making this distinction between moral and natural ability. Some, like Turretin and Gale, regard the inability in a fully modal way, following Augustine's characterization of the four states of mankind in terms of *posse* and *non posse*. Truman, on the other hand, almost always emphasizes a person's willingness or unwillingness to make choices of certain kinds. Edwards seems to have a view nearer to Truman's than to Turretin's. He writes that the ability and inability in question refer to the strength of habits that a person may have, and that such strengths can be various:

> I before observed, that the word "inability" in its original and most common use, is a relative term; and has respect to will and endeavour, as supposable in the case, and as insufficient to bring to pass the thing desired and endeavoured. Now there may be more of an appearance and shadow of this, with respect to the acts which rise from a fixed and strong habit, than others that arise only from transient occasions and causes.... On this account, the moral inability that attends fixed habits, especially obtains the name of "inability."[13]
>
> It can't be truly said, according to the ordinary use of language, that a malicious man, let him never be so malicious, can't hold his hand from striking, or that he is not able to show his neighbour kindness... 'Tis improperly said, that a person can't perform those external

---

12. For further discussion see the exchange between Richard Muller and Paul Helm, Richard A. Muller, "Jonathan Edwards and the Absence of Free Choice: A Parting of the Ways in the Reformed Tradition?," *Jonathan Edwards Studies* 1, no. 1 (2011): 3–22; Paul Helm, "Jonathan Edwards and the Parting of the Ways?," *Jonathan Edwards Studies* 4, no. 1 (2014): 42–60; Richard A. Muller, "Necessity, Contingency and Freedom of Will: In Response to Paul Helm," *Jonathan Edwards Studies* 4, no. 3 (2014): 266–285; Paul Helm, "Turretin and Edwards Once More," *Jonathan Edwards Studies* 4, no. 3. (2014): 286–96; Paul Helm, "Francis Turretin and Jonathan Edwards on Contingency and Necessity," in *Learning from the Past: Essays on Reception, Catholicity and Dialogue in Honour of Anthony N. S. Lane*, ed. Jon Balserak and Richard Snoddy (London: Bloomsbury T&T Clark, 2015), 163–78; and especially Muller, *Divine Will and Human Choice*, 322–24.

13. Edwards, *Freedom of the Will*, 161.

actions, which are dependent on the act of the will, and which would be easily performed, if the act of the will were present.[14]

So there are general and habitual moral inabilities and particular inabilities. And it is perfectly consistent that there is a change between abilities at one time and abilities at another time. Edwards thinks that a natural ability is ability in its proper sense and that moral inabilities are secondary, because it is consistent that a malicious man, for example, can stop himself striking another. In contrast, a legless man is quite unable to walk unaidedly. In the case of moral inability, it is the very will that is necessary and sufficient to do the act. In moral inability, nothing is lacking but the will. Edwards says in that case, echoing Augustine, nothing is wanting but the will. But such wants or lacks may exist in various degrees. Here the views of at least some Reformed orthodox clearly coincide.

The Faculties

The soul possesses the faculties of understanding and will. But these are not two faculties in the old scholastic sense, but rather powers of the soul or of the "heart." It is here that Edwards's turn away from scholasticism is most self-aware, as he followed what Locke had said in his *Essay*:

> God has indued the soul with two faculties, one is that by which it is capable of perception and speculation, or by which it discerns and views and judges of things; which is called the understanding. The other faculty is that by which the soul does not merely perceive and view things, but is some way inclined with respect to the things it views or considers; either is inclined to 'em, or is disinclined, and averse from 'em; or is the faculty by which the soul does not behold things, as an indifferent unaffected spectator, but either as liking or disliking, pleased or displeased, approving or rejecting. This faculty is called by various names: it is sometimes called the *inclination*: and, as it has respect to the actions that are determined and governed by it, is called the *will*: and the *mind*, with regard to the exercises of this faculty, is often called the *heart*.
>
> The exercises of this faculty [the mind] are of two sorts; either those by which the soul is carried out toward things that are in view, in approving of them, being pleased with them, and inclined to them;

---

14. Edwards, *Freedom of the Will*, 162.

or those in which the soul opposes the things that are in view, in disapproving them, and in being displeased with them, averse from them, and rejecting them.[15]

This is elaborated in *Freedom of the Will*, where it is made explicit that Locke was a strong influence. Here is a flavor of this, from part 1, section 1, "Concerning the Nature of the Will." Edwards says that the will is the power of the choice, "that by which the mind chooses or refuses."[16] It is that faculty or power or principle of mind "by which it [the mind] is capable of choosing anything."[17] Refusing is the making of a choice not to have such and such an alternative. Edwards continues, "So that whatever names we call the act of the will by—choosing, refusing, approving, disapproving, liking, disliking, embracing, rejecting, determining, commanding, forbidding, liking, disliking, embracing, rejecting, determining, directing, commanding, forbidding, inclining to or being averse, a being pleased with or displeased with—all may be reduced to this of choosing."[18] What is more, Edwards's hero Locke thinks the same: "The will signifies nothing but a power or ability to prefer or choose."[19] Edwards then offers corrections and tidyings-up of Locke's wording as they occur in his efforts to distinguish between "desire" and "will."[20]

I suppose that here Edwards has chiefly in view what the Reformed orthodox, following a venerable tradition, called the practical reason. However, he does not use the language of either the theoretical or practical reason any more than he distinguishes *contrary* choice from *contradictory* choice. He does use the word "faculty," but (he says) power or principle of mind or inclination would do as well. But he does align the language of choice with the desirable or the good, as the Reformed orthodox also did. "But so much I think may be determined in general without room for controversy, that whatever is perceived or apprehended by an intelligent and voluntary agent which has the nature and influence of a motive to volition or choice,

---

15. Edwards, *Religious Affections*, 96. For comparison, see Locke's chapter "Of Power" in *Essay*, II.xxi (II.193–238).

16. Edwards, *Freedom of the Will*, 137.

17. Edwards, *Freedom of the Will*, 137.

18. Edwards, *Freedom of the Will*, 137.

19. Locke, *Essay*, II.xxi.17 (I.200).

20. For further discussion of Locke's rejection of faculty psychology, see appendix B.

is considered or viewed *as good*; nor has it any tendency to invite or engage the election of the soul in any further degree than it appears such."[21]

Richard Muller says that Edwards "neglects" formal and final causes in his account of causation, abandoning the scholastic understanding of action in terms of fourfold causation—material, efficient, formal, and final. Thus, Muller thinks that this had serious consequences for Edwards's view of freedom.[22] But Edwards can be thought of as providing answers in terms of his own to the four "why" questions posed by the four scholastic terms. For although he does not use the scholastic terms, Edwards repeatedly refers to the *motives* or *preferences* of the mind (efficient causes); what the preferences are, for example, for taking the right hand rather than the left hand turn in the road (material causes); the *ends* or *purposes* of action (final causes); and to *apprehensions*, a way of referring to formal causes.[23]

Edwards's choice of terms may signal his preference for less formal language, while his neglect of other terms may signal his dissatisfaction with the language of scholasticism and with all terms that are as "void of distinct and consistent meaning [as found] in the writings of Duns Scotus, or Thomas Aquinas."[24] Consistent with this view, he pares down the variety of terms used in argument. And he has a set of parallel locutions of his own where he believes their use to be justified. These cover much of the same ground as the scholastic distinctions.

As noted, Edwards favors a unitary view of the mind, as he makes clear when he appropriates Locke's language. This is a view of the mind or self as consisting of modes, similar to what de Moor described, rather than as consisting of part-like faculties, which may be said to be the tendency of the scholastics earlier than de Moor. In this also Edwards is following Locke, who presents a sustained polemic both against the idea of faculties as such as well as ridiculing the possibility of multiplying them. His discussion has one important consequence for the discussion of free will, Edwards's topic. Locke says:

---

21. Edwards, *Freedom of the Will*, 142.

22. Richard A. Muller, "Jonathan Edwards and Francis Turretin on Necessity, Contingency and Freedom of Will: In Response to Paul Helm," *Jonathan Edwards Studies* 4, no. 3 (2014): 272. See also Helm, "Turretin and Edwards Once More."

23. See, for example, Edwards, *Freedom of the Will*, 141–48.

24. Edwards, *Freedom of the Will*, 228.

I leave it to be considered whether it may not help to put an end to that long agitated and, I think, unreasonable, because unintelligible, question, viz. *whether a man's will be free or no*. For if I mistake not, it follows from what I have said that the question itself is altogether improper, and it is as insignificant to ask, whether man's *will* be free, as to ask whether his sleep is swift, or his virtue square: *liberty* being as little applicable to the will, as swiftness of motion is to sleep, or squareness to virtue; and when anyone well considers it, I think he will plainly perceive that liberty, which is but a power, belongs only to agents and cannot be an attribute or modification of the will, which is also but a power.[25]

Edwards shows that he had learned this lesson. For example, in part 1, section 5, of the *Freedom of the Will*, he writes, "For the will itself is not an agent that has a will: the power of choosing, itself, has not a power of choosing. That which has a power of volition or choice is the man or the soul, and not the power of volition itself."[26] And again in part 2, section 1: "I shall not insist on the great impropriety of such questions [of whether the will itself determines all the free acts of the will]; because actions are to be ascribed to agents, and not properly to the powers of agents; which improper way of speaking leads to many mistakes, and much confusion, as Mr Locke observes."[27]

Edwards does not cite any passage from Locke, but expresses the same attitude as Locke more than once: "For the will is not itself an agent that has a will: the power of choosing, itself, has not a power of choosing. That which has the power of volition or choice is the man or the soul, and not the power of choosing. That which has the power of volition or choice is the man or soul, and not the power of volition itself."[28] It is true that Edwards

---

25. Locke, *Essay*, II.xxi.14 (I.199).

26. Edwards, *Freedom of the Will*, 163.

27. Edwards, *Freedom of the Will*, 171. He says nothing about Locke's making fun of the phrase "free will," though it is clear he would concur. When Locke later on, in the *Essay*, IV.xvii, has an extended critique of syllogistic reasoning, which was intrinsic to the scholastic *disputatio*, it looks as if Edwards learned this lesson too. There are many arguments in the *Freedom of the Will* that could be presented syllogistically, but not once does he venture to do so.

28. Edwards, *Freedom of the Will*, 163. To stress the influence of Locke's idea that freedom is a property of the man, not the will, on Edwards's anthropology is not to say that otherwise Edwards would have been opposed to the idea. His fellow New Englander Samuel Willard maintained "that *not the understanding, nor the will in the man, but the whole man is a free*

continues to refer to the "powers" or "faculties" of the soul, but always as powers of the soul, never as the will as a distinct faculty within the soul.

The power of understanding and will are ordered. With the scholastics, both Locke and Edwards assign priority to the understanding. So the powers of the soul, modalities, are not symmetrical, since one is subordinate to the other, serving it. In the second edition of the *Understanding* and subsequently, Locke substituted sections 28–62 for 28–38. The new insertions contained claims about the suspension of the judgment that Edwards opposed.

Locke was known by one or two later Reformed orthodox writers. We noted that de Moor knew of Locke, though there is no evidence of influence. But the Scottish Reformed orthodox theologian Thomas Halyburton (1672–1712) read Locke, and it is fair to say that he had a mixed view of him, criticizing him over his views of the grounding of the divine authority of Scripture.[29]

Isaac Watts (1674–1748) is chiefly remembered for his hymns, but he was a significant influence in eighteenth-century English Dissenting theology. He was educated in Newington Dissenting Academy. His writings illustrate how Locke influenced the Reformed theological tradition in more than one way, being both a latitudinizing influence on English Dissent and (with such as Edwards) a theologically conservative force. Watts published *An Essay on the Freedom of Will in God and in Creatures* in 1732 and *Philosophical Essays on Various Subjects* in 1733. Edwards quotes some of the first book but does not mention Watts as the author. There may be various reasons for this.[30] This is what Watts says:

> There are many instances, wherein the will is determined neither by present uneasiness, nor by the greatest apparent good, nor by the last dictate of the understanding, nor by anything else, but merely by itself, as a sovereign self-determining power of the soul; and that the soul does not will this or that action, in some cases, by any other

---

cause." A Brief Reply to Mr George Kieth (Boston: Phillips, 1703), 15. Perhaps Locke's idea fell on already prepared ground.

29. Paul Helm, "Thomas Halyburton and John Locke on the Grounding of Faith in Scripture," in *Reformed Orthodoxy in Scotland*, ed. Aaron Clay Denlinger (London: Bloomsbury Academic, 2015).

30. For suggestions about this anonymity, see the editor's comments in his introduction to the Yale edition of *The Freedom of the Will.*

influence, but because it will. Thus (says he) I can turn my face to the south or the north; I can point with my finger upward, or downward. And thus, in some cases, the will determines itself in a very sovereign manner, because it will: and hereby it discovers its own perfect power of choice, riding from within itself, and free from all influence or restraint of any kind.[31]

The style is similar to Edwards's and the conceptuality Lockean, but the view of the distinctions between the faculties is that of a scholastic. Watts does not take from Locke what Edwards took, and the claim that Watts makes about the will determining itself is clean contrary to Edwards's own position, as he proceeds to show.[32]

In earlier chapters, we have seen that in their discussion of human freedom, Christian scholastics were polarized between the liberty of rational spontaneity and the liberty of indifference, the liberty of indifference being championed by the Jesuits and the Arminians.

The Affections

In his *Religious Affections*, Edwards is also influenced by Locke's *Essay* in various important ways. In this treatise, the earliest of his three foremost philosophical and theological works (1746), Edwards is more deferential to the Englishman. At the same time, he never mentions Locke by name nor does he quote his words verbatim. Nevertheless, Locke's influence is pervasingly present, as we will see.

Edwards's silence on Locke has led scholars to conclude that the influence of Locke was altogether absent. The editor of the Yale edition of *The Religious Affections*, the late John E. Smith, in his lengthy introduction to the work, only briefly refers to Locke. Why did Edwards avoid making explicit reference to his mentor? A possible answer is that *The Religious Affections* was for domestic consumption, principally for the churches of New England, and it is likely that its author decided that it would be unwise to advertise the identity of John Locke, a broad church Anglican Arminian, on whom he was in fact relying.

---

31. Isaac Watts, *An Essay on the Freedom of Will in God and in Creatures and on Various Subjects connected therewith* (London, J. Roberts, 1732), 25, 26–27.

32. Edwards, *Freedom of the Will*, 196.

The *Affections* was written within the parameters of the Lockean view of the relation between reason and revelation, together with his strictures on "enthusiasm."[33] But Locke's influence went much farther. On a key theme, the character and influence of the affections, Edwards paraphrases Locke extensively, and Locke's influence is certainly as great here as in the better-known references in Edwards's book on the will.

Edwards's Ally, John Locke

When Edwards is characterizing the supernatural character of the Holy Spirit's regenerating work on the soul, he describes it as imparting "what some metaphysicians call a new simple idea" in the mind of the recipient.[34] This is the passage referred to by Smith.[35] "Simple idea" was Locke's term of art for "the materials of all our knowledge."[36] Uninterpreted touches and tastes, for example, are instances of simple ideas. Some have embellished this connection between Locke and Edwards, myself included.[37] According to Edwards, regeneration is the imparting of a new spiritual or supernatural sense, receiving a new simple idea, exercising a sixth sense; and the terminology is clearly Locke's, though very similar language can be found in a Puritan such as Owen.

Edwards, Locke, and Enthusiasm

In *The Religious Affections*, Edwards ratifies Locke's outlook as expressed in the latter's chapter "Of Enthusiasm." This chapter is situated toward the end of book IV of the *Essay*, entitled "Of Knowledge and Opinion," coming immediately after chapter 18, "Of Faith and Reason, and Their Distinct Provinces." It supplements Locke's views in that chapter. His general position on faith and reason is that faith must be "reasonable," that is, it must

---

33. To be found in *An Essay Concerning Human Understanding*, book IV.xviii, "Of faith and reason, and their distinct provinces"; and book IV.xix, "Of Enthusiasm." The second of these was added in the fourth edition (1700).

34. Edwards, *Religious Affections*, 205.

35. John E. Smith, introduction to *Religious Affections*, 2:52.

36. Locke, *Essay*, II.II, "Of Simple Ideas" (I.52).

37. Paul Helm, "John Locke and Jonathan Edwards, a Reconsideration," *Journal of the History of Philosophy* 7, no. 1 (1969): 51–61.

pass the tests of "reasonableness."[38] For example, Scripture is authoritative because the words of prophets, Christ, and His apostles were validated by miracles; and Locke is generally suspicious of claims to have "immediate revelation" from God and advises against placing one's faith in such "enthusiasm." This idea of epistemic tests is prominent in Locke's account of the authority of Scripture. Nonetheless, in the course of opposing enthusiasm in these ways, Locke makes comments in the direction of endorsing the idea of an immediate work of the Spirit, which Edwards appropriated, while he kept within the broad boundaries of what Locke regarded as reasonable.

Here are some of the claims that Locke makes. The enthusiasts behave as follows: "Whatsoever odd action they find in themselves a strong inclination to do, that impulse is concluded to be a call or direction from heaven and must be obeyed."[39] Enthusiasm lays both reason and revelation to one side and "substitutes in the room of them the ungrounded fancies of a man's own brain, and assumes them for a foundation both of opinion and conduct."[40] By contrast Locke writes, "*Revelation*, is natural *reason* enlarged by a new set of discoveries communicated by GOD immediately, which *reason* vouches for the truth of, by the testimony and proofs it gives that they come from God."[41] And further: "So that he that takes away *reason*, to make way for *revelation*, puts out the light of both."[42]

> The question then here is: How do I know that GOD is the revealer of this to me, that this impression is made upon my mind by the Holy Spirit, and therefore I ought to obey it?[43]
>
> If they say that they know it to be true because it is a *revelation* from God, the reason is good; but then it will be demanded how they know it to be a revelation from God. If they say by the light it brings with it, which shines bright in their minds and they cannot resist, I beseech them to consider whether this be any more than what we

---

38. Paul Helm, "Locke on Faith and Knowledge," *Philosophical Quarterly* 23, no. 90 (1973): 52–66. The title of one of Locke's books was *The Reasonableness of Christianity* (1695).

39. Locke, *Essay*, IV.XIX.6 (II.290).

40. Locke, *Essay*, IV.XIX.3 (II.289).

41. Locke, *Essay*, IV.XIX.4 (II.289).

42. Locke, *Essay*, IV.XIX.4 (II.289).

43. Locke, *Essay*, IV.XIX.10 (II.292).

have taken notice of already, viz. That it is a revelation because they strongly believe it to be true.[44]

The strength of our persuasions are no evidence at all of their own rectitude: crooked things may be as stiff and inflexible as straight, and men may be as positive and peremptory in error as in truth.[45]

Light, true light, in the mind is, or can be, nothing else but the evidence of the truth of any proposition; and if it be not a self-evident proposition, all the light it has or can have is from the clearness and validity of those proofs upon which it is received.... For if strength of persuasion be the light which must guide us, I ask how shall anyone distinguish between the delusions of Satan and the inspirations of the Holy Ghost? He can transform himself into an angel of light.[46]

God when he makes the prophet does not unmake the man. He leaves all his faculties in their natural state, to enable him to judge of his inspirations, whether they be of divine original or no. When he illuminates the mind with supernatural light, he does not extinguish that which is natural.[47]

If this internal light, or any proposition which under that title we take for inspired, be conformable to the principles of reason or to the word of God, which is attested revelation, *reason* warrants it and we may safely receive for true and be guided by it in our belief and actions.[48]

So much on the negative side of things, on what does not count as reasonable faith. But holy prophets of old who had revelations from God were in a better position. Locke writes, "Thus we see the holy men of old, who have *revelations* from GOD, had something else besides that internal light of assurance in their own minds to testify to them that it was from GOD. They were not left to their own persuasions alone that those persuasions were from GOD, but had outward signs to convince them of the author of those revelations."[49]

And here is what might be called, somewhat anachronistically, a concession in the direction of Edwards. Locke continues: "In what I have said

44. Locke, *Essay*, IV.XIX.11 (II.293).
45. Locke, *Essay*, IV.XIX.11 (II.293).
46. Locke, *Essay*, IV.XIX.13 (II.294).
47. Locke, *Essay*, IV.XIX.14 (II.295).
48. Locke, *Essay*, IV.XIX.15 (II.295).
49. Locke, *Essay*, IV.XIX.15 (II.295).

I am far from denying that GOD can or doth sometimes enlighten men's minds in the apprehending of certain truths, or excite them to good actions by the immediate influence and assistance of the Holy Spirit, without any extraordinary signs accompanying it. But in such cases too we have reason and the Scripture, unerring rules to know whether it be from GOD or no."[50]

These extracts will be sufficient, I hope, to get Locke's drift in his own words. Note the framework of reason and revelation; the opposition to "enthusiasm"; the references to the terminology of "internal light" and "supernatural light," familiar to readers of *Religious Affections*—at least by the time they reach part III; above all the method of testing claims to be imbued with the Spirit of God in the light of certain criteria, those provided by reason and revelation. The idea of tests or signs is central to *Religious Affections*.

Edwards, Emotion, and Pleasure

So to a large extent Edwards agrees with Locke on reason and revelation, even though their particular judgments about what is reasonable or unreasonable in religion may differ. He also makes the most of Locke's "concession" in the direction of the particular views he holds. His references to a new inward perception, etc.,[51] are in accord with Locke's recognition that God "doth sometimes enlighten men's minds in the apprehending of certain truths...by the immediate influence and assistance of the Holy Spirit, without any extraordinary signs accompanying it."[52] And Edwards broadens Locke's tests to include moral and spiritual fruit. No doubt, theologically speaking, Edwards offered a "puritanized" version of Locke by his more developed appreciation of the connectedness of word and Spirit, which is such a feature of *Religious Affections*.

It is not being argued here that the very fact of the use of tests for the reasonableness of certain phenomena is sufficient to show that Edwards was the follower of Locke and of no one else. Setting up such tests was a part of Puritan practical theology. Edwards has a good example in the case of Thomas Shepard's *Parable of the Ten Virgins*. And it may be that Locke

---

50. Locke, *Essay*, IV.XIX.16 (II.296).

51. Edwards, *Religious Affections*, 205.

52. Locke, *Essay*, IV.XIX.16 (II.296).

gets his own fondness for his tests via English Puritanism. Nevertheless, Edwards follows Locke in respect of reason and revelation.

Edwards's doctrine of the "new sense" as given to us in the *Religious Affections* deliberately meets the Lockean arguments. It is an immediate, supernatural intuition from God, not from man, validated by the reason as such. Locke thinks that such experiences are legitimate, provided that they are subordinated to and informed by revelation. Edwards provides the tests, appealing to reason[53] and revelation to do so, in (as we have seen) a broadly Lockean fashion. For Edwards, Lockean "enthusiasm" is not "spiritual." He dismisses the idea of new revelations and the acquisition of new faculties.[54] No doubt Locke would have regarded the various agitations of the body that Edwards condoned or encouraged—such as those that his wife, Sarah, related to him—as rather unbecoming and even somewhat embarrassing; but he could hardly have argued that in and of themselves they had significant negative epistemological value. But more on Locke's view on bodily agitations is to follow. In any case, as we know, in the main Edwards thought that such agitations were neither here nor there as far as providing evidence of a genuine work of the Holy Spirit.

Working within the Lockean Framework

Let us now see how Edwards works within this Lockean outlook on reason, revelation, and enthusiasm. In part I of *Religious Affections*, there are references to the Lockean view of human nature, particularly Edwards's stress on the unity of the self, which indicates his inclination to dismiss the faculty psychology of his medieval and Reformed orthodox antecedents.

The affections are central to the book, of course. Despite Edwards's Puritan background, the account he gives of an affection was largely the result of direct Lockean influence. Before the long chapter 21 of book II, "Of Power," in Locke's *Essay Concerning Human Understanding*, which Edwards used overtly in his account of human action in *Freedom of the Will*, Locke placed a shorter discussion, chapter 20, "Of Modes of Pleasure and Pain." I will try to display the similarity if not the identity of their views, first by quoting Locke verbatim, and then Edwards.[55] First Locke:

---

53. Edwards, *Religious Affections*, 132.

54. Edwards, *Religious Affections*, 210.

55. Locke's *Essay*, first published in 1689, went through five editions in his lifetime.

1. Amongst the simple *ideas* which we receive both from *sensation* and *reflection, pain* and *pleasure* are two very considerable ones. For as in the body there is sensation barely in itself, or accompanied by *pain* or *pleasure*, so the thought or perception of the mind is simply so, or else accompanied also with *pleasure* and *pain*, delight or trouble, call it how you please. These, like other simple *ideas*, cannot be described, nor their names defined; the way of knowing them is, as of the simple ideas of the senses, only by experience....

2. Things then are good and evil, only in reference to pleasure or pain. That we call good, which is *apt to cause or increase pleasure, or diminish pain in us; or else to procure or preserve us the possession of any other good or absence of any evil.* And, on the contrary, we name that *evil which is apt to produce or increase any pain, or diminish any pleasure in us: or else to procure us any evil, or deprive us of any good.* By pleasure and pain, I must be understood to mean of body or mind, as they are commonly distinguished; though in truth they be only different constitutions of the mind, sometimes occasioned by disorder in the body, sometimes of thoughts in the mind.

3. *Pleasure* and *pain* and that which causes them, good and evil, are the hinges on which our *passions* turn.[56]

Locke then goes on to illustrate this by reference to the affections of love, hatred, and others.

Toward the end of the chapter, Locke makes some remarks on the effects that pleasure and pain may have on the body: "The passions too

---

Edwards is reckoned to have first read the book around 1717. Marsden, *Jonathan Edwards*, 62. The fourth edition of the *Essay* (1700) contained, among other new material, the chapter "Of Enthusiasm," which was retained in the fifth (1706) and subsequent editions. Locke died in 1704. A question is, Was the version of the *Essay* that Edwards read the one that lacked the chapter "Of Enthusiasm," or did he read the fourth or fifth edition? As a student Edwards had access at Yale to the 1690 London edition of Locke's *Essay*, for as we have seen, it was included in the Dummer collection. See Louise May Bryant and Mary Patterson, "The List of Books Sent by Jeremiah Dummer," in *Papers in Honor of Andrew Keogh, Librarian of Yale University, by the Staff of the Library, 30 June 1938* (New Haven, Conn.: privately printed, 1938), 435. More importantly, however, Edwards purchased and used the two-volume seventh edition of the *Essay* (London, 1716). It is listed in his "Account Book" (a register of books that he owned and lent to others). See the Yale edition of Edwards's *Works*, 26:337–38. (I am grateful to Doug Sweeney for this information.) Currently, the most direct route to the seventh edition is the identical fifth edition (1706), 2 vol., ed. John. W. Yolton (London: Dent, Everyman's Library, 1961).

56. Locke, *Essay*, II.XX (I.189). All the italicizations are in the original.

have most of them, in most persons, operations on the body, and cause various changes in it; which, not being always sensible, do not make a necessary part of the *idea* of each passion. For *shame*, which is an uneasiness of the mind upon the thought of having done something which is indecent or will lessen the valued esteem which others have for us, has not always blushing accompanying it."[57]

Locke is claiming the following. First, the ideas of pleasure and pain are important simple ideas—that is, ideas that we cannot understand by their being described, but only by direct experience. Locke is here making a major claim about the philosophical psychology of human action, that actions of aversion are driven by the prospect of pain, and of propensity by the prospect of pleasure. So, secondly, we call that good which is apt to cause pleasure, or to cause its increase. We call that evil which is apt to diminish pleasure or directly cause pain. Pleasures or pains embrace both bodily and mental states of affairs and are the hinges of our action. Thirdly, the prospect of such pains and pleasures are what produce passions such as love and hatred, including both our love of both inanimate and animate things. So pleasure and pain are the motivators of our actions. Fourthly, Locke argues that passions may have effects on the body, and usually do, though not necessarily.

Now we turn to Edwards:

There are some exercises of pleasedness or displeasedness, inclination and disinclination, wherein the soul is carried but a little beyond a state of perfect indifference. And there are other degrees above this, wherein the approbation or dislike, pleasedness or aversion, are stronger; wherein we may rise higher and higher, till the soul comes to act vigorously and sensibly, and the actings of the soul are with that strength that (through the laws of the union which the Creator has fixed between soul and body), the motion of the blood and animal spirits begins to be sensibly altered; whence oftentimes arises some bodily sensation, especially about the heart and vitals, that are the fountain of the fluids of the body; from whence it comes to pass, that the mind, with regard to the exercises of this faculty, perhaps in all nations and ages, is called the *heart*. And it is to be noted, that they

---

57. Locke, *Essay*, II.XX.17 (I.192).

are these more vigorous and sensible exercises outlook, that pleasure and pain.[58]

And later on in the book, Edwards continues, "Nor on the other hand, do I know of any rule any have to determine, that gracious and holy affections, when raised as high as any natural affections, and have equally strong and vigorous exercises, can't have a great effect on the body.... No such rule can be drawn from reason.... None has ever been found in all the late controversies which have been about things of this nature."[59]

Though, as we have seen, Edwards used the Lockean expression "simple idea" later on in *Religious Affections*, he does not do so here. Nevertheless, the Lockean outlook is clearly present. The inclinations of the will are of two sorts: either those which the soul is drawn to some goal, or those which the soul has an aversion to and is disinclined to move toward them. And secondly, when these inclinations reach a certain strength, they give rise to affections and even bodily agitations.

So for both Locke and Edwards, the understanding judges what is good or evil by whether the basic ideas of sensation and reflection, their "simple ideas," are pleasurable or painful. If they are pleasurable, they are good; if painful, evil. That is, of course, good or evil in the estimate of the one who has them. So our passions/emotions are moved by beliefs about the goodness or evil of states of affairs, arising from whether our sensations and reflections are painful or pleasurable. And so our various affections/emotions—love, hatred, and so on—are characterized by distinctive kinds of pleasure and pain. Edwards puts essentially this same point in terms of degrees of pleasedness or displeasedness and notes that these positive and negative qualities have degrees and that the "more vigorous and sensible exercises of this faculty...are called the *affections*."[60] And these affections might be so strong as to affect our bodies.

Finally, these mechanisms, "hinges" as Locke calls them, which Edwards refers to as the "springs" of action, have fundamental effects in our lives.[61] Here's Locke once again: "The uneasiness a man finds in him-

---

58. Edwards, *Religious Affections*, 96.

59. Edwards, *Religious Affections*, 132.

60. Edwards, *Religious Affections*, 97.

61. In discussions such as those of Locke and Edwards, we see the beginnings of modern utilitarianism, as in Jeremy Bentham: "Nature has placed mankind under the governance of

self upon the absence of anything whose present enjoyment carries the *idea* of delight with it is that we call *desire*; which is greater or less, as that uneasiness is more or less vehement. Where, by the by, it may perhaps be of some use to remark that the chief, if not only spur to human industry and action is uneasiness."[62] These words of Locke are taken up by Edwards. Here Edwards is one last time:

> Such is man's nature, that he is very inactive, any otherwise than he is influenced by some affections, either love or hatred, desire, hope, fear or some other. These affections we see to be the springs that set men agoing, in all the affairs of life, and engage them in all their pursuits; these are the things that put men forward, and carry 'em along, in all their worldly business, and especially are men excited and animated by these, in all affairs, wherein they are earnestly engaged, and which they pursue with vigor.[63]

Why do we spring out of bed in the morning? What sets us "agoing"? The answer of Locke and Edwards is, the prospect of the greater pleasures of the body or the mind (or both) being enjoyed by getting up or of pains being averted, than those pleasures to be enjoyed or pains to be averted by staying in bed—even though getting up, considered by itself, may not be very pleasurable. So when Edwards says that "true religion, in great part, consists in holy affections," the doctrine he infers from 1 Peter 1:8, "Whom having not seen you love. Though now you do not see Him, yet believing, you rejoice with joy inexpressible and full of glory," he intends to show the front and central place of the affections in energizing "true religion."[64] "Joy inexpressible" is in Edwards's estimate joy to a high degree, perhaps to the highest degree humanly possible, an exalted pleasurable affection arising from faith in the exalted Savior. And if these affections are strong enough, they will result in effects on our bodies. So not surprisingly Edwards says that such affections are the "springs" of our actions, as Locke had called

---

two sovereign masters, *pain* and *pleasure.*" *Introduction to Principles of Morals and Legislation* (London: T Payne, 1789). But while pleasure of a certain kind might be signs of the moral goodness or badness of an action, Edwards no more than Locke claims that moral goodness *consists in* having sensations of pleasure, or in the maximizing of them.

62. Locke, *Essay*, II.XX.6 (I.190–91).

63. Edwards, *Religious Affections*, 101.

64. Edwards, *Religious Affections*, 96.

them "hinges."[65] So the prospect of pleasure and of pain is at the heart of Edwards's account of action, as they were also for Locke.

Edwards and Practical Reason

One might wonder if these Locke-induced changes in Edwards's outlook were simply skin-deep, a verbal variant of the theological anthropology of Puritanism that he inherited. But to note how different the approaches of these theological forebears were, I will briefly sketch how different Edwards's way of thinking of things looks from first, the Westminster divine Edward Reynolds, and then one whom Edwards endorses or quotes with approval in his footnotes, Owen, who once had a student named Locke. Both Reynolds and Owen had a different way of thinking of the soul and a different estimate of the affections, a different sensibility, than Edwards came to have through Locke's influence.

As we have seen, like Edwards, they thought of the affections as being connected with the will, but the important thing for the Puritans and others is that reason (or the understanding)—in this case the practical reason— should *moderate* the operation of the passions. For it is what we or others do or intend to do or forbear from doing, or which unexpectedly happens to us or others, that brings about affections. Incidentally, Edwards says that affection is "more extensive than passion; being used for all vigorous lively actings of the will or inclination; but passion for those that are more sudden, and whose effects on the animal spirits are more violent, and the mind more overpowered and less in its own command."[66] This is one of the few places where Edwards appears to echo the distinction between affection and passion made by the Puritans and Reformed orthodox in terms of whether or not these phenomena were subject to the control of the practical reason.

This is because for the Puritans and Reformed orthodox, following Aquinas, the faculty of reason or understanding has primacy, whether this is the contemplative or theoretical reason, having to do with the acquisition of truth, or the practical reason, having to do with the choice of ends and with the ways to achieve them. In this tradition—for Reynolds and Owen, and the Reformed orthodox more generally—affections and passions are subrational forces and are to be moderated by the reason.

---

65. Edwards, *Religious Affections*, 100–101.
66. Edwards, *Religious Affections*, 98.

So Reynolds, in his work on the passions and faculties of the soul, has much to say about this both in human behavior generally and in the business of Christian sanctification, while not denying the place of affection and passion in the soul.[67] He writes, "So the agitations of passions, so long as they serve only to drive forward, but not to drown virtue,—as long as they keep their dependence on reason, and run in that channel wherewith they are thereby bounded,—are of excellent service in all the travel of man's life; and such as without which the growth, success, and despatch of virtue would be much impaired."[68] Nevertheless, he continues, "there is in man, by reason of his general corruption, such a distemper wrought, that there is not only crookedness in, but dissension also, and fighting, between his parts…whereby passion, reigning in the lower parts, and being impatient altogether of resistance or control, laboureth to muffle reason, and to obliterate those principles and original truths, whereby their unruliness might be restrained."[69] Note the primacy of reason in this account.

And Owen: As in general the affections and passions should be under the control of the reason, so in mortification

> our love, desire, and delight, will produce a moderation of passions about them, as fear, anger, sorrow and the like; such will men be stirred up unto in these changes, losses, crosses, which these things are subject unto.… When the mind is weaned from the world, and the things of it, it will be sedate, quiet, composed, not easily moved with the occurrences and occasions of life: it is dead unto them, and in a great measure unconcerned in them. This is that "moderation" of mind wherein the apostle would have us excel. (Phil. iv. 5).[70]

Here the emphasis is on the composing of the affections and the setting of the heart on the things above.

The difference, then, is between the Puritan and Reformed orthodox view that affections are a consequence of the will, which is to be subordinated to the reason or understanding, and the Lockean and Edwardsean view that the pivotal sensations, pleasure and pain, are the movers of the

---

67. Reynolds, *Treatise on the Passions and Faculties of the Soul*, in *Works*, vol. 6, ch. 6.

68. Reynolds, *Treatise on the Passions and Faculties of the Soul*, in *Works*, 6:47.

69. Reynolds, *Treatise on the Passions and Faculties of the Soul*, in *Works*, 6:50.

70. John Owen, *Evidences of the Faith of God's Elect*, in *The Works of John Owen*, ed. W. H. Goold (Edinburgh: Banner of Truth, 1966), 5:448–49.

will, the springs or hinges of all action. The idea of their correction by reason is almost entirely absent. But of course given Edwards's more unitary view of the self, the understanding and the affections must be closely identified. Both views, the Puritan and the Edwardsean, hold that the actions are executed *sub specie boni.* But for Locke and Edwards, that goodness is pleasure or the lessening of pain. For the Puritans, it may be various—for example, following a sense of duty or the dictates of conscience because you believe it is the voice of God, or that the action—for example, viewing a painting or singing a song, pleasing you and not myself, putting out the trash—are goods in themselves, or a necessity. That's another story, worth narrating in detail. But without such further explanation, the differences can still be made out starkly.

Personal Identity

Finally, we will glance at Edwards's endorsement of Locke's theory of personal identity in his last great work, that on *Original Sin* (1757), a book that was intended by Edwards to go beyond the churches of New England to Europe, to the fashionable Deists, whose tenets were, in Edwards's view, the root cause of those theological ills that were besetting New England. The book was intended as a blow at the root of these tenets, and Edwards was happy to use Locke explicitly and overtly in his project. For the Deists thought of Locke as *their* ally, but Edwards didn't agree. Locke was *his* ally.

Locke's view of personal identity was molded by his forensic interest in the person. He was concerned with "that consciousness which draws reward or punishment with it." Because of this interest, his thought about the soul had to have a strong epistemological dimension. If a person is responsible for something that occurred in the past, then there must be a way or ways of tracing a line from his present to his past. For Locke, that line was traced by memory. Memory is the criterion of personal identity in this forensic sense. In precisely what sense the employment of memory in these ways so as to secure, as Locke thought, the forensic connection presupposes the soul in some other, deeper sense is a further interesting question.[71] But this issue is not of direct interest to us now any more than it was to Locke. He writes:

---

71. Paul Helm, "Locke's Theory of Personal Identity," *Philosophy* 54, no. 208 (1979): 173–85.

To find wherein *personal identity* consists, we must consider what *person* stands for; which, I think, is a thinking intelligent being that has reason and reflection and can consider itself as itself, the same thinking thing in different times and places; which it does only by that consciousness which is inseparable from thinking and, as it seems to me, essential to it: it being impossible for anyone to perceive without perceiving that he does perceive…. For since consciousness always accompanies thinking, and it is that that makes everyone to be what he calls *self*, and thereby distinguishes himself from all other thinking things: in this alone consists *personal identity*, i.e. the sameness of a rational being. And as far as this consciousness can be extended backwards to any past action or thought, so far reaches the identity of that *person*: it is the same *self* now it was then, and it is by the same *self* with this present one that now reflects on it, that that action was done.[72]

Locke's forensic interest in all this comes out plainly in words such as these:

In this *personal identity* is founded all the right and justice of reward and punishment: happiness and misery being that for which everyone is concerned for *himself*, not mattering what becomes of any substance not joined to or affected with that consciousness.[73]

But is not a man drunk and sober the same person? Why else is he punished for the act he commits when drunk, though he be never afterwards conscious of it? Just as much the same person as a man that was and does other things in his sleep is the same person as is answerable for any mischief he shall do in it. Human laws punish both, with a justice suitable to their way of knowledge; because, in these cases, they cannot distinguish certainly what is real, what counterfeit; and so ignorance in drunkenness or sleep is not admitted as a plea…. But in the Great Day, wherein the secrets of all hearts shall be laid open, it may be reasonable to think no one shall be made to answer for what he knows nothing of, but shall receive his doom, his conscience accusing or excusing him.[74]

For Locke, it would appear that the identity of the human soul through a period of time is compatible with considerable changes in consciousness,

---

72. Locke, *Essay*, II.XXVII.9 (II.280–81).

73. Locke, *Essay*, II.XXVII.18 (II.287).

74. Locke, *Essay*, II.XXVII.22 (II. 288–89).

just those changes which memory is capable of picking up. We know that a person is the same person as at some previous time if there is sameness of consciousness, like the behavior of cells in a growing tree. Locke explicitly draws the parallel: "Different substances, by the same consciousness (where they do partake in it) being united into one person, as well as different bodies by the same life are united into one animal, whose *identity* is preserved in that change of substances by the unity of one continued life."[75]

A person and a tree have a similar kind of identity, identity through change and continuity, losses as well as gains. In the sections prior to discussing personal identity, when he is concerned with the identity of living things such as trees, Locke seems at times to advocate an even stronger thesis. He appears to claim not merely that the continuous identity of a tree is compatible with great change in the physical composition and organization of the tree from seedling to sapling to mature tree, but that continuous identity *requires* there to be such changes. He writes:

> In the state of living creatures, their identity depends not on a mass of the same particles but on something else. For in them the variation of great parcels of matter alters not the identity: an oak growing from a plant to a great tree, and then lopped, is still the same oak; and a colt grown up to a horse.... Though in both these cases there may be a manifest change of the parts, so that truly they are not either of them the same masses of matter, though they be truly one of them the same oak, and the other the same horse. [76]

However, the key factor, as far as the telling of our particular story is concerned, is that for Locke awareness of personal identity through time is not awareness of something which has strict or absolute conditions of identity. Rather, it is the awareness of features of mental organization, compatible with and indeed requiring change over time. For what makes for the identity of living things across time is unity of organization, whether physical organization in the case of trees and animals, or mental organization in the case of persons.

For his argument in *The Great Christian Doctrine of Original Sin*, Edwards adopted these parts of Locke's anthropology that we have noted. Edwards writes:

---

75. Locke, *Essay*, II.XXVII.10 (I.281).

76. Locke, *Essay*, II.XXVII.3 (I.276).

Thus a tree, grown great, and an hundred years old, is one plant with the little sprout, that first came out of the ground, from whence it grew, and has been continued in constant succession; though it's now so exceeding diverse, many thousand times bigger, and of a very different form, and perhaps not one atom the very same.... So the body of man at forty years of age, is one with the infant body which first came into the world, from whence it grew; though now constituted of different substance, and the greater part of the substance probably changed scores (if not hundreds) of times.... And if we come even to the *personal identity* of created intelligent beings, though this be not allowed to consist wholly in what Mr Locke supposes, i.e. same consciousness; yet I think it cannot be denied, that this is one thing essential to it. But 'tis evident that the communication or continuance of the same consciousness and memory to any subject, through successive parts of duration depends wholly on a divine establishment.[77]

A little later on, Edwards refers to "created substance,"[78] and it is likely that this is the other essential factor for personal identity besides same consciousness. However, what Edwards takes from Locke is the idea that personal identity through time is not the unity of a simple and imperishable soul, but the unity of mental organization that the memory is aware of. Though Edwards does not say so, it is plausible to suppose that the target which (with Locke's help) he has in his sights is the idea of the natural indestructibility of the soul considered as a simple, indivisible substance, is the form of a human being. If the soul is naturally indestructible, then a soul existing at t_1 will exist at all subsequent times unless God annihilates it. For Edwards, this was precisely to view God's relation to the soul the wrong way round.

Let us suppose, for a moment, that personal identity through time was strict and not loose. That is, that A is a person if and only if A is a metaphysically simple individual, a soul, and A's identity from time to time consists solely in being that soul through that time. Any change that A undergoes as a soul is accidental to his being that soul, and hence to his being A. Then there is only one possible way for A's life to be temporally extended—namely, by his soul, the soul that he is, being extended. Such an

---

77. Jonathan Edwards, *The Great Christian Doctrine of Original Sin*, ed. Clyde A. Holbrook vol. 3, *The Works of Jonathan Edwards* (New Haven, Conn.: Yale University Press, 1970), 399.

78. Edwards, *Great Christian Doctrine of Original Sin*, 400.

extension of A's soul is necessary and sufficient for the extension of A. It is Locke's denial of such a thesis that seems to have so attracted Edwards.

So Edwards adopts the Lockean view. It is not all he has to say about the soul, however. For that self to continue through time, it has to be upheld by God from moment to moment, and, according to his doctrine in the *Great Christian Doctrine of Original Sin*, recreated by God *ex nihilo* from moment to moment.

Edwards's approach to the soul is very different from scholastics such as Voetius. He is less concerned with its essence, its substance, than with its observable properties indicative of change, as Locke was. This is what Edwards took from Locke. But the same sort of result could have been obtained by a hylomorphist probing of the consequences of the vegetative and sensory faculties, the will and the emotions. The interesting point is that by and large the significance of these changes as such, their implications for personal identity, fell outside the interest of the Reformed orthodox. These were manifestations of the soul, whereas Edwards, not going as far as to think of that substance as "something, I know not what" was less interested in the soul as an underlying, hidden substance than its being a Lockean person immediately upheld by God's power from moment to moment.

CHAPTER 9

The Last Word

I suggest that what we have been tasting and testing is a rich literary tradition in which the powers of human nature are opened up. The faculty psychology that was at the root of this endeavor persists in popular language until the present time. It is an excellent example in Reformed theology of the cooperation, or copartnership, of nature and grace, where nature is understood not as autonomous, secular nature but as created nature. Later Reformed suspicions of nature and grace, that it leads to a dichotomy of opposition between the two, do not stand scrutiny. Both nature and grace were regarded by Reformed orthodoxy as two gifts of the one Creator, who redeems what He created but is fallen. Grace depends on nature even as it renews it.

So for the Reformed philosophers of our period, there was no such dichotomy. And their faculty psychology was an expression of created nature, which Calvin did not spurn, even though he was more in the tradition of Christian Platonism. The Reformed orthodox, more consistently Aristotelian than Calvin, developed sophisticated analyses of human powers; and in their soteriology (not central in this book) they furthered our understanding of regeneration, for example. Catholic Christianity is not gnostic or docetic. And faith seeks understanding. In appropriating the scholastic tradition—in which many of them had been educated—for Christian theological purposes, the Reformed orthodox (including the Puritans) were not capitulating to paganism or to rationalism. This can be illustrated further by noting two features of their work.

One is that they clearly show that what they took from scholasticism is an array of conceptual distinctions, many of which we have seen at work. These distinctions were used to defend theological positions flowing from the New Testament. So, for example, they regimented the powers of the human soul as depicted in Scripture: the "heart," mind, will, memory, emotions, and so on. And these are found in a variety of causal relations—material, efficient, formal, and final.

The attitude of the Reformed orthodox to scholasticism was critical in the best sense. This can be seen in the second point: their careful adaptation of that tradition when the Scriptures required it. Aristotle had no notion of the conscience. But the New Testament clearly has. So Aquinas developed one. His proposal was accepted, but it led to some discussion of whether conscience was a separate faculty or an aspect of the understanding. More centrally, the Reformed scholastics took up different views, distinctively Christian positions, modifying scholasticism where necessary. Similarly, Aristotle had no conception of a resurrection, and so his hylomorphism was initially developed as an account with mortalist assumptions. But Aquinas not surprisingly developed an account of the soul which survived death but did so in an incomplete state because it became bodiless at death, awaiting the resurrection of the dead. So Aquinas introduced the idea of a *substantial unity* of soul and body. So the soul surviving death lacked its body and was incomplete without it, for in death it came to lack a substantial part, this anomaly being rectified in resurrection. This was explicitly adopted by Reformed scholastics such as the elder Voetius and others.

What this shows is that the doctrinal contours of Scripture, and particularly of the New Testament, were respected. When the data of revelation required it, they invariably trumped the original pagan outlook of Aristotle.

As for other philosophical influences in the seventeenth century and later that we have noted, in this book I have not taken sides over them. Whatever their influences, they did not have the effect of turning their adherents from faculty psychology entirely. For all Edwards's stress on the unity of the self, he continued to refer to the faculties and to their relations. His unified view of the self was in any case anticipated by earlier writers, such as his fellow New Englander Samuel Willard. In his admiration for Locke, Edwards came under the influence of an early, mild Enlightenment influence. He turned this to the support of the theology of Calvinism, something that Locke himself could not have envisaged. But there was a price to be paid for this. Siding with "Mr. Locke" made one emphasize epistemology to a greater degree than had the scholastics. We can see this in his treatment of personal identity. The extent of the influence of Locke on

Edwards is still a matter of debate, but we have seen in the previous chapter that it was considerable. In appendix A, we note that in the nineteenth century, Herman Bavinck, the leading theologian of Dutch Neo-Calvinism, rather surprisingly perhaps, followed the contours of scholasticism in outlining his view of human psychology.

Herman Bavinck's Psychology

If we think of the last phase of Reformed orthodoxy, considered as a continuous movement, to end with the death of Bernardinus de Moor, a professor of theology at Leiden, in 1780, then there is only a lifetime between that event and the birth of the distinguished Reformed dogmatician Herman Bavinck (1854–1921). By the time of Bavinck's birth, however, a very different theology affected the Reformed churches. Besides the full impact of Descartes and Spinoza, there was the effect on theology of the Copernican Revolution of Immanuel Kant, which changed the character of Christian theology, including that of Reformed theology, through Friedrich Schleiermacher and others. As a result, the University of Leiden to which Herman Bavinck went as a student (1870–1874) had a sharply different character from the Leiden of old, a liberally religious and theological agenda that was antipathetic to the old ways and which the young Bavinck found hard to stomach.

But Bavinck's mature theology harkened back to that of Reformed orthodoxy as well as taking account of contemporary changes. This included his attitude to and understanding of anthropology.

We will first consider the sources of Bavinck's anthropology and its consequent character from the clues given in a small book of his, *Beginselen der Psychologie* (The foundations of psychology).[1] Though it has been translated into English, it has never been published in English.[2] Alongside this, there are three pieces of Bavinck's translated into English which are

---

1. Herman Bavinck, *Beginselen der Psychologie* (Kampen: Kok, 1923).

2. Herman Bavinck, "The Foundations of Psychology," trans. Jack Vanden Born (MA thesis, Calvin College, 1981).

also on the topic of psychology,[3] and there is a resemblance between parts of these and parts of the book.

This book is interesting because of the prestige of Bavinck as a theologian and his cultural situation as a Neo-Calvinist of the second half of the nineteenth century and beyond, whose lineage lay in the Reformed church in Holland and its confessional theological outlook. Besides which, he was clearly a person who attempted to keep up to date on any discipline which might have a bearing on Christian theology.

The book has a structure that reflects faculty psychology as we have met it, together with an inquisitiveness regarding new developments in psychology, with judgments on several then-modern psychologists. It has three chapters that may be said to concern the faculties (the soul, its knowing faculty, and its desiring faculty) and a chapter on the freedom of the will. But the detailed scholastic terminology of his theological forebears is largely absent. Bavinck thinks this approach is important when taken together with empirical psychology, presumably as providing a conceptual framework for empirical research.

Bavinck's life work, as far as writing was concerned, was his *Gereformeerde Dogmatiek* (*Reformed Dogmatics*), the four volumes of which appeared respectively in 1895, 1897, 1898, and 1901.[4] Writing to Abraham Kuyper on September 10, 1897, about this work, at the completion of the second volume, Bavinck stated that he would put together two more volumes. He continued, "I still need to limit things at every turn. The doctrine of man is incomplete. Therefore in a couple of months I shall publish a small, separate work, *Beginselen der Psychologie*.[5] The copy is ready, and the first proofs have been set."[6] Bavinck developed the desire to enlarge and republish it, which he never was able to complete. A second edition was published in 1923 under the supervision of Valentine Hepp (1879–1950), his successor at the Free University of Amsterdam, who implemented

---

3. These are "Trends in Psychology," "The Unconscious," and "Primacy of the Intellect or the Will" in a selection of Bavinck's essays. *Essays on Religion, Science, and Society*, ed. John Bolt, trans. Harry Boonstra and Gerrit Sheeres (Grand Rapids: Baker Academic, 2008).

4. Translated into English as *Reformed Dogmatics*, ed. John Bolt, trans. John Vriend, 4 vols. (Grand Rapids, Baker, 2003–2008).

5. I am indebted to Jack Vanden Born for the use of this translation, for his introduction to it, and for various notes.

6. Bavinck, "Foundations of Psychology," vii.

Bavinck's plans as far as these went at the time of his death. It is this edition that was translated into English as "The Foundations of Psychology" by Jack Vanden Born as a dissertation written toward a 1981 Calvin College M.C.S. Surprisingly, perhaps, as a result there is very little on psychology in Bavinck's *Reformed Dogmatics*.

It is suggested that there were three reasons for the separate book. Bavinck was interested in and concerned over the theoretical foundations of experimental psychology, which had begun to develop in the nineteenth century. So his treatment begins with a survey of the history of psychology which culminates in reflection on the trends current in Holland and in Europe more generally. Secondly, he kept up with the culture of his day, as well having an abiding interest in Christian education. He was active in speaking to various groups and so reflecting on the sort of psychology that teachers were being offered as part of their training. Finally, Bavinck himself suggested that coming to the place in his writing of his *Dogmatics* where the doctrine of man might be expected, he put a good deal of the excess of his anthropological material in this separate book, which also would attract a wider readership. The doctrine of man in volume 2 of his *Dogmatics* is scantier than one might expect, confined as it is to discussion to the creation of mankind in the image of God. This must be the "incompleteness" which Bavinck mentioned to Kuyper. It was completed, or at least supplemented, by the material in *Beginselen der Psychologie*.

It may be that Bavinck moved further away from scholastic anthropology after the original publication of *Beginselen der Psychologie* in 1897; and so had he lived longer, he may have written a different book than the partly revised book which formed the second edition. According to Jack Vanden Born, Valentine Hepp wished that this had been so, and Cornelius Jaarsma (1897–1966) of Calvin College also believed so on the basis of the character of another book of Bavinck's, *Der Overwinning der Ziel* (1916).

My own impression is that in the *Beginselen*, Bavinck was satisfied with the general outlook of faculty psychology. Whatever more was needed, the faculty approach was on the right track. When the book was written and had been partly revised for the second edition, though it was not scholastic in form, the substantive view that Bavinck presents in the book *requires* at least the outlines of the faculty (*viermogen*) psychology. Bearing in mind the *homunculus* tendency of the treatment of separate faculties and the "powers of the soul" view of them, it is the "powers" view that attracted

Bavinck, I believe, and I will try to show this. His emphasis in the book is on the wide variety of psychological data present in the human mind, and then their grouping, very broadly, under the heading of "knowing" and "willing"; and an account is needed of the separate characteristics of each. His views are not an exercise in faculty psychology from their first word, but his adherence to its pattern is made clear by the last word. He is never afraid of using the word "faculty," which appears in various contexts throughout the book.

Before saying more about the presentation of Bavinck's view, it is necessary to say something on the first, introductory chapter, which is a compressed history of psychology, ending up with a more detailed though still summary account of contemporary trends in Holland and more widely in Europe. Bavinck emphasizes the well-known point that by the beginning of the nineteenth century psychology was being separated from philosophy to become a subject in its own right, whose methods of enquiry were empirical in one way or another. Bavinck was particularly interested in the position of Johann Friedrich (1776–1841), Kant's successor at Königsburg.[7] In Friedrich's view, psychology must become a positive science using mathematical techniques. Others also attempted to develop a psychology based exclusively on the phenomena of the consciousness, "psychologism," which took various forms. Some of these were direct intellectual successors of Locke and Hume, such as John Stuart Mill, for whom even logic was a branch of psychology.[8]

At the outset, Bavinck commits himself to a very integrated form of soul-body interactionism, in which "nothing happens in the psyche in which the body does not participate, nor vice versa." The psyche possesses different powers and carries out different activities.[9] Thus understood, psychology is the "science of the powers and activities of the human mind,"[10] based on the distinction between the subject and its objects. Here and throughout the

---

7. See discussion on Bavinck, "Foundations of Psychology," 32.

8. Wilhelm Maximilian Wundt (1832–1920) was a German physician, physiologist, philosopher, and professor, known today as one of the founding figures of modern psychology. Wundt was influenced by the views developed by J. S. Mill from John Locke. Bavinck, "Foundations of Psychology," xvi, 38–40. See Mill's *A System of Logic, Ratiocinative and Inductive* (London: George Routledge and Sons, n.d.), II.iv.

9. Bavinck, "Foundations of Psychology," 2.

10. Bavinck, "Foundations of Psychology," 3.

book Bavinck is concerned about the dangers of a reductionist approach to psychology, the elimination or bracketing from consideration of the bearer of the phenomenal mental activity, the soul itself, and an exclusive concentration on the phenomena of the consciousness.[11]

Other than regarding it as a "mystery," Bavinck is not troubled by this soul-body interactionism, and though he hardly mentions hylomorphism, there are occasional suggestions of that position.[12] He endorses the scholastic distinctions between the *anima vegetativa*, *anima sensitive*, and *anima intellective*, but comments on the disjointedness of the approach,[13] and the fact that it is based on outdated physiology. For Descartes, the *res cogitans* and the *res extensa* are intimately joined up. In its scholastic form, there is a multiplicity of distinctions, but no explanations. "None of this takes away, however, that this psychology provides a better and deeper insight into the nature of psychic-life and the mutual connections of the activities within it than does the psychology of more recent times."[14] The author welcomes its emphases if only because of its resistance to reductionism.

Chapter 1 is entitled "The Psyche or Soul." If there is a dualism between the soul and the body, this does not mean that there is an antagonism between the two. Rather, they are made for each other.[15] Bavinck rejects materialism and pantheism. Each person is distinct from others, the product of many factors, but each has its own individuality and character, "a secret, hidden, unexplainable being," and certainly not the mechanical result of material forces.[16] The soul is spiritual, with the capacity for knowing, for representing the world in various ways, for willing, and also with the capacity to rise above the world of time and space and sense. In human beings, the spirit is organized as a soul, which is "the life principle of a material organism."[17] Again, there are touches suggestive of hylomorphism[18] and the assertion that soul and body "are as earnestly united as is

---

11. Bavinck, "Foundations of Psychology," 5.
12. Bavinck, "Foundations of Psychology," 5.
13. Bavinck, "Foundations of Psychology," 3.
14. Bavinck, "Foundations of Psychology," 16.
15. Bavinck, "Foundations of Psychology," 16.
16. Bavinck, "Foundations of Psychology," 26.
17. Bavinck, "Foundations of Psychology," 30.
18. Bavinck, "Foundations of Psychology," 30.

the figure and the marble in a statue"[19]—like the form and matter of the human being. Consider this passage:

> In that humans are souls, they are related to plants and animals. Man is an animal, a sensual animal-like being. This was generally known long before Darwin. If man can be said to be like animals it is also possible to ascribe a soul to animals and plants. Plants, humans, animals are all physical beings that live. But the soul is differently developed in each. In a plant the soul has an organizational and formable power which shapes and sustains the plant, but it has neither consciousness nor will. In animals the soul is not only organizational but also sensitive: it perceives, has consciousness, memory, judgment, understanding to a degree, anger, instinct, desire. But in man the soul reaches its highest development, with reason and will. Man is rational.[20]

He proceeds to discuss the faculties, groups of psychic events that cannot be understood in virtue of some lower common denominator. Bavinck provides a historical review of them,[21] including the influence of Christianity in moving the Greeks' exclusive dominance of the intellect to include the will.[22] He takes Descartes to propound a development of the faculty approach. The Enlightenment philosophers made understanding the essence of humanity.[23] Feelings were sublimated. Romanticism and sentimentalism were the reaction, introducing a faculty of feeling.[24]

Bavinck held that "feeling" is significantly ambiguous. To start with, it may be associated with bodily states or with intellectual states of various kinds. Sometimes, as with Schleiermacher, it is feeling prior to all thinking and willing, a direct, unmediated sense of dependence on God. In other cases, feelings are desires—that is, they have objectives concerned with the satisfaction of appetite, whether intellectual or bodily. There is an "about-ness" of such feelings, an intentionality, giving them a distinctive temper. Often there is general confusion between these two sorts of feeling, a perception of consciousness or an intentional condition. Feeling cannot be

---

19. Bavinck, "Foundations of Psychology," 31.
20. Bavinck, "Foundations of Psychology," 31.
21. Bavinck, "Foundations of Psychology," 31.
22. Bavinck, "Foundations of Psychology," 42.
23. Bavinck, "Foundations of Psychology," 44.
24. Bavinck, "Foundations of Psychology," 46.

a separate faculty.[25] Bavinck spends a lot of time on this, going into it in more detail than on anything else, no doubt reflecting his concern with the prevalence of Romanticism. As with feelings and Romantic psychology, so with the will and voluntaristic psychologies.[26] Reductionism of various kinds fails, and in Bavinck's estimate of the soul's activities, distinct faculties are needed to express the manifoldness of the soul's life.

Bavinck thus defends what might be called a "faculty approach" to human psychology. Thoughts, identified as a result of observation of oneself and others, preserve it against reduction, either in materialistic or psychologistic terms. By way of comment on this, Bavinck only says, "The doctrine of the soul and its faculties only opens the possibility for explaining psychic events but does not yet present the explanations."[27] Faculty psychology is an attempt to arrange the mental life. To explain it, an account of its causes and the regularities that can be formulated are needed. This is as yet undeveloped. It is not clear what the character of such nonreductionistic explanations are to be.

A general discussion of these matters leads to chapter 3, "The Knowing Faculty." Here again a concern with reduction is in view, that of a person to his circumstances. The debate about innatism had led "sensualists" to oppose intellectualists. Each position, empiricism and rationalism, may be criticized from the standpoint of the other. This leads, not surprisingly, to a discussion of Kant's mediating strategy, in which the phenomena of the mind are ordered in terms of a set of synthetic *a priori* ideas constitutive of the human mind. But Kant's error lay in "his ascription of only subjective, phenomenal significance to the *a priori* elements."[28] And on the subjective side of things, a psychic event must be distinguished from the stimulation of a nerve, as perceiving is distinct from sensing.[29] Kantianism led to an agnosticism regarding the soul. But Bavinck held that knowledge of the soul emerges *to the individual in the course of time.* Both subjective and objective awareness have their existence from the Creator.

---

25. Bavinck, "Foundations of Psychology," 50–51.
26. Bavinck, "Foundations of Psychology," 57.
27. Bavinck, "Foundations of Psychology," 61.
28. Bavinck, "Foundations of Psychology," 72.
29. Bavinck, "Foundations of Psychology," 79.

In Cartesian vein, Bavinck observes that thinking is essential to humans. However, he rejects the idea of innate knowledge,[30] but believes that human beings are born with potentialities, abilities, to see, to use reason, to perceive, to know, and so on. Knowledge is not built up on sensations but also from an intuitive discernment of law, logic, arithmetic, and the physical laws. We can develop habits and sensibilities, the difference between the outside world and the inner conscious awareness of the states of the self. The change from stimulation to sensation is a mystery. The transition from passive sensation to active perception involves attention and judgment, and the individual is aware of the external and internal worlds. Bavinck further discusses the consciousness, self-consciousness, and the unconscious.[31] At this point, he discusses the vegetative power of the soul rather in the manner of hylomorphism, which mostly proceeds unconsciously, as do the working of habits unless interrupted in some way. Memory and representation and imagination are facets of the knowing faculty; likewise, understanding and reason, which involve perception, abstraction, and aesthetic judgment.[32] Conscience is similar across cultures and eras and is God-given.[33] Bavinck has further comments on aesthetic judgment and on self-awareness, which is a condition of language use.[34]

In chapter 4, "The Desiring Faculty," Bavinck discusses the will and the emotions. The will is continuous with physical desire, an extension of it, where our desires are for goals identified by our reason and chosen by the will. Desiring has to do with the good or evil of things desired. So the intellect is involved in desiring and its attainment or failure.[35] This faculty is not narrow: "Desire, will, drive, temperament, appetite, non-appetite emotion or passion belong to the desiring faculty." From time to time Bavinck stresses the vegetative life of the soul, which brings about strivings within a physiological system. And reflex actions are naturally involuntary. Skills can be learned and then are maintained automatically by the mind and the body

---

30. Bavinck, "Foundations of Psychology," 74.

31. Bavinck, "Foundations of Psychology," 80. For more on the unconscious, see Bavinck, *Essays on Religion, Science and Society*, ch. 10.

32. Bavinck, "Foundations of Psychology," 98.

33. For more of Bavinck on the conscience, see "Conscience," trans. Nelson D. Kloosterman, *Bavinck Review* 6 (2015): 113–26.

34. Bavinck, "Foundations of Psychology," 109.

35. Bavinck, "Foundations of Psychology," 119.

at a subconscious level. And in growing up, desire manifests itself before our consciousness. Such subconscious drives have much to do with self-preservation. So self-love produces drives, of which the will is an extension.

In human beings, desire arises from instinct, but it is more than that.[36] It is distinguishable from acquired drives, which are often conditioned by customs. A desire is distinguished from a drive because it usually has objectives, being attached to a certain kind of representation. Desiring leads to a consideration of emotions.[37] Emotions are generated through the prospect of success, leading to hope or failure in desires leading to joy or despair, arising from the awareness of success or failure. The harder the objective is to achieve or to avoid, the more intense the feeling. Bavinck follows "recent psychology" in distinguishing between emotions and passions, to which he adds moods and feelings.[38] Moods are more general, sometimes hard to explain, and arise from general states. Feelings may have a more specific source. Emotions may be more intense and have bodily effects. These all depend on the knowing or desiring faculty. The differences between moods and emotions may be only a matter of degree. Emotions are not immediately forced on us but arise through the impact of a wide variety of sources on our beliefs and on our beliefs about our beliefs.

Bavinck is keen to stress the role of the will. There is a will of desiring and a will of enjoying, and he thinks that traditional Christian psychology stresses the latter. Emotions are not simply uninteresting byproducts of human changes. "In the human world they are the weightiest factors and strongest powers we know."[39] He thinks that willing is the highest activity of the desiring faculty. It is the apex of a hierarchy of changes that may be called "desires," higher therefore than the "lower activities of the desiring faculty."[40] We are enslaved if desire dominates; freedom comes from the exercise of the will, at least with regard to those matters that are under our control. It does not evolve from desiring but is a "new action," in those matters that arise from the understanding, particularly where good and evil are concerned, that is, from the practical reason. But decisions as to

---

36. Bavinck, "Foundations of Psychology," 127.
37. Bavinck, "Foundations of Psychology," 132.
38. Bavinck, "Foundations of Psychology," 133.
39. Bavinck, "Foundations of Psychology," 141.
40. Bavinck, "Foundations of Psychology," 146.

what to do are quickly taken, many of them. Decision differs from execution, which may be laborious. The will has to do with those matters that the subject regards as good, or as a means to a good. The will processes what the soul receives from all its manifold sources, directing and not acting *de novo*. Bavinck stresses the limits to the soul's control of itself. "In sum, power of the will is rather scanty."[41]

This leads to the final chapter, a shortish treatment of the freedom of the will, not containing any surprises.[42] It is noteworthy as containing the only places where Bavinck utilizes scholastic distinctions verbatim, between the *libertas exercitii* (freedom as between willing and not willing), *libertas discretionis* (willing as between course A and course B), and *libertas contrarietatis* (the choice between two courses that are contrary to each other). This was the sense, Bavinck notes, that was at issue between Augustine and the Pelagians.[43] But as regards freedom in the wider sense, "there were those who defined God's foreknowledge in order to preserve a full and free will for man, but most seemed to somewhat thoughtlessly to maintain God's foreknowledge and also hold that this did not absolutely determine events in advance."[44] Freedom of the will excludes its coercion. The only question is an ethical one, the relation between free will and responsibility. The issue here is between those who see freedom in terms of indifference, or in rational self-determination, here using the traditional scholastic terms. Those favoring determinism appeal to the nature of the rational will and the connections between reason and action. Indeterminists think of the will as capable of equipoise between alternatives, a unique position and power of the will. Bavinck takes the view of his Reformed forebears. He thinks that the difficulty is exacerbated by a *homunculus* view of the will, as independent, distinct from all causal factors. But the will is not like that. It is "the desiring faculty in its highest development."[45] Understanding is involved in freedom, not mere will. So the will is "rational desiring," though this phrase does not appeal to some rational norm, but simply to the significant employment of the reason.

---

41. Bavinck, "Foundations of Psychology," 150.
42. Bavinck, "Foundations of Psychology," 152.
43. Bavinck, "Foundations of Psychology," 152–53.
44. Bavinck, "Foundations of Psychology," 153.
45. Bavinck, "Foundations of Psychology," 155.

Summing Up

In the space he gave himself, Bavinck provided an informative survey of psychological data with a historical orientation and sustained polemic against various kinds of reductionism influential in his day. The psychological data are organized loosely around the idea of faculties in a fairly conventional manner. The faculties are psychologically incomplete, utilizing distinctions, but not venturing explanations of the data. It is not made clear what exactly Bavinck means by such explanations in a situation in which he stresses the individuality and uniqueness of the human person and the mysteriousness of the interaction between soul and body. This is especially difficult to envisage given the categorical difference between the mental and the physical, even though he did not characterize the boundaries of the dualism in Cartesian terms, but he preferred, for example, to note the continuity between bodily and rational appetites in a way reminiscent of hylomorphism.

John Locke's Critique of Faculty Psychology

We noted in chapter 8 John Locke's criticism of faculty psychology in his *Essay Concerning Human Understanding*, which exercised an influence on Edwards and had a more general influence as well. What follows is a brief discussion of what Locke wrote at greater length in criticism of faculty psychology.[1] Locke criticized it by way of developing its weakness as the basis for causal account of human action. Such a critique coheres with his view of the mind as a *tabula rasa* and with a more unitary character of the self. In his long chapter "Of Power,"[2] in a rather rambling discussion, two arguments against the position can be distinguished.

First is his argument from the indefinite multiplication of faculties. He writes,

> For if it be reasonable to suppose and talk of *faculties* as distinct beings that can act (as we do, where we say the *will* orders, and the *will* is free), it is fit that we should refer to a speaking *faculty*, and a walking *faculty* and a dancing *faculty*, by which those actions are produced, which are but several modes of motion, as well as we make the *will* and *understanding* to be *faculties* by which the actions of choosing and perceiving are produced, which are but several modes of thinking. And we may as properly say that it is the singing *faculty* sings, and the *dancing* faculty dances, as that the *will* chooses, or that the understanding conceives; or, as is usual, that the *will* directs the understanding, or the understanding obeys or obeys not the *will*: it being altogether as proper and intelligible to say that the power of

---

1. The usual approach to Locke's view of the faculties is touched on in various brief discussions in Perler, *Faculties*, 98–99.

2. Locke, *Essay*, II.xxi.

speaking directs the power of singing, or the power of singing obeys or disobeys the power of speaking.[3]

That is, to postulate a faculty as the source of the power of the understanding or the will is to warrant a faculty for every human power. It becomes an instance of circular reasoning, of defining a faculty by its effect. In his play *The Imaginary Invalid*, Molière offered the explanation of the sleep-inducing property of opium to cause sleepiness as arising from its "*virtus dormitiva*," its sleep-inducing power. The explanation is tautological, being simply a repeat of what needs explaining in the first place.

Locke deplores such circularity because he believes that faculties are introduced for the purpose of psychological explanation. Then indeed the invocation of faculties would be ridiculously redundant. It does not advance an explanation to say that dancing is caused by a dancing faculty, or that we speak because we have a speaking faculty. However, the first business of introducing faculties was classificatory, to distinguish between different (sets of) powers of the mind, the intellectual, the volitional, the affective, and so on. The faculties are not in themselves explanations, though the powers of a faculty may be part of a much more complex view of causation such as that using the Aristotelian fourfold causation—particularly the formal cause of an action and its efficient cause. The individual skills come first, and the faculty of the will or of the understanding are generalizations of sets of them.

So, do appeals to one faculty or another have any explanatory value, or are such appeals simply circular reasoning posing as an explanation? If the agent in the course of an hour chooses to do a number of different things, it makes perfect sense to postulate a faculty which "houses" the common features of such different willings, and similarly with the understanding. In fact, while it may be unilluminating to postulate many faculties, grouping similar activities makes some sense. It makes sense to understand that a choice is a willed activity and not an activity of the understanding, for example. Locke passes over the fact that "faculties" are introduced as a result of observation. They are not part of a theory devised *a priori*.

The sort of explanations that the faculty psychologists are familiar with are the various different activities being classified of the understanding or

---

3. Locke, *Essay*, II.xxi.17 (I.200–1).

the will, say. Such classifications are based on observable goings-on in one-self and others and on conceptual distinctions. That is why Aristotle's work is said to be a mix of what is nowadays called psychology and philosophy. It is classificatory, forming the mass of data into various observable types and postulating causal connections between them. However, such a pro-cedure does not favor scientific explanations which attempt reductionistic, overarching explanations of many events into one causal type, such as the association of certain ideas to other ideas.

The distinctions between the vegetative, sensible, and rational faculties, or souls, is simply an extension of such classificatory thinking, compar-ing humans with the higher animals, having to do with activities of the sensitive parts and roles of the body, unified in one faculty, a faculty which itself has to do with the growth and running of the body, which is a nec-essary presupposition of the operation of the senses and of the mind and its thinking. And likewise with the sensible and rational souls. Dualistic accounts are based on the body and the mind having different categories, like those of extension and thinking in Descartes.

We do not talk of a dancing faculty or a speaking faculty. But we do think of people having dispositions or propensities to speak or dance, among other things. And as a consequence we are not surprised to see people learning to speak or to dance. Or perhaps it is the other way round. Men and women speak and dance, and so we reckon that they have dis-positions—or potencies, as the scholastics might say—to do so. Such dispositions are not supposed to be exclusively concerned with one activity, with dancing but not with riding, or marching, for example. Such disposi-tions or potencies are less grand or general than faculties, but are similar in other respects. Learned activities are based on inherent abilities, which then may be stored in the memory and reproduced at will as long as they are in good repair, once we leave infancy and before we decay in old age.

Second, Locke thinks that such an approach relies on another mistake, that of thinking of the faculties as themselves independent human-like agents, *homunculi*.[4] Were such activities as walking and dancing said to have their own distinctive and exclusive powers, then the point would be

---

4. A *homunculus* is the Latin for "little man," from the diminutive form of *homo*, a man. Anthony Kenny, "The Homunculus Fallacy," in *The Legacy of Wittgenstein* (Oxford: Blackwell, 1984).

well taken. There is no reason to think that there are such powers, treating the will, for example, as an agent in its own right. A will does not itself have a will. Even if scholastics were guilty of this *homunculus* fallacy in respect of the will, referring to it as free or otherwise, they in general have not favored the proliferation of faculties, though William of Ockham is said to have recognized fifteen faculties, but he seems at this point to have been thinking of faculties in a different sense. As we have noted, scholastics following Aristotle referred to the vegetative, sensory, and rational faculties. These are rather different from the distinction between the will and understanding, which are distinctions within the rational faculty. Many nonscholastics have used that faculty terminology of the very general activities of appraising and formulating goals and pursuing those goals. These, which came to be called the faculties of the understanding and the will, are what Locke was being critical of. They are very wide and general in their scope, and if they are themselves treated as subjects (substances), agents in their own right, this is only because such language is shorthand for a basic activity of the soul or self that is being referred to.

This way of thinking was modified somewhat with the advent of Descartes's mind-body interactive dualism, but not completely eliminated by it. Descartes's view that the body, spatially extended, is a separately behaving mechanical pump that can be explained in its own terms meant that the human soul is deprived of the vegetative powers which it has according to hylomorphism. It is the body which has vegetative powers, for example. Nonetheless, Descartes is well known for upholding the closeness of the interaction between body and soul, much closer than the analogy of a pilot in a ship.[5] Nor did Descartes repudiate the language of distinct "faculties" operating in the soul, some of which depended on the interaction with the body, the consciousness of bodily feelings, such as tiredness and hunger and physical pain, but no longer called by him the sensitive soul. For Descartes, the rational faculty is the only resident of the soul alone, but of course needing the body to express its reasonings and willings.

Locke seems to think that the elimination of references to distinct faculties helps to solve the problem of "free will" by eliminating the phrase:

---

5. *Meditation* VI: "That I am not only lodged in my body as a pilot in a vessel, but that I am very closely united to it, and so to speak so intermingled with it that I seem to compose with it one whole." Descartes, *Philosophical Works*, I, 192.

[The] *will* being nothing but a power in the mind to direct the operative faculties of a man to motion or rest, as far as they depend on such direction: to the question, What is it that determines the will? The true and proper answer is, the mind. For that which determines the general power of directing, to this or that particular, is nothing but the agent itself exercising the power it has that particular way. If this answer satisfies not, it is plain the meaning of the question, *What determines the will?* is this: What moves the mind, in every particular instance, to determine its general power of directing to this or that particular motion or rest? And to this I answer: The motive for continuing in the same state or action is only the present satisfaction in it; the motive to change is always some *uneasiness*: nothing setting us upon the change of state, or upon any action, but some *uneasiness*. This is the great motive that works on the mind to put it upon action, which for shorthand's sake we will call *determining of the will*, which I shall more at large explain.[6]

But as one might surmise, the different views in the debate on free will are relocated from the will to the person. So one can have a determinist view of a person, such as the view of Locke and Edwards, or a view of a person as possessing the power of indifference, like the Jesuits and Remonstrants, and of indifference simply, "as long as the intellect remains doubtful and uncertain whither to turn itself," as some at least of the Reformed orthodox held.[7]

---

6. Locke, *Essay*, II.xxi.29 (II.206).

7. Turretin, *Institutes of Elenctic Theology*, 1:665.

Faculty Psychology and Contemporary Psychology

In this appendix I refer to two very different contemporary philosophers. The first is a dualist, who covers ground also covered by faculty psychology, albeit in his own way, but in a way that is not inconsistent with faculty psychology. The second is a materialist who nevertheless believes that the idea of faculties is helpful in developing a computational theory of the mind.

Richard Swinburne's Mind-Body Dualism

A contemporary mind-body dualist such as Richard Swinburne (b. 1934) has an unwitting sympathy and convergence with the faculty psychology of the scholastics, though not of Aristotelian fourfold causation, in *The Evolution of the Soul*.[1] He offers a robust and sophisticated version of dualism, and he holds that it cannot be accounted for by the evolution of the body over uncountable millions of years. Whatever its present relation to the body, the mind is not a product of a body. Rather, the soul is the product of the direct, personal agency of God, who

> intentionally keeps the laws of nature operative (i.e conserves those natures which are causally effective, in substances which have them), and also brings it about that there is linked to the brain of an animal or man a soul which interacts with it in a regular and predictable way.... God, being omnipotent, would have the power to produce a soul thus interacting, to produce intentionally those connections which, we have seen,[2] have no natural connection. And God would have a reason for so doing—to give to the souls of men beliefs,

---

1. Richard Swinburne, *The Evolution of the Soul*, rev. ed. (Oxford: Clarendon Press, 1997).

2. This is a reference to Swinburne's discussion of the relation of the soul to the body in *Evolution of the Soul*, ch. 10.

thoughts and sensations caused by brain-states in regular ways, allow man to acquire knowledge of the world and to make a difference to it by choice—good things which allow men to share in the creative work of God himself.[3]

Swinburne also notes in this section the coherence of this view with the doctrine of the creation of souls known as creationism, as opposed to traducianism. Besides this, he also recognizes the difference between theoretical and practical reason.

Later in the book, Swinburne devotes chapter 14, "The Structure of the Soul," to the soul being comprised, "structured" of thoughts, purposes, desires, and beliefs, with a will and emotions, though he has little to say about the emotional side of things. In his view, each of the elements of the soul's structure represents a grouping of psychological powers, based on observation and conceptualization. Besides having animal powers, humans have the capacity for rationality, a complex and logical structure that is lacking in any nonhuman animal. Humans also have capacity for moral concepts, enabling them to make moral discriminations. And they have free will; their actions "are not predetermined by brain states, and so in a crucial sense, humans have free will"; and their souls have "a character which does not arise from the brain state to which it is linked."[4]

So what we are seeing is that a dualist with no axe to grind for faculty psychology nonetheless offers an account of mental structure that is similar to it. Of course there are matters discussed and modes of presentation treated in this book that are not those discussed by faculty psychologists in the seventeenth century, but could have been. For example, Swinburne points to the fact that our beliefs are distinguishable as sets that stand or fall together, rarely ever as singular beliefs. This is not a point that Reformed faculty psychology makes, but it is entirely consistent (so it seems) with what they hold. The same applies for features of the soul such as drives, phobias, and the unconscious.[5]

---

3. Swinburne, *Evolution of the Soul*, 198–99.

4. Swinburne, *Evolution of the Soul*, 203.

5. For Bavinck's view, see "The Unconscious," in *Essays on Religion, Science, and Society*. Interestingly there is a discussion of allergies in Joseph Truman's *Discourse of Natural and Moral Impotency*. See chapter 5 of the present volume.

Jerry Fodor and "Faculty Psychology"

Jerry A. Fodor (b. 1934) is a materialist of sorts, certainly not a dualist. And yet he uses the idea of faculty psychology in trying to "model" the mind and especially its cognitive powers in an effort to provide a basis for further thinking of the mind computationally. However, Fodor is thinking of a faculty in a rather different sense than historically understood, though his sense is derived from it. His book is entitled *The Modularity of Mind: An Essay on Faculty Psychology.*[6] Fodor revisits historical faculty psychology to try to throw light on the computational mechanisms that would provide an account of the workings of the mind, particularly of the characteristic cognitive powers of the mind, at the most basic level. From a dualistic perspective, this is a bottom-up approach which a dualist could not entertain. However, it is hard to see how this program can be developed without taking the cues from body and soul together. Nevertheless, what Fodor says about an understanding of a faculty has an independent interest. How should a dualist think of the "shape" of the structure of the mind? Is it possible to go much further than such as the Reformed orthodox went?

Here we briefly review the accounts of "mental structure" that Fodor offers in the first chapter of his book, bearing in mind the caveats above and noting the speculative character of what he says. Could what he hopes will one day be said about the brain be true of or plausibly said of the faculties of the mind?

Fodor is one of the group who reject the prevailing associationist outlook of those who, following David Hartley and David Hume (who were of course mentalists) in the eighteenth century, thought of the human mind as bereft of any innate ideas. This tradition has culminated in experimental psychology of the Skinnerian kind, in which the contents of the mind are the sum of its responses to environmental stimuli of various kinds. Historically, this stems from Locke's rejection of innate ideas. It is a propositional account of knowledge. So Fodor associates with Noam Chomsky's (b. 1928) "neo-cartesian" account of knowledge, in particular his view that the mind has a structure or "architecture."[7]

---

6. Jerry A. Fodor, *The Modularity of Mind: An Essay on Faculty Psychology* (Cambridge, Mass.: MIT Press, 1983).

7. Noam Chomsky, *Aspects of the Theory of Syntax* (Cambridge, Mass.: MIT Press, 1965).

Chomsky's starting point is that the mind has an intrinsic structure, rich and diverse, a body of information.[8] But Fodor holds that Chomsky's approach is structurally defective. Take memory, for example. This is not lists of propositions and the rules that govern them and what is involved in their "figuring out."[9] Rather, memory is an innate capacity of a different kind, a sort of mechanism with operations of its own, employing what the memory "stores" in appropriate actions with varying degrees of success. Fodor thinks that propositional structures à la Chomsky may be part of the picture, one sort of faculty, but there are others. So an appropriate faculty psychology question is, What are the mechanisms of memory use? If we use our memories, what is the mechanism not that we consciously use, such as "searching," but which must operate for efficient use? Even Locke had use of these, and so do the faculty psychologists, though they don't explore them. These are what Fodor calls "interacting component mechanisms."[10] Such mechanisms are topic invariant; and in making judgments, exercised in perceptual recognitions, for example, they work with whatever the topic is that we have memories of. The same faculty is at work, the faculty of judgment or that involves judgment.[11] This is what Fodor calls a "horizontal" faculty.

We have seen the repeated tendency among faculty psychologists to think of faculties as discrete powers of the soul. So there is one faculty, the understanding, for example; and it understands hosts of different matters, covering different topics. All memories are stored together. Or if several "rooms" are occupied, then there is a common space in which they are sorted or stored by age or topic. So the memory performs certain kinds of function, in doing so crossing subject domains. A content specific memory would not be "horizontal," but vertical.[12]

This is the second idea of mental structure, a vertical faculty. By this[13] Fodor means that the mind is a bundle of what we can call aptitudes of different kinds, of fundamental powers. So the psychologist Franz Joseph Gall

---

8. Fodor, *Modularity of Mind*, 7.

9. Fodor, *Modularity of Mind*, 8.

10. Fodor, *Modularity of Mind*, 11.

11. Fodor, *Modularity of Mind*, 11–12.

12. Fodor, *Modularity of Mind*, 13.

13. "Horizontal" and "vertical" are Fodor's terms.

(1758–1828)[14] thought of the mind as a set of structures distinguishable into functionally discrete subsystems, these being skill-specific. An account of such competencies or proclivities routinely involves the combination of the cognitive and volitional features of the mind. So for Gall, there is not just the faculty of perceiving, but perceiving in football ("reading" a game), and botanical perception (having an eye for the make-up of a flower), and so on. So on the idea of vertical faculties, there is no faculty of perceiving as such. Similarly with the faculties of memory, judgment, and the like. This idea of a faculty may seem to carry the consequence that a good memory for dates will be a good memory for names, or recipes, and whatever else the person turns his attention to. But Fodor thinks that this assumption of equal memory strength seems dubious.[15]

In his exploration of the idea of a faculty, Fodor reckons that such a view (associated with Gall) has strengths and weaknesses, but that it may be part of a view of the mind which has both vertical and horizontal faculties. Fodor particularly stresses that what can be taken from such a vertical approach is the idea of their being associated with neural structures and computational autonomy. And there may be proclivities that are not learned, but are handed down genetically.[16]

A further way of conceiving the mind's structure is the widespread view that for a long time preceded Chomsky's innatism—namely, associationism, developed by David Hartley. This view was dismissive of faculty psychology and accepted Locke's arguments against faculties. Fodor endorses Locke's answer to his own *reductio ad absurdum* of faculty psychology—namely, that is *the man* who sings or dances, not his singing faculty or dancing faculty. Such reductions to absurdity require an understanding of faculties, and a version of mind-body dualism, which was the view of the Reformed orthodox, but which Fodor rejects.

Associationism allows for a set of elements out of which psychological structures are constructed.[17] So it is a "profoundly reductionist impulse" in which faculties explain nothing but mental data, and their relations explain everything. Memory is constructed out of the "force and vivacity of certain

---

14. Gall is best remembered these days for phrenology. An overview of his approach is given by Fodor, *Modularity of Mind*, 14–23.

15. Fodor, *Modularity of Mind*, 17.

16. Fodor, *Modularity of Mind*, 22.

17. Fodor, *Modularity of Mind*, 27.

ideas," as Hume implausibly claimed.[18] This was a simpler sort of explanation than the invocation of memory as a set of powers of the faculty of understanding—hence its initial attraction. The fundamental powers of the soul are not several, but one: the capacity to form associations between ideas, so providing a fresh rendering of the various powers of the faculties, that is, a rational reconstruction of them.[19] This dispenses with the idea of mental structure or architecture intrinsic to Fodor's approach to the mind. So admitting some version of faculty psychology is intrinsic to the computational approach to the mind that Fodor advocates.

Fodor's work in *The Modularity of Mind* is a good example of the continued interest in faculty psychology even by one who does not share its metaphysical outlook.

---

18. Fodor, *Modularity of Mind*, 28.
19. Fodor, *Modularity of Mind*, 29.

Bibliography

à Brakel, Wilhelmus. *The Christian's Reasonable Service*. Translated by Bartel Elshout. Edited by Joel R. Beeke. 4 volumes. Grand Rapids: Reformation Heritage Books, 2012.

Alvarez, Diego. *De auxiliis divinæ gratiæ et humani arbitrii viribus et libertate, ac legtimâ ejus cum efficaciâ eorumdem auxiliorum concordiâ libri XII*. Rome, 1610.

Ames, William. *Conscience with the Power and Cases thereof*. N.p., 1639.

Aquinas, Thomas. *Summa Theologiae*. Various translators. New York: McGraw-Hill, 1967–1980.

Aristotle. *De Anima*. Edited by Christopher Shields. Oxford: Oxford University Press, 2016.

Arminius, Jacobus. *Opera theologica*. Multiple volumes. Leiden, 1629.

Arrowsmith, John. *Armilla Catechetica or A Chain of Principles*. Cambridge: John Field, 1659.

Augustine. *City of God*. Translated by John Healey. Edited by R. V. G. Tasker. London: J. M. Dent & Sons, 1945.

———. *Confessions*. Translated by Henry Chadwick. Oxford: Oxford University Press, 1991.

———. *Letters*. Volume 1 in *The Nicene and Post-Nicene Fathers*. Edited by Philip Schaff. Grand Rapids: Eerdmans, 1971.

———. *On the Catholic and the Manichean Ways of Life*. Edited by R. J. Deferrari. Washington, D.C.: Catholic University Press, 1947.

———. *On the Grace of Christ, and on Original Sin*. Volume 5 in *The Nicene and Post-Nicene Fathers*. Edited by Philip Schaff. Grand Rapids: Eerdmans, 1971.

———. *On the Trinity*. Translated by A. W. Hadden. Edinburgh: T&T Clark, 1873.

————. *Tractate LX, on John 13:21*. Volume 4 of *The Nicene and Post-Nicene Fathers*. Edited by Philip Schaff. Grand Rapids: Eerdmans 1994.

Baron, Robert. *Metaphysica Generalis*. Leiden: F. Moyard, 1654.

Bavinck, Herman. "Conscience." Translated by Nelson D. Kloosterman. *Bavinck Review* 6 (2015): 113–26.

————. *Essays on Religion, Science, and Society*. Translated by Harry Boonstra and Gerrit Sheeres. Edited by John Bolt. Grand Rapids: Baker, 2008.

————. "The Foundations of Psychology." Translated by Jack Vanden Born. MA thesis, Calvin College, 1981.

————. *Reformed Dogmatics*. Translated by John Vriend. Edited by John Bolt. 4 volumes. Grand Rapids: Baker, 2003–2008.

Beeke, Joel R. *Assurance of Faith*. Frankfurt-am-Main: Peter Lang, 1991.

Bentham, Jeremy. *Introduction to Principles of Morals and Legislation*. London: T Payne, 1789.

Bernard, John. *Christian See to thy Conscience or A Treatise of the nature, the kinds and manifold cases of conscience...* London: imprinted by Felix Kingston for Robert Milbourne, 1631.

Buddeus, Franciscus. *Institutiones Theologiae Moralis*. Lipsiae: Thomae Fritsch, 1727.

Bunyan, John. *The Works of John Bunyan*. Edited by George Offor. 2 volumes. Glasgow: Blackie and Son, 1857.

Burgess, Anthony. *The Doctrine of Original Sin Asserted & Vindicated against the Old and New Adversaries Thereof*. London, 1658.

Calvin, John. *The Bondage and Liberation of the Will*. Translated by G. I. Davies. Edited by A. N. S. Lane. Grand Rapids: Baker, 1996.

————. *Commentary on the First Book of Moses Called Genesis*. Volume 1 in *Calvin's Commentaries*. 22 volumes. Grand Rapids: Baker, 1979.

————. *Commentary on the Psalms*. Volume 19 in *Calvin's Commentaries*. 22 volumes. Grand Rapids: Baker, 1979.

————. *Institutes of the Christian Religion*. Translated by Henry Beveridge. Various editions.

————. *Letters*. Translated by David Constable. Volume 3 in *Selected Works of John Calvin*. 7 volumes. Edited by Henry Beveridge. Grand Rapids: Baker, 1983.

————. *Psychopannychia*. Volume 3 in *Tracts and Treatises*. In *Selected Works of John Calvin*. 7 volumes. Edited by Henry Beveridge. Grand Rapids: Baker, 1983.

————. *Sermons on Genesis 1–11.* Translated by Rob Roy Macgregor. Edinburgh: Banner of Truth, 2009.

————. *Sermons on the Hundred and Nineteenth Psalm.* Audubon, N.J.: Old Paths, 1996.

Cameron, John. *Praelectiones de Ecclesia.* Edited by F. Spanheim. Geneva: Jacob Chouet, 1642.

Charnock, Stephen. *The Complete Works of Stephen Charnock.* 5 volumes. Edinburgh: Banner of Truth, 1985.

Chomsky, Noam. *Aspects of the Theory of Syntax.* Cambridge, Mass.: MIT Press, 1965.

Cleveland, Christopher. *Thomism in John Owen.* Burlington: Ashgate, 2013.

Cooper, John W. *Body, Soul and Life Everlasting.* Grand Rapids: Eerdmans, 2000.

Cross, Richard. *Duns Scotus on God.* Aldershot: Ashgate, 2005.

Davenant, John. *Animadversions Written by the Right Reverend Father in God, John, Lord Bishop of Salisbury, upon a Treatise intitled Gods Love to Mankind.* Cambridge: printed by Roger Daniel, Printer to the University, 1641.

————. *An Exposition of the Epistle of St. Paul to the Colossians.* 2 vols. Translated by Josiah Allport. London: Hamilton, Adams, and Co., 1831.

Davies, Brian. *Aquinas.* London: Continuum, 2002.

Dekker, Eef. "Was Arminius a Molinist?" *Sixteenth Century Journal* 27, no. 2 (1996): 337–52.

de Molina, Luis. *Molina on Divine Foreknowledge: Part IV of the* Concordia. Translated and introduced by Alfred J. Freddoso. Ithaca: Cornell University Press, 1988.

de Moor, Bernardinus. *A Continuous Commentary on à Marck's* Compendium of Christian Theology. Leiden, 1761–1771.

Descartes, René. *Descartes' Conversation with Burman.* Translated with introduction and commentary by John Cottingham. Oxford: Clarendon Press, 1976.

————. *Meditations on First Philosophy.* In volume 1 of *Philosophical Works of Descartes.* Edited by G. R. T. Ross and Elizabeth Haldane. 2 volumes. Cambridge: Cambridge University Press, 1911.

Donnelly, John Patrick. "Calvinist Thomism." *Viator* 7 (1976): 441–55.

Edwards, Jonathan. *Freedom of the Will.* Edited by Paul Ramsey. Volume 1 in *The Works of Jonathan Edwards.* 26 volumes. New Haven, Conn.: Yale University Press, 1957–2008.

———. *The Great Christian Doctrine of Original Sin.* Edited by Clyde A. Holbrook. Volume 3 of *The Works of Jonathan Edwards.* 26 volumes. New Haven, Conn.: Yale University Press, 1957–2008.

———. *Religious Affections.* Edited by John E. Smith. New Haven, Conn.: Yale University Press, 1959.

Fenner, William. *The Souls Looking-Glasse, Lively representing its estate before GOD: With a Treatise of Conscience: Wherein the Definitions thereof are unfolded, and several Cases resolved.* London: printed by T. R. & E. M. for John Rothwell at the Sun and Fountain in Paul's Church-yard, 1652.

———. *A Treatise on the Affections.* London: printed by A. M. for J. Rothwell, 1650.

Field, David. *Rigide Calvinism in a Softer Dresse, The Moderate Presbyterianism of John Howe 1630–1705.* Edinburgh: Rutherford Studies in Historical Theology, 2004.

Flavel, John. *Pneumatalogia, a Treatise of the Soul of Man, the Second Edition.* London: printed by J. D. for Tho. Parkhurst at the Bible and Three Crowns near Mercers Chappel in Cheapside, 1698.

Fodor, Jerry. *The Modularity of Mind: An Essay on Faculty Psychology.* Cambridge, Mass.: MIT Press, 1983.

Gale, Theophilus. *The Court of the Gentiles, Part I Of Philologie* (Oxon: Printed by Hen. Hall for Tho. Gilbert, 1669); *Part II Of Philosophie* (London: Will Hall for Tho. Gilbert, 1671); *Part III The Vanity of Pagan Philosophy* (London: A. Maxwell and R. Roberts, for T. Cockeril, at the sign of the Atlas in Cornhil hear the Royal Exchange, 1677); *Part IV Of Reformed Philosophie* (London: for John Hill at the Black Lyon in Fleetstreet, and Samuel Tidmarsh at the King's-Head in Cornhill, 1678).

Gaukroger, Stephen. *The Emergence of a Scientific Culture: Science and the Shaping of Modernity 1210–1695.* Oxford: Oxford University Press, 2006.

Geach, Peter. *God and the Soul.* London: Routledge and Kegan Paul, 1969.

Gill, John. *The Cause of God and Truth.* London: Thomas Tegg & Son, 1838.

Goodwin, Thomas. *An Unregenerate Man's Guiltiness before God in respect of Sin and Punishment.* London, 1692.

Gootjes, Albert. *Claude Pajon (1626–1685) and the Academy of Saumur.* Leiden: Brill, 2014.

Goudriaan, Aza. *Reformed Orthodoxy and Philosophy, 1625–1750.* Leiden: Brill, 2006.

————. "The Synod of Dordt and Arminian Anthropology." In *Revisiting the Synod of Dordt (1618–1619)*, edited by Aza Goudriaan and Fred Lieberg. Leiden: Brill, 2011.

Hale, Matthew. *A Discourse of the Knowledge of God and of Ourselves*. London: printed by B. W. for William Shrowsbury, 1678.

Helm, Paul. *Calvin at the Centre*. Oxford: Oxford University Press, 2010.

————. "Francis Turretin and Jonathan Edwards on Necessity and Contingency." In *Learning from the Past*, edited by Jon Balserak and Richard Snoddy. London: T&T Clark, 2015.

————. *John Calvin's Ideas*. Oxford: Oxford University Press, 2004.

————. "John Locke and Jonathan Edwards, a Reconsideration." *Journal of the History of Philosophy* 7, no. 1 (1969): 51–61.

————. "Jonathan Edwards and the Parting of the Ways?" *Jonathan Edwards Studies* 4, no. 1 (2014): 42–60.

————. "Jonathan Edwards, John Locke and Religious Affections." *Jonathan Edwards Studies* 6, no. 1 (2016): 3–15.

————. "Locke on Faith and Knowledge." *Philosophical Quarterly* 23, no. 90 (1973): 52–66.

————. "Locke's Theory of Personal Identity." *Philosophy* 54, no. 208 (1979): 173–85.

————. "*Reformed Thought on Freedom*: Some Further Thoughts." *Journal of Reformed Theology* 4, no. 3 (2010): 185–207.

————. "Structural Indifference and Compatibilism in Reformed Orthodoxy." *Journal of Reformed Theology* 5, no. 2 (2011): 184–205.

————. "Thomas Halyburton and John Locke on the Grounding of Faith in Scripture." In *Reformed Orthodoxy in Scotland*, edited by Aaron Clay Denlinger. London: Bloomsbury Academic, 2015.

————. "Turretin and Edwards Once More." *Jonathan Edwards Studies* 4, no. 3 (2014): 286–96.

————. "Vermigli, Calvin et l'éthique d'Aristote." In *Contre vents et marées*. Edited by Jean-Philippe Bru. Aix-en-Provence, France: Kerygma, 2014.

Heppe, Heinrich. *Reformed Dogmatics Set Out and Illustrated from the Sources*. Translated by G. T. Thomson. London: George Allen and Unwin, 1950.

Heyd, Michael. *Between Orthodoxy and Enlightenment: Jean-Robert Chouet and the Introduction of Cartesian Science in the Academy of Geneva*. The Hague: Martinus Nijhoff, 1982.

Hopkins, Samuel. *The Life and Character of the Late reverend, learned and pious Mr Jonathan Edwards*. Boston: S. Kneeland, 1765.

Junius, Franciscus. *The Mosaic Polity*. Translated by Todd M. Rester. Edited by Andrew McGinnis. Grand Rapids: CLP Academic, 2015.

Kant, Immanuel. *Religion within the Limits of Reason Alone*. Translated by T. M. Green and H. H. Hudson. New York: Harper and Row, 1960.

Kenny, Anthony. *Descartes, A Study of His Philosophy*. New York: Random House, 1968.

———. "The *Homunculus* Fallacy." In *The Legacy of Wittgenstein*. Oxford: Blackwell, 1984.

Lane, Anthony. *John Calvin: Student of the Church Fathers*. Grand Rapids: Baker, 1999.

Le Blanc de Beaulieu, Louis. *Theses Theologia Varii Temporiblus in Academia Sedanensi*. London, 1675.

Locke, John. *An Essay Concerning Human Understanding*. 5th ed. Edited by John Yolton. 2 volumes. London: Dent and Co., 1961.

Maccovius, Johannes. *Scholastic Discourse: Johannes Maccovius (1588–1644) on Theological and Philosophical Distinctions and Rules*. Edited, translated, and introduced by Willem J. van Asselt and others. Apeldoorn, Netherlands: Instituut voor Reformatieonderzoek, 2009.

Marsden, George. *Jonathan Edwards, a Life*. New Haven, Conn.: Yale University Press, 2009.

Midgley, Mary. *Beast and Man: The Roots of Human Nature*. London: Routledge, 2002.

Mill, John Stuart. *A System of Logic, Ratiocinative and Inductive*. London: George Routledge and Sons, n.d.

Mosley, Nicholas. *Psychosophia, or Natural and Divine Contemplations on the Passions and Faculties of the Soul of Man*. London: printed for Humphrey Mosley, 1653.

Muller, Richard A. *After Calvin: Studies in the Development of a Theological Tradition*. New York: Oxford University Press, 2003.

———. *Dictionary of Latin and Greek Theological Terms*. Grand Rapids: Baker, 1985.

———. "Divine Covenants, Absolute and Conditional: John Cameron and the Early Orthodox Development of Reformed Covenant Theology." *Mid-America Journal of Theology* 17 (2006): 11–56.

———. *Divine Will and Human Choice*. Grand Rapids: Baker, 2017.

―――. "John Gill and the Reformed Tradition: A Study in the Reception of Protestant Orthodoxy in the Eighteenth Century." In *The Life and Thought of John Gill (1697–1771), A Tercentennial Appreciation*, edited by Michael A. G. Haykin. Leiden: Brill, 1997.

―――. "Jonathan Edwards and Francis Turretin on Necessity, Contingency and Freedom of Will: In Response to Paul Helm." *Jonathan Edwards Studies* 4, no. 3 (2014): 266–85.

―――. "Jonathan Edwards and the Absence of Free Choice: A Parting of the Ways in the Reformed Tradition?" *Jonathan Edwards Studies* 1, no. 1 (2011): 3–22.

―――. "'Not Scotist': Understandings of Being, Univocity, and Analogy in Early-Modern Reformed Thought." *Reformation & Renaissance Review* 14, no. 2 (2012): 127–50.

Owen, John. *The Works of John Owen*. Edited by W. H. Goold. 16 volumes. Edinburgh: Banner of Truth, 1966.

Pasnau, Robert. *Aquinas on Human Nature*. Cambridge: Cambridge University Press, 2008.

―――. "Olivi on Human Freedom." In *Pierre De Jean Olivi (1248–1298)*, edited by Alain Boureau and Sylvain Piron. Paris: Librairie Philosophique, J. Vrin, 1999.

Pemble, William. A *Summe of Moral Philosophy*. Oxford: printed by John Lichfield, 1632.

―――. *Vindiciae Gratiae, A Plea for Grace, More Especially Grace and Faith*. In *The Workes of that Late Learned minister of God's Holy Word, Mr William Pemble*. Oxford: printed for Henry Hall, for John Adams, Edw. and John Forrest, 1659.

Perkins, William. *A Discourse of Conscience*. Cambridge: John Legate, printer to the Universitie of Cambridge, 1596.

Perler, Dominik, ed. *The Faculties*. Oxford: Oxford University Press, 2015.

Pictet, Bernard. *Christian Theology*. Translated by Frederick Reyroux. Philadelphia: Presbyterian Board of Publications, n.d.

Plato. *The Republic*. Translated by Robin Waterfield. Oxford: Oxford University Press, 1993.

Purnell, Robert. *A Little Cabinet Richly Stored with all sorts of Heavenly Varieties, and Soul-reviving Influences*. London: R.W., 1657.

Rex, Walter. *Pierre Bayle and Religious Controversy*. The Hague: Martinus Nijhoff, 1965.

Reynolds, Edward. *A Treatise on the Passions and Faculties of the Soul*. In *The Whole Works of the Rt. Rev. Edward Reynolds*. Volume 6. Edited by Alexander Chalmers. London: B. Holdsworth, 1826.

Ryrie, Alec, and Thom Schwanda, eds. *Puritanism and Emotion in the Early Modern World*. London: Palgrave, Macmillan, 2016.

Saarinen, Risto. *Weakness of Will in Renaissance and Reformation Thought*. Oxford: Oxford University Press, 2011.

Schuurman, Paul. *Ideas, Mental Faculties, and Method: The Logic of the Ideas of Descartes and Locke and Its Reception in the Dutch Republic (1630–1750)*. Leiden: Brill, 2004.

Stapfer, Johann Friedrich. *Institutiones Theologiae Polemicae Universae*. 4th ed. Zurich, 1746–1753.

Stevenson, Leslie. *Seven Theories of Human Nature*. Oxford: Oxford University Press, 1974.

Strang, John. *De Voluntate et Actionibus Dei circa Peccatum*. Amsterdam, 1657.

Suarez, Francisco. *De Anima*. In vol. 3, *Opera Omnia*. Madrid: Fundacion Xavier Zubiri. Translated by Sydney Penner. http://www.sydneypenner.ca/SuarTr.shtml#anima.

Sudduth, Michael. *The Reformed Objection to Natural Theology*. Farnham: Ashgate, 2009.

Swinburne, Richard. *The Evolution of the Soul*. Rev. ed. Oxford: Clarendon Press, 1997.

Synopsis Purioris Theologiae. Edited by Dolf te Velde. Leiden: Brill, 2014.

Sytsma, David. "Calvin, Daneau and *Physica Mosaica*: Neglected Continuities at the Origins of an Early Modern Tradition." *Church History and Religious Culture* 95, no. 4 (2015): 457–76.

———. "The Logic of the Heart: Analyzing the Affections in Early Reformed Orthodoxy." In *Church and School in Early Modern Protestantism*, edited by J. J. Ballor, David S. Sytsma, and Jason Zuidema. Leiden: Brill, 2013.

———. "The Portraiture of Thomist Anthropology: John Weemes' Reformed Portrait of the Image of God." ThM thesis, Calvin Theological Seminary, 2008.

Tertullian. *On the Testimony of the Soul and On the "Prescription" of Heretics*. Translated by T. Herbert Bindley. New York: E. S. Gorham, 1914.

Teste, R. "Soul." In *Augustine through the Ages*. Edited by Allan. D. Fitzgerald. Grand Rapids: Eerdmans, 1999.

Truman, Joseph. *A Discourse of Natural and Moral Impotency*. 2nd ed. London: printed for Robert Clabel, 1675.

Turretin, Francis. *The Institutes of Elenctic Theology*. 3 volumes. Translated by G. M. Giger. Edited by James T. Dennison Jr. Phillipsburg, N.J.: P&R, 1992–1997.

van Asselt, Willem J. "Andreas Rivetus (1572–1651) International Theologian and Diplomat." In *The Theology of the French Reformed Church from Henry IV to the Revocation of the Edict of Nantes*, edited by Martin J. Klauber. Grand Rapids: Reformation Heritage Books, 2014.

———. *An Introduction to Reformed Scholasticism*. Translated by Albert Gootjes. Grand Rapids: Reformation Heritage Books, 2011.

van Asselt, Willem J., J. Martin Bac, and Roelf T. te Velde, eds. *Reformed Thought on Freedom: The Concept of Free Choice in Early Modern Reformed Theology*. Grand Rapids: Baker, 2010.

van den Brink, Gerrit A. "The Act or Habit of Faith? Alexander Comrie's Interpretation of Heidelberg Catechism Question 40." In *Scottish Reformed Orthodoxy*. Edited by Aaron C. Denlinger. London: Bloomsbury Academic, 2015.

van Ruler, J. A. "New Philosophy to Old Standards: Voetius' Vindication of Divine Concurrence and Secondary Causality." *Netherlands Archief voor Kergeschiedenis* 71, no. 1 (1991): 58–91.

Venning, Ralph. *Sin, the Plague of Plagues*. London: John Hancock, 1669.

Vermigli, Peter Martyr. *A Commentary on Aristotle's Nicomachean Ethics*. Volume 9 in The Peter Martyr Library. Edited by Emidio Campi and Joseph C. McLelland. Kirksville, Mo.: Truman State University Press, 2006.

———. *Philosophical Works*. Volume 4 in The Peter Martyr Library. Edited by Emidio Campi and Joseph C. McLelland. Kirksville, Mo.: Truman State University Press, 1996.

Voetius, Gisbertus. "Concerning Practical Theology." In *Reformed Dogmatics*, edited by John W. Beardslee III. New York: Oxford University Press, 1965.

Warfield, B. B. *The Plan of Salvation*. Grand Rapids: Eerdmans, n.d.

Watts, Isaac. *An Essay on the Freedom of Will in God and in Creatures and on Various Subjects connected therewith*. London: J. Roberts, 1732.

———. *Philosophical Essays on Various Subjects*. 5th ed. London: printed for J. Murgotroyd, 1793.

Weemes, John. *The Portraiture of the Image of God in Man, in His Creation, Restauration and Glorification.* London: printed by T. C. for John Bellamie, 1632.

Willard, Samuel. *A Brief Reply to Mr George Kieth.* Boston: Phillips, 1703.

————. *A Compleat Body of Divinity.* Boston: B. Green and S. Kneeland for B. Eliot and D. N. Henchman, 1726.

Zachman, Randall C. *The Assurance of Faith: Conscience in the Thought of Martin Luther and John Calvin.* Minneapolis: Fortress Press, 1993.

Zwingli, Ulrich. *Commentary on True and False Religion.* N.p., 1525.

Index